Foreign Policy of India and West Asia

Change and Continuity

Foreign Policy of India
and
WEST ASIA

Change and Continuity

Edited by

Fazal Mahmood
Centre of West Asian Studies,
Aligarh Muslim University (AMU), Aligarh

and

Rafiullah Azmi
Centre for West Asian Studies,
Jamia Millia Islamia (JMI), New Delhi

New Century Publications
New Delhi, India

NEW CENTURY PUBLICATIONS
4800/24, Bharat Ram Road,
Ansari Road, Daryaganj,
New Delhi - 110 002 (India)

Tel.: 011-2324 7798, 4358 7398, 6539 6605
Fax: 011-4101 7798
E-mail: indiatax@vsnl.com • info@newcenturypublications.com
www.newcenturypublications.com

Editorial office:
LG–7, Aakarshan Bhawan,
4754-57/23, Ansari Road, Daryaganj,
New Delhi - 110 002

Tel.: 011-4356 0919

First Published: **2014**

ISBN: **978-81-7708-381-1**

Published by New Century Publications and printed at Salasar Imaging Systems, New Delhi.

Designs: Patch Creative Unit, New Delhi.

PRINTED IN INDIA

About the Book

West Asia, stretching from Iran to Turkey, has loomed large for the Indian foreign policy makers irrespective of its politically turbulent nature. Since Independence in 1947, India has tried to build good relations with West Asia. Both India and West Asia are endowed with vast resources of varied nature which make the relationship highly desirable. India as an emerging Asian power, with a large population and economic potential, can play a vital role in the development of West Asia. On the other end of the spectrum, West Asia has the potential to meet the growing energy requirements of India. The bonds between India and West Asia have gone beyond oil and expatriates, encompassing almost all important dimensions of bilateral relationships.

The present book is an attempt to explore and analyse India's multi-faceted engagement with West Asia from an interdisciplinary perspective. The book examines the relations between India and West Asia in all their ramifications. The academics from Aligarh Muslim University, Aligarh, Jamia Millia Islamia, New Delhi and Jawaharlal Nehru University (JNU), New Delhi have contributed to this volume. Research papers included in the book relate to energy security, migration, bilateral trade, diplomatic relations, India's policy on Palestine, and the issue of terrorism.

About the Editors

Dr. Fazal Mahmood is Associate Professor (Geography) at the Centre of West Asian Studies, Aligarh Muslim University, Aligarh. He obtained his M.Sc., M.Phil. and Ph.D. degrees from the same university. He has published more than 20 articles on different geo-political aspects of West Asia in reputed national and international journals. Specializing in social, political, economic and tourism geography with special reference to West Asia, he has attended and presented papers at various national and international conferences/seminars.

Dr. Rafiullah Azmi is currently teaching at the Centre for West Asian Studies, Jamia Millia Islamia (JMI), New Delhi. Before joining JMI, he worked at the Institute for Defence Studies and Analyses (IDSA), Delhi. He obtained his Ph.D. degree from the School of International Studies, Jawaharlal Nehru University (JNU), New Delhi. His areas of research interest include US involvement in West Asia, security of the Gulf region, and India's relations with Gulf countries. He has published a book and also contributed chapters in edited books, besides several articles in reputed journals. He has traveled to UK, UAE, Sultanate of Oman, Iran and Turkey in connection with research work.

Contents

Contributors

Javed Ahmad Khan	Associate Professor, Centre for West Asian Studies, Jamia Millia Islamia, New Delhi.
Mohammad Iqbal	Professor, Department of Economics, Aligarh Muslim University, Aligarh.
Rafiullah Azmi	Centre for West Asian Studies, Jamia Millia Islamia, New Delhi.
Prakash C. Jain	Professor (Retd.), Centre for West Asian Studies, Jawaharlal Nehru University, New Delhi.
Anisur Rahman	Associate Professor, Academic Staff College, Jamia Millia Islamia, New Delhi.
Shamir Hasan	Chairman, Centre of West Asian Studies, Aligarh Muslim University, Aligarh.
Mohammad Gulrez	Professor, Centre of West Asian Studies, Aligarh Muslim University, Aligarh.
Jawaid Iqbal	Associate Professor, Centre of West Asian Studies, Aligarh Muslim University, Aligarh.
Khurshid Imam	Assistant Professor, School of Languages, Jawaharlal Nehru University, New Delhi.
Bansidhar Pradhan	Professor, Centre for West Asian Studies, Jawaharlal Nehru University, New Delhi.
Akhtar Nazmi	Assistant Professor, Centre for West Asian Studies, Jamia Millia Islamia, New Delhi.
A.K. Pasha	Director, Gulf Studies, Centre for West Asian Studies, Jawaharlal Nehru University, New Delhi.
Fazal Mahmood	Associate Professor, Centre of West Asian Studies, Aligarh Muslim University, Aligarh.

Preface

Ever since independence, India's relations with West Asia have occupied an important position from political, economic and cultural points of view. Geography has been a prominent factor in influencing India's relations with West Asia since early times. The region of West Asia stands as a bridge between India and Europe, Africa and Central Asia through land as well as sea routes. Apart from historical and cultural links, the presence of vast quantities of oil and natural gas reserves makes the region very important for India.

There was first a shared heritage of anti-colonial struggle, with a special fellow feeling for the peoples of West Asia. Subsequently, West Asia became crucial in India's striving for a strategy of non-alignment symbolized by Nehru's rapport with Nasser. Palestine became a focal issue in India's foreign policy.

India got involved in West Asian affairs first through the Khilafat movement and later through the Palestine issue. At the time of Indian independence, the contours of the emerging international order had already become quite clear. The Cold War between the two superpowers was a reality to which every nation had to respond in a way that best served its national interest. India's West Asian policy, during the Cold War years operated within the given international context. Nehru's non-aligned initiatives in West Asian and Sub-Saharan Africa, Indira Gandhi's activist Palestine policy and the decision to establish close relations with Iraq were the best available option for India during the Cold War when the basic thrust of the country's foreign policy was based on ideological issues of the time like anti-imperialism, non-alignment and anti-colonialism.

The end of the Cold War and the subsequent disintegration of the Soviet Union brought about radical changes in the international power configuration which had far reaching implications for the conduct of relations among nations. The ideas of free market and economic liberalization became a major tendency the world over and the thrust shifted to economic co-operation in view of the increasing sway of globalization. Each nation had to adjust to this new reality by bringing about necessary changes in its foreign policy, both at the broader as well as regional levels. India was no exception to that.

Both India and West Asia are endowed with vast resources of varied nature which make the relationship highly desirable. India as an emerging Asian power with a large population and economic potential can play a vital role in the development and growth of West Asia. West Asia, on the other, has the potential to meet the growing global demand of energy. Its cheapest cost of production of oil and gas and the overall well developed energy exploring infrastructure makes it a valuable partner for economic ties. In fact, resource diversity enhances the opportunity of economic, political and strategic alignments between them.

The importance of West Asia in India's overall energy security framework is likely to increase manifold in the coming years. West Asia also provides an attractive market for several Indian commodities like tea, rice, wheat, pulses, meat, wood products and light engineering goods. Bilateral trade between India and West Asia turns into billion of dollars. Finally, the presence of hundreds of thousands of Indian workers in the region is also an important aspect in Indo-West Asian relations. The expatriate workers are a major source of India's foreign exchange earnings through remittances in hard currency. The cultural relationship between India and West Asia, in which Islamic culture and Arabic and Persian served as bridges, is now supplemented by the huge stream of temporary migrants that India sends to the Gulf. There is, therefore, new cultural interaction not witnessed before, with subtle shift of Indian Muslims from the Iranian to the Arab cultural tradition.

The present book examines the relations between India

and West Asia in all their ramifications.

I take this opportunity to place on record my deep sense of gratitude to Professor Irfan Habib, Emeritus Professor of History at the Centre of Advanced Study of History, AMU, Aligarh, for his moral support and constant encouragement in the preparation of the present study. I am equally indebted to Professor Shireen Moosvi of the Centre of Advanced Study of History, AMU, Aligarh and Professor Ali Mohammad, Department of Geography, AMU, Aligarh for their generous help and support.

Thanks are also due to the following scholars for their help and co-operation at every stage of the completion of this work: Professor Shamir Hasan, Professor Mohammad Gulrez, Professor Nizam Ali, Dr. Mohammad Iqbal, Dr. Javed Iqbal, Professor Mohammad Azhar, Mr. Shamim Akhtar and Mr. Ashraf Husain.

Aligarh/New Delhi

Fazal Mahmood
Rafiullah Azmi

Part I
India-West Asia Economic Relations

1

West Asia's Current Economic Inclination towards India

Javed Ahmad Khan

Arab businessmen and investors in recent years have shown extraordinary optimism about business prospects despite concerns about terrorism, and political risks. According to a survey of 140 senior Arab executives interviewed in 14 countries by PricewaterhouseCoopers and the Dubai-based Moutamarat group, released at the World Economic Forum in Davos, Switzerland, about 83 percent of them saw conditions improving further over the next year. This was basically to show that the general level of confidence in the Arab world in the non-oil sectors is very high and these countries are aiming to achieve growth through alliances and joint ventures.

With the introduction of economic and political reforms in the region, the increasing role of the private sector in the infrastructure of GCC countries, as well as a rapid rise in the number of privatizations, has seen the number of developmental projects growing into an industry worth US$ 100 to 150 billion globally.

GCC Eyes the Asian Market

But the most noteworthy phenomenon is their recent drive is to woo Asian investments as most of the Gulf States, in order to broaden their economic bases have started a push to attract direct investment from Asia's regions. Two major factors point toward this shift. First, the resurgent Gulf economies are flush with money from oil sales and need fresh pastures to invest and diversify. Secondly, the increase in

Asia's oil consumption with both energy-starved China and India, needing the fuel to boost their growth engine. Asia consumes 30 percent of world's oil. GCC oil exports to Asia are two-thirds of its output and Asian oil consumption will be more than double by 2020. Additionally, more than half of total GCC exports go to Asian countries while a third of GCC imports are from Asia.

Under the new global market development, the oil rich Arab Gulf States are showing their inclinations towards the Asian and East Asian countries where India is emerging their vital economic partners. The existence of this new phenomenon is mainly due to the economic and political reforms that are taking place in the Arab world. But another important factor is the anti-West feeling in these countries particularly after the September 11, 2001 attacks, US occupation of Iraq and the style of Western worlds fight against 'Islamic terrorism' and these altogether prompted Arab world to seek geo-strategic and economic cooperation from their traditional Asian partners.

But the two major positive developments in this regard point toward this new shift. First, the resurgent Gulf economies are flush with money from oil sales and need fresh pastures to invest and diversify. Secondly, the increase in Asia's oil consumption with both energy-starved China and India needing the fuel to boost their growth engine. Clearly, economic integration between Asia and the GCC is increasing and the Asian market is becoming a major target for GCC oil exports. Thus there can be seen the rising optimism among business executives for the prospects of their companies despite concerns about terrorism, and according to a survey by the PricewaterhouseCoopers and the Dubai-based Moutamarat group, Arab companies were willing to open up their markets, at a time when global corporations are looking for new opportunities. [1]

This paper aims to focus on the Arab world's new 'Look East Policy' towards the Asian region especially of their seeking geo-strategic and economic collaboration with the India. Here, the anti-West feelings in the Arab world are seen as one of the major factor behind this inclination. The paper basically points that there is now an atmosphere of interdependence on each other's market in recent years. Finally, it is argued that the current Indo-Gulf economic relations is more realistic and hence durable than the relations of 1980s and early 1990s because of the prevailing politico-economic factors that have surrounded these Gulf States.

India an Attractive Market for GCC

The major trend of the Arab Gulf's economic inclination towards India could be seen in the first GCC-India Industrial Conference that was held in February 2004 and also known as 'Mumbai Declaration'. This was the first time that the ministerial and business delegations from the Gulf States came together to search the potential Indian market. They discussed under the theme 'Opportunities and Challenges in the 21st Century', focused on four select priority areas covering GCC and India: (i) trade, (ii) investments, (iii) industrial cooperation including small and medium enterprises (SMEs), small-scale industries (SSIs), and (iv) transfer of technology including information technology. India and the GCC member-states also signed the framework agreement on economic cooperation in August 2004. The salient features of this include that both sides agreed to consider ways and means for expanding and liberalizing their trade relations including initiating discussions on the feasibility of a free trade area (FTA) between them and to make arrangements for setting up joint investment projects and facilitating corporate investments in various fields. [2]

An India-AGCC joint commerce and trade committee has defined the contours of a preferential/free trade agreement with the AGCC, which accounts for about 11 percent of India's exports. The framework agreement with the AGCC is aimed at exploring opportunities in areas of oil and gas, knowledge-based products, education, health and other investments.

Again, during December 9 to 11, 2005, the Indo-Gulf Partnership Summit, on "Challenges and Emerging Opportunities: India and the GCC Countries" suggested the formation of a Gulf-India free trade area to facilitate trade between the two regions. Several free trade zones were already operating successfully within the Gulf area and by 2007, it was proposed to be Greater Arab free trade area. The Associated Chambers of Commerce and Industry in India (ASSOCHAM), in fact called for an immediate implementation of the framework agreement on economic cooperation signed between Gulf Cooperation Council (GCC) member-states and India. [3]

In this context, both sides appreciation to each other's economy sounds positive trends for the future relation. GCC has greatly acknowledged India's achievements in developing and sharing leading edge technologies in the fields of Information and Communications Technology, biotechnology, space, etc. On other hand, India has appreciated GCC's economic integration efforts, including the realization of a GCC Customs Union, GCC Common Market and GCC-Monetary Union with a single currency. [4]

The GCC is in the midst of a period of exceptional economic performance. The aggregate GDP for the GCC is expected to rise by 24.8 percent in 2005 and 7.5 percent in 2006, to a total of US$ 627 billion in 2006.The rationale is that the exceptionally large oil export receipts will lead to substantial fiscal stimulus in the region which will result in huge government spending in the six member GCC region. According to the report, high oil prices have facilitated increases in government spending and bolstered confidence, stimulating a surge in activity in the non-hydrocarbon sectors. This reflects a number of key developments, including increased intra-regional capital flows, as reflected in a property boom and a run-up in equity prices; and a region-wide acceleration in project implementation.

The non-oil exports will mainly be in the form of re-exports with the UAE continuing to be the main centre for re-exports in the region, owing to its world class ports, though Kuwait will play a growing role because of the ongoing infrastructure development in neighbouring Iraq. Other non-hydrocarbon exports are also expected to perform well, owing to the increases in manufacturing output, though they will account for only around 7 percent of total exports. [5]

Under this background, India's economic relationship with the oil rich Arab Gulf states is undergoing a new change. The Arab Gulf states are opening up on an unprecedented scale to foreign investments in both their oil and non-oil sectors, for which India is a natural partner. Indian manufacturers and traders are moving with increasing confidence into the Gulf markets where Indian brands are starting to gain recognition as competitors to Western names. Proof of this can be seen especially in the area of trade.

As one recent estimate published in *Khaleej Times* shows that including crude oil and petroleum products, India's imports from the West Asia increased from US$ 5.4 billion in fiscal year 1996-97 to approximately US$ 27.5 billion in fiscal year 2004-05. In the other direction, India has become a substantial and increasingly important exporter to the region. India's exports to the region increased from US$ 3.0 billion in 1996/97 to US$ 12.0 billion in 2004-05.

Within the region, the UAE is by far the most important destination, receiving Indian exports worth US$ 7.1 billion in 2004-05. Overall, India appears to have a sizable and increasing trade deficit with the Arab Gulf, currently of the order of US$ 15 billion a year. The West Asia is probably the first region to experience directly the growing confidence and outreach of Indian manufacturers and traders. India's strength as a service and technology provider, its geographical proximity, and its cultural affinity with the Middle East, make it a natural economic partner for the region. [6]

Anti-West Feelings in the Arab World

Since the early 2000s, some radical shift by these States

can be seen especially from their traditional allies; the United States and Western European countries to the Asian countries in a bid to secure their future markets and also strengthening diplomatic relation with the Asian countries. These Gulf regimes are also eager to reduce their security dependence on US and are now discussing to set up new security system. [7]

But the notable development with regard to Gulf's inclination towards India is that in recent years Arab feels being persecuted and harassed particularly after 9/11 terrorist attacks. This insecurity is rampant due to organized attacks against Islam and Arabs as people of this region are still molested in their own land and elsewhere. Further, with a view to rising Arab terrorist activities, the restrictive US visa policies are putting a dent in trade and investment flows between the United States and the Arab world. According to a study released by a business group, the National US-Arab Chamber of Commerce, the September 11, 2001, attacks on New York and Washington could be costing the United States at least US$ 5 billion in lost revenue from Arab countries. [8]

Consequently, the discrimination in the United States and Europe has compelled Arabs to flock to the Gulf and this is again enriching this region through the increased flow of tourism and money exchange. The evident fallout of Arabs not being able to establish businesses abroad or send their children to the Western countries has also seen that Arab businesses have begun to flourish and local educational institutions have started attracting more students. This is seen to have a long-time affect on the region's economy, tourism etc. [9] Also, Arab money and revenue from surging oil prices has mostly flowed into stock exchanges and real estate in the Gulf region after attacks for fear that foreign assets would be frozen as part of a crackdown on militants. [10]

Moreover, in this anti-West feelings, the popular campaign against US products has gained momentum in the Arab World and till the mid of 2005, the effectiveness of the campaign was such that, according to one US report, issued by the US National Council for US-Arab Relations, that stores selling American consumer products such as cars, drinks and foodstuff in the Gulf area lost nearly 40 percent of their customers because of the campaigns. [11] In fact, putting the ideological rivalry aside, the 9/11 compelled the so-called 'fundamentalist' Saudi Arabia to move towards the Russia for its economic development programme. Russia's transportation giant, Russian Railways, has been invited to participate in the 1,200 km. long railroad project that would connect the Kingdom's east and west coast regions. Among the countries being considered for such joint investment, is India.

Under this new anti-West climate, the Gulf and other Arab countries are also looking for investment opportunities in other Asian countries where China and India figure prominently. Although it is a debatable issue as to how far India has been successful to seek advantage of this new situation. However, the geo-political relations between India and West Asia, long discouraged by US during the Cold War period, have begun germinating specially since the last one decade. In fact, India counts to one of the favourite destination of these oil rich Gulf States. Besides various bilateral agreements during the years, the earlier visit of Iranian President Ali Muhammad Khatmi as chief guest at the India's Republic Day in 2002 and now of King Abdullah of Saudi Arabia in 2006 point towards the importance the two major Gulf States have given to India.

The Saudi market, which is mostly oriented to America and Europe, is finding new opportunities of investments in the India. Saudi Arabia's protected but growing economy is opening to the outside world after joining the World Trade Organisation in December 2005. Saudi Arabia's WTO entry is expected to boost foreign investment worth US$ 624 billion, providing funds for diversification of the country's booming oil-based economy. It has also softened regulations to woo foreign investors. Applying the same liberalized policies since last one and half decades, India is witnessing rapid economic growth and technological superiority. The two countries are expected to benefit to each other's economy in the days to come. [12]

Similarly, Dubai's government has started a push to attract direct investment from Asia's manufacturers, as it tries to broaden its economic base. According to industry leaders speaking at a *MEED* forum on project finance in the Arab World new projects in the GCC—already at a record high—are expected to continue to grow by up to 50 percent in 2006. Here, it can be argued that plenty of new investment opportunities exist in India for Gulf corporate majors and vice versa. Following the decisions of several Emirate states to permit foreign ownership of real estate, there has been substantial interest on the part of Indian investors in purchase of houses and apartments in the UAE. In the last few years, about a third of all investment in real estate in the UAE has originated from the Indian subcontinent.

While speaking on 'Economic diversification and political reforms in the Arab world and its impact on India', at the Confederation of Indian Industry's (CII) Partnership Summit in Kolkata, Chairman of the Galadari Group UAE, Mohammed A.R. Galadari, has rightly said that 'it is time for India to stop treating the Gulf region merely as a lucrative destination for its work-force and upgrade relations to a new realistic level. What he in fact wanted that India must do immediately to take full advantage of the economic diversification and political reforms under way in the Arab world. For the region will have a significant impact on India as a number of Indians residing and doing businesses in the Arab region will interact more closely with the governance process, depending on the pace of reforms. But above all India must be a friend to the Arab region—much more than an economic partner". [13]

Likewise, major investments from UAE into India in recent years are notable such as the Hyderabad Convention Centre by Emaar Properties, Dubai and the purchase of Thomas Cook by Dubai Investment Group and the RAK Ceramics plant in Andhra Pradesh. Emaar has, in fact, firmed up plans to invest US$ 1.2 billion in Punjab in various real estate projects like residences, roads, shopping malls, golf courses and a sports complex of global standards in Chandigarh. [14]

Thus, the central to India's booming trade ties with the Gulf region is the UAE, which has emerged as its third largest trade partner after the US and China. The two-way non-oil trade surged some 60 percent in 2004-05 fiscal year to US$ 12 billion with exports recording a 50 percent growth at US$ 7.2 billion and imports posting 120 percent rise to US$ 4.7 billion. The increasing role of the private sector in the infrastructure of GCC countries, as well as a rapid rise in the number of privatizations, has seen the number of projects grow exponentially. [15] Emaar-MGF Land Private Limited, a joint venture company formed by Emaar Properties PJSC—the world's largest listed real estate company, and MGF Developments Limited of India have come into India's largest FDI in real estate amounting to over half a billion dollars for projects with a capital outlay of US$ 4 billion (₹ 18,000 crore). The projects are planned for Delhi, Andhra Pradesh, Karnataka, Tamil Nadu and Maharashtra. [16]

Plenty of new investment opportunities exist in India for Gulf corporate majors and vice versa. Since 2002, following the decisions of several emirates to permit foreign ownership of real estate, there has been substantial interest on the part of Indian investors in purchase of houses and apartments in the UAE. In the last few years, about a third of all investment in real estate in the UAE has originated from the Indian subcontinent.

Though substantial oil and gas reserves of the GCC region play a vital role in fulfilling India's energy needs and are integral to country's energy security, in recent ties, India-GCC trade having become extremely diversified is not limited to oil and oil products only. GCC-India trade, which totalled US$ 12.5 billion in 2001-02, touched US$ 145.72 billion by 2011-12. India's exports were valued at US$ 45.36 billion, while imports were put at US$ 100.35 billion for 2011-12. Major commodities exported to GCC member states from India include gems and jewellery, textile products, metal manufactures, machinery and instruments, iron and steel etc., while major non-oil items imported from GCC countries include gold, organic and inorganic chemicals, non-ferrous metals etc.

The Persian Gulf is also a major source of hard currency remittances for India from its expatriate labour. The Indian expatriate communities themselves are important contributors to the Gulf economies. These communities originated primarily as traders and retailers, usually under sponsorships and partnerships with Gulf nationals. Although most Indian expatriates do not have permanent residence or citizenship in the Gulf states, in practice most have been settled for many years and even for generations. By our estimates there are now at least 5 million Indian expatriates in the AGCC states, of whom about 2.5 million are in the UAE and about 1.5 million in Saudi Arabia. India is an awakening giant.

Defence and security relations between India and the GCC, long discouraged by Washington during the Cold War period, have begun germinating since the early 1990s. India is considering training a larger number of GCC military officers at several of its defence establishments by tailoring special Arab language courses for them.

The Indian Navy (IN), however, has played the most crucial role in developing security relations with the GCC. It executed a hydrographic survey of Oman+s coastline between 1993 and 1994—the first ever by India of any foreign state—and in 1995 conducted its first regional exercise with the UAE navy, signalling closer ties with the Gulf countries. Further reaffirming India's strategic thrust into the Arabian Gulf region, the IN held its first naval exercises with Kuwait and neighbouring Iran in June 1998. It also held one-day manoeuvres with the navies of Saudi Arabia and Oman in what officials term as 'initial' move to counter neighbouring Pakistan's established influence with these Islamic countries.

India's only aircraft carrier, INS Viraat, also visited Abu Dhabi and other UAE emirates last year before going in for a major, two-year refit to extend its operational life.

Military analysts said India's decision to hold joint exercises with Iran, despite Washington's bid to isolate Tehran, was an assertion of New Delhi's independent foreign policy initiative. For Iran, these manoeuvres were an indication to the West that despite its pariah status it continues to influence regional security matters. India's military relations with Iran have grown since the early 1990s with reciprocal visits by service chiefs of staff.

A stable and prosperous Gulf will also become an important market for India's manufactured goods and cultural products. The prospects of energy and economic integration between the Gulf and India will have significant consequences for the geopolitics of the region.

India has also started wooing GCC investors. The Associated Chamber of Commerce and Industry (ASSOCHAM) invited the ambassadors and economic counsellors of nearly 22 Arab countries in Kerala's commercial capital of Cochin in January 2006. This was the first time that such a gathering of Arab countries took place in Kerala. [17] Nearly 200 top industrial and business houses of the country, including the Singhanias, Tatas, Birlas, Reliance, Hindustan Lever and Thapars, are expected to attend the meeting, according to the ASSOCHAM chief. [18]

Rising Oil Revenues

In recent years, the exceptionally large oil export receipts is projected to lead to substantial fiscal stimulus in the region which is projected to result in huge government spending in the Gulf region. The GCC states, which are pumping about 30 percent of total world oil output, are forecasted to earn record earnings in the years to come.

Since the Gulf states have already earned record oil revenues, the economists and policy makers are now suggesting that Gulf states should avoid repeating the mistakes of the oil boom in the 1970s and early 1980s when they wasted a golden opportunity to diversify and reform their economies. Now, one of their main challenges is to involve private sectors in new industries and develop a services sector which could absorb their growing populations. [19]

As a market Saudi Arabia boasts probably the best "collateral" in the world—25 percent of the world's proven oil reserves. And this from an explored area covering only a quarter of the country. The Kingdom's daily oil income, according to the Middle East Association, has increased from US$ 196 million in August 2004 to US$ 630 million in August 2005. This has led to an unprecedented budget surplus and levels of liquidity in the country. In the 2005 budget for instance some SR 75.5 billion was earmarked for capital expenditure mainly in education and health sectors. The value of actual construction contracts awarded in the Kingdom in the first six months of 2005 totalled SR 61.5 billion. This compared to SR 45.8 billion for the whole of 2004. Future project expenditure, according to figures from National Commercial Bank (NCB), is estimated at US$ 326 billion for the period 2005-2010.

The oil and gas sectors are also planning massive expansion with Saudi Aramco planning to spend US$ 46 billion over the next five years. At least six mega oil and gas projects are planned to push production capacity to 12 million barrels per day. Saudi Basic Industries Corporation (SABIC), now a major global petrochemicals player is also planning a major expansion with much greater private sector involvement.

India is the second largest trading partner in the Arab Gulf Cooperation Council region after the USA. During 2003-04, while India's exports to GCC were US$ 7.02 billion, imports from GCC, excluding oil, was US$ 3.25 billion. The UAE is the second largest importer of Indian goods, after the US and Saudi Arabia is the 16th largest destination of Indian goods.

India probably has substantial, exports of services to the

Middle East. Service companies in the region are outsourcing on an increasing scale, and India, with low labour costs and strong language skills, is a natural beneficiary of this trend.

Huge opportunities for setting up educational institutions and collaborations also exist, particularly because of the big expat Indian population. Indian educational institutions like IITs and IIMs are well-known brands and have a bright future in the Gulf. At India Economic Summit 2004, it was suggested that the Arab world should look at India for investments in hi-tech technologies and expertise. Indian IT related exports to the West Asia have touched to US$ 17.21 billion in 2004-05 with rate of growth to 41 percent (45 percent in dollar terms).

Recently, Satyam Computer Services has launched a programme to develop an Arab workforce in the region is involved in classroom training and on-the-job training to the youngsters. Likewise, Wipro Infotech, has been chosen by Thuraya Satellite Communications for Business Intelligence and Data warehousing solution. Greaves Cotton Limited, India's leading engineering company also launched a major export thrust in the Gulf region. [20] In June 2004, Dubai Internet City set up the Dubai Outsource Zone as a specialised free zone dedicated to companies providing outsourcing services.

In May 2005, Indian builders who are currently conducting a road show, organized by Arabian Trade Show in association with the Housing Development Finance Corporation Ltd. (HDFC) and the Alireza Group's Rezayat Trading Co. Ltd., in different parts of the Kingdom. [21] Similarly, Ducab, the leading manufacturer of power cables in the Arab world, is eyeing a manufacturing base in India to meet the requirements of the regional market. Company is targeting institutional customers with large infrastructure projects like metro rail, airport upgradation and power generation, transmission and distribution, instead of the retail segment. Ducab has already supplied cables to the Delhi Metro Railway Corporation (DMRC) and the proposed metro rail project in Bangalore could open up a potential business for the company. [22]

GCC countries now realize that their future economic security depend only on their ability to manage oil resources effectively and to engage in successful regional integration.

Oil and Gas Market

In the globalize world energy market, Indo-Gulf relation has taken a significant turn in the sense that conventional view of intra-regional trade, the heavy energy dependence and its impact on geo-politics and economy, fear of energy supply disruption, all seems to be diminishing under new environment. This can be seen especially in the context of Asian Oil Market conference in June 2005, which India successfully organized in New Delhi and in which oil minister's of Asian and Gulf countries examined the market situation from the consumers and producer's perspectives. This also marks a significant development in the area of Indo-Gulf energy relation.

Saudi Arabia pumps 60 percent of its overseas sales to Asia and is looking for new opportunities across the region to secure an outlet for its supplies. Asia imports more than two-thirds of its daily oil needs with about 80 percent coming from the Middle East. The fear of oil supply during the Gulf War I (2003) was in fact the most worrying aspects. Warning that oil and gas supplies could be seriously disrupted in the wake of a conflict, Foreign Minister Yashwant Sinha was balanced in his reply. While conceding that New Delhi had "high stakes" in that region, he said India imported most of its crude from the Gulf and there were 3.5 million Indians there who repatriated savings of US$ 7-8 billion annually. Endorsing India's policy, Sinha said any military action would send oil prices spiralling up.

In the fiscal year 2004-05, India imported 105 million tons of crude oil and petroleum products at a cost of US$ 29.8 billion a 45 percent increase over the bill for the previous year. Since 2000, India has stopped publishing data on the sources of its oil imports. The Gulf region provided about 65 percent of India's oil imports. We are now heading towards interdependency. This mean 'the fear of oil dependency on this volatile region would not be same as it was in 1970s or 1980s. In fact, the concept of oil supply disruption is not any issue, as for India's future economic relations with the region is concerned.

Another important development in Gulf hydrocarbon sector can be seen in the re-opening of oil and gas fields to the international oil companies (IOC), Previously too, IOCs were in the Gulf countries, but the main dominance was of US and Western oil companies. This time, conscious of the Western biased attitudes towards the Arabs, Gulf is trying not to be wholly dependent on Western oil companies. This became possible also because now the de-regulated global oil market has provided them the cheaper companies from Asian countries.

This intra-regional cooperation in the WTO regime provides new space of economic cooperation and the oil and gas, the so-called 'sensitive items' would not pose much threat to India. Our petroleum minister is now a relaxed man, as he is invited to explore the Gulf oilfields where both India's public and private sector companies are presently engaged. Moreover, Gulf countries now find India as their future secured market as the country's energy demand is escalating day-by-day.

A new element in the trade equation is the import of natural gas into India from the Middle East. Early in 2005, India agreed to import 7.5 million tons of liquefied natural gas annually from Iran over a 25 year period. The Indian government is also close to realising the long-standing project to build a pipeline from Iran, which could start supplying India with natural gas by 2010. Finally, the Dolphin project, conceived in 1999, envisages the construction of a pipeline to carry dry natural gas from Qatar to the UAE and Oman, and ultimately to Pakistan and India.

Conclusions

With the political and economic reform undergoing in the Gulf region, their inclination towards Asian market is unprecedented. Here, India is becoming a favourite destination of their trade and investment. India has begun new initiative towards an economic cooperation agreement with the Gulf countries for ties in trades and services.

The Gulf is going to become India's most important economic partners in the areas of trade, investments and joint ventures with about 3.5 million Indians—workers and professionals—presently engaged in the economic development of the Gulf region.

The region has now become the second largest zone for Indian exports, after the USA. India's trade with the Arab world has touched US$ 39 billion—about 5 percent of India's GDP. India's exports to the West Asian region have recorded successive increases over the last five years. The current year has seen a 63 percent increase in exports to West Asia.

India's new 'look-west' initiative towards the GCC members is projected to bring the economies of the Gulf closer to India. In July 2005, a meeting of the Trade and Economic Relations Committee, chaired by Prime Minister Manmohan Singh, also directed the ministries of commerce and external affairs to conclude the free trade agreement with the GCC.

This post-9/11 pictures also question on India's interest and idealism with regard to India's foreign policy in the region. For, India's main worry with the Arab Gulf states has been of their undemocratic governments, which can spark off terrorism at any time. But, the new initiative towards the Islamic world is seen as an important step in India's foreign policy, as one analyst has rightly pointed out that 'sensing the new opportunities, India has begun to shed its traditional inhibitions and step forward to a new engagement with the Islamic world'. [23]

End Notes

1. In the survey, 140 senior executives were interviewed in 14

countries and findings were that about 83 percent saw conditions improving further over the years. See, 'Business Confidence Rising in Arab World', *Gulf Daily News*, 28th January 2006.

2. The agreement was signed by Kuwait Foreign Minister Mohammed Al-Sabah Al-Salem Al-Sabah on behalf of GCC and the Indian Minister of Commerce and Industry Kamal Nath on August 25, 2005. See, *Arab News*, 20th November, 2004.
3. *Khaleej Times,* 9th June, 2005.
4. *Khaleej Times,* 17th November, 2005.
5. *Khaleej Times*, 3rd September, 2005.
6. 'Middle East Benefits from India's Economic Boom', *Khaleej Times*,13th January, 2006.
7. The ideas were floated during a weekend conference under the theme, "Security and Dialogue in the Gulf', held in Bahrain. Speaking at the meeting, Saudi Foreign Minister Saud al-Faisal criticized US policy in Iraq and stressed the need for a security system in the Gulf, based on four pillars: the countries of the Gulf Cooperation Council (GCC), Yemen, Iraq and India.
8. *Arab News,* 26th May, 2005.
9. Mahmoud Ali, *Khaleej Times,* 11th September, 2004.
10. *Khaleej Times,* 2nd February, 2005.
11. *Khaleej Times*, 19th May, 2005.
12. Tariq Alhomayed, Why do Saudis travel to India and China? Sharqul Awsat, 23rd January, 2006.
13. S.N.M. Abdi, 'India must give high priority to Gulf states', says Galadari, *Khaleej Times*, 20th January, 2006.
14. Gulf's interest in India can be gauged from the fact that UAE Minister for Economy and Planning, Shaikha Lubna Al Qasimi, took time off to come to Kolkata to address the Indian Industry's (CII) Partnership Summit, *Khaleej Times,* 21st January, 2006.
15. "Major Dubai Drive to Woo Asia Investments", *Gulf Daily News,* 28th January, 2006.
16. www.menareport.com., 21/12/05.
17. *Khaleej Times*, 5th December, 2005.
18. *Khaleej Times,* 5th December, 2005.
19. The GCC has a total population of about 35 million, one-third of them foreigners. With an annual population growth as high as 3.5 percent, the number of nationals entering the labour market continues to soar each year and the ability of states to provide jobs to their citizens has been diminishing.

20. *Khaleej Times,* 12th January, 2005.
21. K.S. Ramkumar and Syed Abdallah Rizvi, *Arab News,* 17th May, 2005.
22. *Khaleej Times,* 6th July, 2005.
23. C. Raja Mohan, *The Hindu,* see online; http://www.meadev.nic.in/OPn/2000may.

2

India's Economic Relations with Iran

Mohammad Iqbal

Before the dawn of definitely recorded history one can trace the intimate connection between the Iranians and the ancestors of the present day Hindus, who once lived together as important branches of the Aryan family and enjoyed a basic identity of race, religion, language, customs and culture in general. However, after generations of amicable co-existence they happened to be divided by disagreements on religious matters, and a large group resolved the dispute by coming down and settling near the river Sindhu or Indu, from which these were known subsequently Hindus. India is shown in Iranian works, while Iran appears more frequently in Indian myth and legend, poetry, drama and fiction. In fact the historical connection between India and Iran begins with the conquest of Punjab and Sindh by Darius Histaspes in 512 B.C.

Pre-Revolution Period

Iran formerly known Persia has been an ancient cradle of civilization and vital transit zone between India and the Near East. The fabulous Persia of olden times declined into a state of economic stagnancy for many centuries while the world advanced. Only after the discovery of oil in commercial quantities of Masjid-i-Sulaiman in 1908 and subsequently its export especially after the World War II and Nationalization of Iranian oil industry in 1951, Iran has done tremendous economic progress.

During 1959-72, Iran maintained an outstanding record of sustained economic growth and balance of payments stability. Iran's gross domestic product achieved a growth rate of about

14.7 percent in 1976-77 over the preceding year. [1] Looking into the sectoral growth one notice, "Industry achieved a growth rate of 16 percent at constant prices, due to full utilization of available labour and productive capacity". [2] It recorded an average rate of GNP growth of 9.2 percent in real terms during the period 1959-72. Besides overall economic growth, per capita real income also increased, in spite of higher rate of growth of 2.7 percent per annum.

The style of government in the constitutional monarchy, the strategy f development in one of the richest third world countries, hectic military build-up by this powerful state in West Asia—all these made this a unique country in this region. The Shah in his speech [3] in 1975 observed that the key to the country's success in achieving high rates of growth was that its officials managed to keep the country a few steps ahead of current developments over her neighbours.

India and Iran possessed long standing ties in economic, social, cultural and political fields. The people in both the countries have descended from the Aryan race. In the early decades prior to 1945, India's bilateral relations were not quite considerable. The 1971 War with Pakistan made our relations with Iran rather low. But in 1974, these relations took a dramatic upturn, and a number of commercial and collaboration agreements were signed. The government at that time gave an impetus to these relations and obviously the areas of agreement were expanding.

India and Iran at that time came closer to one another in many ways. It was observed, "From a traditionally agricultural state Iran has been transformed into one in which no single sector has such a great predominance over the others". [4] There exists a great scope in Iran for India's advanced technology in the field of industry and agriculture. Iran launched an extensive scheme of six reforms including the land reform during Shah's time in 1963. Iran has good agriculture potential, rich soil and abundant water resources, However, deficiency is realized in advanced agricultural technology. It, therefore, offers a good scope of economic cooperation.

Iran had to be dependent on industrialized countries for various items and the leading suppliers of these items during Shah's time were US, West Germany, Japan, UK, France, Italy and the former Soviet Union and EEC countries. It was observed, "Iran's imports of goods during 1976-77 were expected to be worth some US$ 15,000 million. By 1983, this figure could reach US$ 29,000 million. The US is the leading supplier, with 19.6 percent of the total imports and West Germany second (17.3 percent). Japan is in third place (15.9 percent) followed by the UK, (8.8 percent) France, Italy and the Soviet Union. The EEC countries together account for nearly 42 percent of Iran's total imports". [5]

Both the countries i.e. India and Iran had similarity of political and economic views and complete understanding on various issues. The late Shah of Iran giving an interview to the TV observed that he had brought a message of friendship from a country which had 3,000 years of historic bonds and friendship with India. The Shah of Iran expressed willingness to offer generous aid for the speedy completion of the second phase of the Rajasthan canal project. He said, it was up to the Government of India to accept the offer in any manner it liked. He further said if we cooperate on this project, it would not only be a good bilateral thing to do but almost serving humanity.

At that time Indo-Iranian joint venture was launched in Iran for the production and exports of automotive shock absorbers. Besides financial participation to the extent of 25 percent of equity, the Indian firm Escorts was to provide technology as well. The project was likely to be fully commissioned by 1982 and its production capacity of shock absorbers was supposed to reach 1.5 million per annum. The said project after fulfilling Iran's requirements, was expected to export its items to neighbouring countries. India and Iran had satisfaction at the progress of their bilateral relationship in economic and cultural fields and there was great urge to explore further avenues for expanding bilateral cooperation between two countries.

The Shah of Iran offered huge Iranian investment programme when the Indian delegation led by the then Prime Minister, Mr. Morarji Desai and Iranian delegation led by the Iranian Monarch held a meeting on 3rd February, 1978. This offer to boost the bilateral relations between India and Iran was likely to create basis for multilateral and regional cooperation. Indo-Iranian Joint Commission was coordinating the economic cooperation between the two countries. This Commission was functioning satisfactorily and as wished by the two sides this institution was expected to be made "more decisive". Joint communiqué in connection with close bilateral relations of India and Iran said this was precious gift of history.

In response to this agreement Iran was to make available to India additional quantities of crude oil annually at the OPEC price on credit, the rupee equivalent of which was to be used for financing the second stage of the Rajasthan canal, an alumina project based on eastern coast deposits of bauxite and a paper and pulp factory in this connection said the rupee equivalent of these instalments or the lump sum as the case might be was to be refunded in India as required, whether for investments or expenditure or could be used to finance the approved project.

The possibilities of Indo-Iranian collaboration in trade and industrial development were extremely good. Iran was fully aware of stupendous development task ahead and conscious of the difficulties in asking its new products. It was noticed that Iran's import trade was expanding at a tremendous rate and there was growing need to tap this huge Iranian market. India's share in Iran's import trade was negligible. However, in 1974, a number of items like tea, sugar, cement, woven fabrics, woven fabrics of jute, jute yarn, iron and steel, pipes and tubes, cycle and cycle parts etc. were supplied to Iran. At official level, there was no bias or resistance in Iran against increasing trade with India. However, at business level, because of West's better and longer experience with the parties in the developed countries there was a psychological bias in favour of the West.

Since Iranian markets were extremely price conscious there was a great need for offering really competitive price. For marketing products in Iran, Indian exporters were bound to train sales to meet the requirements of buyers. This required an aggressive marketing technique. It offered large opportunities where Indian firms could undertake jobs either as prime contractors or sub-contractors.

Plans for economics development of both the countries provided an excellent opportunity for mutually beneficial co-operation in accordance with their respective capabilities and capacities. The possible areas of cooperation between India and Iran during Shah's time included rural electrification generation and transmission of power, development of railways, rehabilitation of tracks, construction of railway lines, consultancy services, technical assistance, supply of railway equipment and construction materials and participation in the construction of industrial estates, new townships, housing, ship-building, repair of ships etc.

From the beginning of his reign in 1941, the Shah throughout his reign from 1941-1979, aimed at bringing the country overnight into the category of advanced countries and to eradicate backwardness in all fields to achieve this goal he contacted mostly with Western countries specially America for their cooperation, though the Shah made agreements even with the former U.S.S.R. as well. On the other hand, Iran's political and strategic importance as super most before former super powers America wanted to prevent Iran from falling under former U.S.S.R. domination and to have a regular source of oil supply. Iran purchased huge quantity of arms from America to defend monarchy against foreign aggression mainly from U.S.S.R. and to curb domestic opposition.

The Shah's concentration on purchase of arms and expenditure on military outweighed economic and social ones.

Despite of all these things the Shah used oil revenues to finance successive economic development plans for rapid industrialization. Its unprecedented rate of economic growth compared favourably with that of most developing and even some developed countries. The country's ambitious industrialization projects, its decreasing agricultural productivity and increase in real income led to increase in imports. Iran imported machinery, capital goods and consumer goods. [6] in view of Shah's programme for modernization and westernization, adoption of monarchical policies was taken by the public of Iran as bias and anti-Islamic and anti-socio-cultural and entirely Western motivated.

The people turned against the Shah's policies of modernization, westernization and Shah's tilt towards America. The fanatic religious groups turned against the spreading of western culture in Iran. All these things led to sudden cut burst of revolution in 1979 which led to the ouster of the Shah and emergence of religious group under the leadership of Ayatollah Khomeini. After the end of monarchy, the Islamic Republic was established in Iran in 1979. During Shah's policies of rapid industrialization, agriculture was neglected while the fact is that nearly 30 percent of agricultural area is irrigated mostly in the hilly margins between desert and mountains. [7]

In the year 1965, the first joint venture was set up between India and Iran under which development of Madras Oil Refinery was done. Indian Ministry of Petroleum held 50 percent equity while National Iranian Oil Company (NIOC) held 15 percent and other private sector banks etc. held 35 percent. This Refinery had a production capacity of 2.8 million tons and was further extended to 3.5 million tons per annum in 1974. [8] The name of Madras Refinery Ltd. was changed to Chennai Petrochemical Corporation Ltd. In the year 1974 Iran-o-Hind Shipping Company Ltd. (IHSC) was formed.

During the seventies India had a number of consultancy and project export. Under the Colombo Plan, India extended facilities to two trainees from Iran who came to study the cooperative marketing courses in India at various Indian cooperative training institutions during 1974. India provided 32 training places in Iran after spending a total of US$ 51,000 for this purpose. During 1975 and 1976, two training places were provided to Iran under Colombo Plan agreement. Under this plan India gave aid to Iran from 1950 to 1976 worth about ₹ 1,137 thousand. [9]

During 1973 and 1974, four [10] Indian experts were working in Iran. India had another project in Iran which was related to feasibility cum-cost-study of new railway line in Iran for a total length of 340 kilometres costing about ₹ 23 lakh. India extended educational help to Iran and allotted 21 seats for engineering courses and six seats for medical course in various Indian universities for Iranian students. In 1975, a consultancy programme and an important agreement was signed for the development of Kudremukh iron ore mines. Under this programme, Iran had agreed to give a significant amount of US$ 630 million.

In return, subsequently, Iran was to buy 150 million tons iron ore from India over a period of 20 years. [11] Iran had already advanced US$ 225 million and the project was completed in record time and within stipulated cost. This Kudremukh Iron Ore Company Ltd. was established in April 1976. It was expected to produce 7.5 million tons of iron ore concentrate per annum. India managed to settle the dispute pertaining to this 12 year old dispute over a US$ 250 million debt to Iran and to supply iron ore to Iran for 15 years. [12]

Pakistan Factor

Indo-Iranian relations since 1947 are qualitatively different from earlier phases but traditional relations did persist. These bilateral relations got altogether new dimensions after the World War II in view of complex international relation system. In the era of fresh milieu, geography, strategic location, endowment of rich natural resources, economy acquired new significance. The factors like ideological competition, inter-dependence, Cold War and perceptions of political leaders played an important role in relations between India and Iran. These factors along with certain indigenous issues greatly affected India's relations with Iran. When Pakistan emerged as new state, India lost its age-old territorial contiguity with Iran. Emergence of Pakistan and territorial loss of India, Pakistan held about 590 miles of common border with Iran. Pakistan stood not merely geographically between India and Iran but it also served to be a determining factor in Indo-Iranian relations. [13]

Iran had its tilt towards Pakistan and Iran was the first country to extend recognition to the state of Pakistan. Iran established diplomatic relations in May 1948. The Shah was the first head of the State to pay a state visit to Pakistan in March 1950 and consequently a treaty of friendship was signed between Iran and Pakistan. However, we cannot ignore an Air Transport Agreement in November 1948 and the visit of an Iranian Mission to India in December 1949 which came to explore the prospects of bilateral trade. The foundation for modern relations between India and Iran was provided after independence when the first ever treaty of commerce and navigation was signed between India and Iran in 1954. It served to be the basis of all other agreements signed in 1961, 1963 and 1968. Another Landmark in India's relations with Iran was the Shah's second visit to India in 1964. [14}

Post-Revolution Scenario

Mohammad Reza Shah Pahlavi was ruling in Iran since 1941, when revolution took place in the country the Shah left Iran for Egypt on 16th January 1979 and Ayatollah Khomeini returned to Tehran on 1st February 1979 and the Islamic Republic was established in the country.

After the revolution and change in Government in Iran, the agreements and protocols signed by the Shah's government with different countries were cancelled. As a result, India lost a substantial part of its trade with Iran. There erupted war between Iran and Iraq in September 1980 which continued for about eight years.

During the War, Iran's major focus of attention was on military industry and obviously economic progress was overshadowed by the procurement of war goods.

India's economic and trade cooperation was greatly affected by this war and India had to suffer because of higher prices of oil as a result of war between both of its partners namely Iran and Iraq.

However, in 1987, Dr. Ali Akbar Vilayati came to India to attend the meeting of Indo-Iranian Joint Commission. Both the countries decided to pick up specific projects for economic cooperation and transfer of technology.

Iran after revolution adopted a policy of "Neither East-Nor West" and a policy of cooperation based on mutual respect for the territorial integrity of their countries. During the War, Esfahan and Ahwaz Steel Complex, which were using iron ore from Kudremukh mines, were bombarded and sustained damages. However, later on, long standing issues pertaining to Kudremukh were resolved and memorandum of understanding was signed between the two countries.

During the period of Iran-Iraq War, few Indian delegations paid visit to Iran but this could not bring about a significant break through in India's economic India and Iran was signed for cooperation in the field of petrochemical industry.

Moreover, under this programme, cooperation was expected in plant operations, research and development, bilateral trade, joint ventures, information exchange and regional cooperation. In the period of reconstruction Iran was in need of technology to repay the petroleum industry which had sustained irreparable damages. This opened doors for vast opportunities for India to help Iran and earn foreign exchange.

India took effective steps to expand economic ties with Islamic Republic of Iran through the Joint Economic Commission. In 1992, the Indian Trade Promotion (ITPO) participated in the international trade fair held in Tehran. In this fair, ITPO displayed traditional and non-traditional goods with vast scope in Iran. The major items displayed in this fair included machine and hand tools automobiles and their spare parts, farm machinery and the implements, electric motors chemicals, fuel injection equipments, cement plants, food items etc. In 1992, India won contract for projects to the tune of US$ 1 billion from Iran. Efforts were made by India to strengthen trade and cooperation in industry, science and technology, agriculture, rural development, transportation and communication etc. India won another contract worth US$ 700 million to set up a major thermal power project in Kerman. In 1993, steps were taken to strengthen bilateral relations between the two countries—India offered to Iran for engineering and technological expertise for the Iranian oil and natural gas sector.

There exists tremendous scope of economic cooperation with Iran. Another memorandum of understanding was signed to enhance bilateral cooperation in surface transport, science and technology. There exists great scope for cooperation in areas like metallurgy, oil and petroleum, bio-technology, electronics, computer, communication, energy including research in these areas. Both the sides agreed to explore possibilities for setting up bilateral scientific and technological research centres in leading scientific areas. India also agreed to collaborate in projects like developing and constructing ports, roads, rail roads, air links and infrastructure to develop economic and commercial links with the Central Asian region.

Some Indian companies were already engaged in the Ahwaz Bander Elam signalling project. India exports to Iran consisted of items like processed minerals, machinery and instruments, primary and semi-finished iron and steel, organic and inorganic chemical, manufacture of metals, rubber and manufactured products, paper wood products, man made yarn fabric, transport equipments, tea and iron ore. Three items like machinery and instruments, drug pharma and fine chemicals and iron accounted for export to Iran worth US$ 19.2 million, US$ 26.5 million and US$ 24.56 million respectively. These three items constituted 35 percent of the total exports to Iran.

Recently, there has been an upsurge in Iran's imports from India of five, items namely machinery and instruments, primary and semi-finished iron and steel, organic and inorganic chemicals, drug pharma and fine chemicals and processed minerals. Other commodities which earn sizeable foreign exchange are rubber manufacture products, transport equipments, paper wood products, man made yarn fabric and tea. On the contrary, major imports of India from Iran include oil, non-ferrous metals, fruits and nuts, organic chemicals, inorganic chemicals, pulses, sulphur and un-casted iron pyrites, artjel, resins and plastic material etc., metal ferrous ores and metal scrap.

India adopted policy with regards to Iran for promoting close economic and commercial relations, bilateral agreements coordination of actions and in particular in intra-governmental Joint Commission, working of the technical assistance programme geared to the possibilities of utilizing the maximum of India's technical advancement, extending support for economic collaboration and cooperation at regional and international level, securing joint ventures, joint-project, consultancy services projects, soft loans etc., export of skilled, semi-skilled and non-skilled manpower. A comprehensive training programme of Iran-o-India Cement Engineering Consultancy Company was organized in Tehran in 1977.

A joint venture consultancy company was set up in 1996 between ACC India and Pars Khuzestan of Iran. A Memorandum of Understanding pertaining to bilateral cooperation in veterinary field was signed which also included a protocol on health requirements for meat exports. Under this protocol, the two countries undertook to exchange experts, information and expertise in the areas of veterinary and to furnish each other the information on health care of livestock in both the countries. [15] Bharat Heavy Electrical Ltd. set up a major thermal power project in Kerman at the cost of US$ 700 million bearing the capacity of 810 KW. India also won a contract worth US$ 200 [16] million for setting up a major sugar project in Khuzestan.

With regard to Iran's intention to link the Central Asian region, officials of Indian Railway Construction Corporation (IRCON) undertook a detailed study in this respect. Subsequently two countries worked on the two railway links in eastern Iran measuring 700 km. south-east to northern Iran Bafq Mushhad railway line and 500 km. east-west Kerman Zahedan track and service. Both these tracks were meant to provide new land routes to the fast developing Central Asian Republics through Iran. Another contract worth US$ 25 million was signed between Indian Railway Construction Company and Iranian Railways for Ahwaz Bander Elam signalling project. [17] In 2002, an agreement was signed between India and Iran to boost and concretize scientific cooperation.

Under this agreement both identified areas of collaboration which include information and communication technology, food technology, pharmaceutical research, energy, environment and sustainable development. It also included some specific areas like software, medical and agricultural technology, metallurgy, oil and petrochemicals and alternative sources of energy. In response to this a joint committee for achieving objectives laid down in the agreement was to meet in Tehran and New Delhi. This was supposed to implement joint projects, training of scientific personnel visits and exchange of experts, holding scientific technology workshops, sharing experiences in technology infrastructure and technological documents and information as well as experiences with regard to women entrepreneurship and rural technology. [18] In 1986, India signed few agreements with Iran to set up small-scale industries and undertaking road and railway construction and various employment oriented rural development programme.

The programme continued throughout 1990s. In 1991, the

Indian Petrochemical Corporation Ltd. (IPCL) won US$ 4.4 million contracts to train personnel of the Iranian National Petroleum Company (NPC) to develop their petrochemical industry. The whole programme was completed in ten phases as under each phase 30 trainees were trained by Indian experts. The Engineers India Ltd. provided management and co-ordinating services including planning, rescheduling, cost control and construction management. It further won a US$ 2 billion prestigious management services contact.

This contract was obtained for complex of Tabrez Petrochemicals in Iran against stiff international competition. This assignment was of over US$ 17 million in terms of services cost alone. Under this programme, 100 experts of various engineering disciplines were sent. [19] An Indian private sector company Tata Consultancy Engineers (TCE) won a contract from Iran to render project management service for Tanvir's 3,390 MW Gilan combined cycle based power plant at Rasht in Gilan Province of Iran. In the same year, it obtained another contract worth about US$ 1.4 million plus expenses for similar project management services for the 425 MW Grab Thermal Power Project at Hamadan. [20]

During 1980-88, Iran-Iraq War, India adopted a conscious approach towards Iran and Iraq as both being India's trading partners. India before this war was receiving 70 percent of her total oil imports from Iran and Iraq. During this War, India had to suffer a great loss in terms of higher oil prices. Somehow or the other India managed to regain the previous position in Iranian market and supplied a number of traditional and engineering goods to Iran. However, trade of Iran as a whole had declined due to shortage of funds.

After the revolution, India was the first country to send an official delegation to Iran. Thereafter in 1983, a new Indo-Iran Joint Commission was formed. It was followed by sending a 15 member delegation of the Federation of Indian Export Organization (FIEO) to Iran for exploring potential to capture Iranian market. In 1987, a joint commission between India and

Iran agreed to expand their industrial cooperation in small scale industries like cement plant, textile machinery, automotive sector, road construction and the foundry and steel sector. [21] In 1987, Dr. Ali Akbar Vilayati came officially to attend the Indo-Iranian Joint Commission meeting who besides discussing international and mutual concerns, reiterated Iran's policy and expressed the view that Iran regarded India as one of the influential members of the Non-Aligned Movement and attached greatest significance to its relations with India. [22]

India's relations with Iran grew more important during 1990s as Iran needed technical help for their reconstruction drive and India found new market after the collapse of U.S.S.R.

There has been a significant increase in Indian exports to Iran, however still much headway has to be done in this respect to fully exploit the opportunities existing in Iran. There have been some reasons for decline in India's share like delay in delivery from India, differences between samples and specifications and the actual goods exported, lack of understanding between the Iranian exporters and importers in both the countries etc., malpractices, delays, poor quality, lack of export culture and poor marketing efforts.

End Notes

1. *West Asia Diary,* July 30-August 5, 1997, p. 616.
2. Ibid., p. 616.
3. *Kayhan International,* May 1975, p. 1.
4. Julian, Bharier, *Economic Development in Iran 1900-1970,* Oxford University Press, Toronto, 1971, p. 61.
5. *The Middle East and North Africa 1977-78,* "An Annual Survey and Who's Who", Europa Publications Limited, London, p. 347.
6. Ramazani, R.K., *The United States and Iran,* Praeger Publisher 1982, pp. 69-70.
7. *The New Encyclopaedia Britanica,* Vol. 5, 15th Edition, Chicago 1987, p. 335.
8. Singh, Darshan "Appraisal of Iran President Rafsanjani's Visit to India in April 1995", *India Quarterly,* No. 51 (2-3), ICWA Publications, New Delhi, pp. 125-126.

9. Colombo Plan Consultative Committee Report, p. 343.
10. Vohra, Dewane, *India Aid Diplomacy in the Third World*, Vikas Publication, New Delhi, 1978, p. 149.
11. Ministry of External Affairs (MEA), *Annual Report*, New Delhi, 1975-76, pp. 206-207.
12. "India Treaty to Take Part in West Asia Talks" *The Business and Political Observer*, New Delhi, 4th February 1992.
13. Khan, Javed Ahmed, *India and West Asia*, Sage Publications, New Delhi, 1999, p. 183.
14. Abidi, A.H.H., "Relations between India and Iran", *The Iranian Journal of International Affairs*, Vol. VII, No. 4, Tehran, 1997, p. 878.
15. *Commercial and Economic Report*, Embassy of India, Tehran, May 1998.
16. "India, Iran sign MoU to Boost Ties", *The Business and Political Observer*, New Delhi, 12th November, 1992, p. 5.
17. Khan, Javed Ahmed, No. 13, p. 188.
18. *Monthly Newsletter*, Vol. XL, No. 2, Indian Investment Council, New Delhi, 25th Febraury, 2003.
19. "IPCL Bags US$ 4.4 Billion Project in Iran", *The Business and Political Observer*, New Delhi, 2nd August, 1991, p. 11.
20. Khan, Javed Ahmed, No. 13, p. 188.
21. Khan, Javed Ahmed, No. 13, pp. 182-183.
22. "India, Iran Discuss Trade Technology Transfer", *The Economic Times*, New Delhi, 20th February, 1987, p. 8.

3

Iran-Pakistan-India Gas Pipeline and Indo-Iran Relations

Rafiullah Azmi

Over the last few years, energy security has become a new buzz word. Energy security has become of paramount concern and has acquired great salience as part of the over all national security dynamics. Gas is steadily emerging as a popular source of energy. In response to the growing gap between the demand and supply, India began to gear its effort to address this critical factor in order to maintain the momentum of its economic development. It began to explore various avenues and options. Diversification was adopted to prevent any future shock of supply disruption as the Gulf region regarded very volatile and instable. Despite the best effort to diversify the source of energy import, the Gulf region remained an important source not only in case of oil but also in gas as well, and it is projected to maintain this position in the foreseeable future. Among the Gulf countries, Iran is reported to have the largest reservoir of gas. Though gas could be transported by the tanker but pipeline has emerged as better and economical option due to advancement in the technology. In this respect, Iran-Pakistan-India (IPI) Gas Pipeline has assumed great significance. It is believed that the project besides meeting India's requirement of the gas would also play a great role in promoting regional cooperation.

The project was mooted in the early 1990s but could not get materialized for various reasons, but mainly due to mistrust between India and Pakistan. The recent US opposition to the IPI gas pipeline has made situation more complex and uncertain. The central thesis of the study is that interdependency and inter-linkage will help to promote a conducive atmosphere between India and Pakistan which may ultimately lead towards regional economic integration which is the need of the hour in the highly impoverished South Asian region. Another premise of the study is that successful completion of the project would leave consequences beyond South Asia. It will also act as regional bridge between South and West Asia. Over the time if countries, such as China, join, then region will be locked into a regional energy grid.

The third thesis of this paper is that the domination over the critical raw material and market had historically been an important factor that leads towards colonization of many part of the world by the European powers. This geo-strategic game of domination and hegemony has not ended, only its mechanism has changed. The present attempt of the US to dominate over the supply of energy resources, particularly gas is the continuation of the same story or trend and thus not a new phenomenon.

The IPI Gas Pipeline though envisaged in the early 1990s but could not get materialized due to mutual hostility between India and Pakistan. However, with the latest meeting between the official of India and Iran in New Delhi towards the end of December 2005, the project has been revived and it is hoped that it will be given final shape by the middle of this year.

The IPI gas pipeline, though envisaged in the early 1990s, could not get materialized due to various complexities and problems. The proposal to construct IPI gas pipeline project was mooted in 1989 when major oil and gas discoveries were made in its territory, adjoining the state of Qatar. The planned pipeline, termed as the "peace pipeline", would be about 2,670 km. long. It would cost about US$ 7 billion. As transit country, Pakistan would be beneficiary as it would get royalties amounting to US$ 1 billion a year. The pipeline would connect the Assalwyen (South Pars) gas and oil fields in southern Iran to the Hazira-Vijaipur-Jagdishpur (HUJ) pipeline in India, with an immediate focal point in Multan.

Three parallel tracks of bilateral negotiations between India and Iran, Iran and Pakistan and India and Pakistan over a period of time have created a situation where three countries had scheduled to hold a trilateral ministerial level discussion in March 2006. Various forms of project restructures and price mechanism are being considered to make this pipeline project a reality because these two factors are equally if not more important, though they have not received much media attention like geo-political factors. After the third round of meeting of the India-Iran Special Joint Working Group (SJWG) on the IPI project in New Delhi between 28-29 December 2005, positive indication has emerged that blueprint of the pipeline project would be given final shape early this year for implementation. [1]

The proposed pipeline has been hanging fire for one and a half decades. The project, which is economically very viable and urgently needed earlier, became victim of the Indo-Pakistan mutual hostility and now a new factor of the US opposition has also been added.

Trends in the Energy Sector

Over the last few years, Asia has emerged as the largest consumer of the energy resources because economies of some of the Asian countries like India, China and Malaysia have grown and are still growing at considerably higher rate. This position was earlier held by the USA and Europe.

Another important trend is that use of gas is becoming more widespread in various sectors of the economy and therefore generating phenomenal increase in its demand. Due to technological changes and environmental concerns, gas is steadily becoming more popular as a fuel. It is now the number one choice for use in power generation because of the advancement in combined cycle gas turbine technology. Advancement in technology has raised the prospect of an abundance of low cost natural gas and also the transportation of the gas carrier. Trans-national pipe lines and LNG plants have made it possible for gas to be delivered around the world at a very low cost and thus helping natural gas to compete successfully with other resources such as coal and oil. Thus in the last few years, gas consumption has grown more than 50 percent. [2]

In the meanwhile, Indian economy began to grow at much faster rate after the beginning of the liberalization. The fuelled the demand for more energy resources. [3] Energy security became a new buzz-word. In its quest for energy security, India regards Iran and Russia as two important partners. Despite the best effort to diversify the sources of energy import, the Gulf remained an important source not only in case of oil but also in gas as well, and is projected to maintain this position in the foreseeable future. Among the Gulf countries, Iran is reported to have the largest reservoir of gas. [4]

Though gas could be transported by tankers but pipeline has emerged as a more better and economic option due to advancement in the technology. In this respect IPI gas pipeline has assumed great significance. It is believed that the project besides meeting India's requirement of the gas would also play a great role in promoting regional cooperation. [5] From the Iranian perspective, the Indian initiative or regional cooperation dovetails with its own policy on shifting its oil and gas trade to the Asia region so as to reduce its market dependence on the west. In this backdrop, both countries—India and Iran—began to take initiative to further strengthen their ties in every spheres in the 1990s. A series of high level exchanges took place in this period. [6]

The IPI gas pipeline project became one of the important components of this relationship. There were certain developments, which brought Iran and India closer. Market (globalisation and liberalization) and geopolitical (the emergence of the Taliban in Afghanistan) factors forced both Iran and India to explore avenues of mutual benefit or cooperation in the 1990s. After the 1979 Iranian Revolution, it had to face great hostility from the US and the West. However, break up of the USSR threw up opportunities for Iran. It became part of both the areas of the Persian Gulf and Central Asian and Caspian Sea hub. Without Iran's cooperation, transportation of the Caspian Sea gas became very difficult. (The emergence of Taliban in Afghanistan as a factor could be highlighted in details because it led to the convergence of the strategic interests of Iran and India).

Advantages of IPI Gas Pipeline

1. The pipeline would ensure the demand for Iranian gas free from market fluctuations and other extraneous considerations, which will ensure in assured income and the growth of its economy.
2. The import of natural gas from Iran is a vital element in India's quest for energy security. It will ensure the smooth supply of the gas at a reasonable price to meet its steadily growing requirement, which is very important to maintain the momentum of its economic growth. [7]
3. Likewise, the pipeline would also be beneficial for Pakistan, as it would help to meet its increasing energy requirement and also to earn good money in the form of the transit fee.
4. The pipeline project will open up a new and potentially exciting chapter in the bilateral relations between India and Pakistan as inter-dependency and inter-linkages will help to promote a conducive atmosphere between these two countries which may ultimately lead towards regional economic integration which is the need of the hour in the highly impoverished South Asian region.
5. The successful accomplishment of the project, it is hoped, would have consequences beyond South Asia. It will act as a regional bridge between South and West Asia. If countries such as China joins and it is also extended towards the Caspian Sea, then an energy grid will be created linking vast region from the Gulf-South Asia-

Central Asia to China, which would lower costs of transportation of gas all round. [8]

6. However, the most important benefit considering the long-term implications would be that it may jeopardize the hegemonic and geopolitical game of the US. In order to pursue its design in the Gulf region, the US wants to perpetuate its control in some form or the other over its key source-oil and gas.

Impediments

Ever since the project was floated, the historical baggage of unpleasant and acrimonious relationship between India and Pakistan had its impact on it. India expressed reservations about the possibility of disruption of the gas supply by Pakistan, which was understandable considering the nature of relationship between them. However, since he took the reins of the country in October 1999. General Musharraf has been consistently advocating for the construction of the pipeline. To allay Indian fears, Pakistan has said it was ready to give any kind of guarantee. In the meanwhile, Indo-Pak relationship, despite occasional hiccups, began to improve. There are various reasons for that which need not to be explained here in detail because this issue is beyond the scope of the present paper.

The project gained momentum after the assumption of office by the United Progressive Alliance (UPA) led by the Prime Minister Manmohan Singh. It figured prominently at the meeting of foreign ministers of India and Pakistan in New Delhi in early September 2004 as well as the landmark summit between General Musharraf and Dr. Singh on September 25, 2004 on the sidelines of the UN General Assembly Session in New York. "It was felt that such a project could contribute to welfare and prosperity of the people of both the countries and should be considered in the larger context of expanding trade and economic relations between India and Pakistan", the joint Press statement said.

However, the real turning point came in early 2005, when

India decided to de-link the proposed pipeline to progress on "Other issues" between New Delhi and Islamabad. The Union Cabinet asked on February 10, 2005 the Ministry of Petroleum to explore and examine various aspects of the project and reach an early solution. [9] For the first time, an attempt was made to de-politicise the pipeline project from Indo-Pak relations on other issues. The pipeline was no longer linked to issues such as Pakistan giving reverse transit to Indian goods to Iran and Central Asia as well as grant of the Most-favoured Nation Status by Pakistan to India. Thus, the pipeline project was placed in the over all context of bilateral economic relations but not be linked to progress on other issues. However, when the prospect for the materialization of the project became bright another factor the US opposition has come to play a role.

US Geo-Politics of Energy

The turning point came when India and Iran along with Pakistan began to seriously consider the construction of the pipeline. The US Secretary of State Condoleezza Rice for the first time publicly aired her concerns about the prospective deal during her visit to New Delhi in March 2005. In order to wean away India from the Project, the US offered "The energy dialogue" to explore the avenues of cooperation to meet India's growing energy needs. [10]

It is widely believed that India-US civilian energy deal of July 2005, which was further strengthened following the signing of agreement in New Delhi on 2nd March 2006 by President Bush and Prime Minister Manmohan Singh, is one of the components of this strategy. The suspicion regarding India's intention about its commitment to the project arose when the Indian Prime Minister Manmohan Singh spoke in an interview to the Washington Post during his visit to Washington in July 2005 about the financial obstacles the construction of the pipeline might encounter.

Though India has officially reiterated its position that India is fully interested in this project but confusion still persists due to reports emanating from the US sources that India has given assurance to the US that the project will not materialize. [11]

The US opposes the gas-pipeline deal on several counts:

1. In the US perception, it would help ease Iran's economic difficulties because of the handsome revenues it would generate. The US is concerned about the bonanza that oil-rich countries, including Iran are reaping due to skyrocketing global oil prices.
2. The pipeline would set a dangerous precedent for other countries to follow as Iran is suitably placed as the natural transit corridor for the transport of Caspian Sea oil and gas. The US has, therefore, gone overboard to draw transit routes for Caspian oil that by-pass Iranian territory. The Prime example of this approach has been the construction of the Baku-Ceyhan oil pipeline. In this case, the US made an extraordinary effort to route the pipeline-towards the Turkish port of Ceyhan, so the Iranian territory was avoided. In this politically driven deal, the companies involved had to spend million in extra costs to construct the pipeline through unfriendly terrain and conflict prone zones. [12]
3. Another important reason of the US opposition is that the pipeline would help anchor friendly ties among Iran, Pakistan and India. This would greatly undermine US Strategic leverage with India and Pakistan against Iran in the future.
4. The fourth and most important reason of the US opposition is that it considers Iran and impediment in its geo-strategic design to maintain its domination over the Gulf region. Despite very critical cooperation extended by Iran in Afghanistan and to some extent in case of Iraq, the US is now training its guns on Iran. After destroying Iraq, it has now turned its attention towards Iran: the second most important country in what President Bush calls "the axis of evil". [13] So it is now bent upon dubbing Iran as the

enemy of peace, threat to the security and stability of not only to the Gulf region but even beyond that (to Israel which is the creation of the West and continues to get full backing from US) and a country which does not respect the will of the "international community" and therefore need to be punished. The agenda and method adopted in the case of Iraq is now being repeated in case of Iran (so the controversy over nuclear issue, etc.), which is however, beyond the scope of the present paper.

Prospects

Since the US expressed its strong opposition against the pipeline project, it has become a matter of great debate in India.

Though India has reiterated time and again its full commitment to the successful completion of the pipeline project, India's vote in favour of the US and EU-3 backed resolution at the International Atomic Energy Agency (IAEA) in Vienna in September 2005 [14] and February 2006 over the alleged nuclear weapon programme of Iran and the deal between the US and India over civilian nuclear cooperation has polarized the opinion in India.

A very vigorous debate is going on various nuances of this issue. India tried to delink both the issues—India's vote in Vienna and civilian nuclear deal with the US. India maintained the deal with the US on the nuclear cooperation as part of its long-term strategy of energy security.

However, regarding India's seriousness to the commitment of the gas pipeline, Indian officials refer to the Prime Minister's speech of August 15 to buttress their argument that India is still interested in the project. Referring to the on going discussion on the gas pipeline from Iran to India via Pakistan, the Prime Minister Dr. Manmohan Singh said in his speech on Independence Day "Once this is completed, we will be able to address a major constraint affecting our economy". [15] Manmohan Singh conveyed the fullest support of the Indian

Government to the project when Amanullah Khan Jadoon, Minister of Petroleum and Natural Resources, Pakistan called on him in New Delhi in February 2006. [16]

Many of the issues casting shadow over this important project is becoming gradually clear, more so after the conclusion of Bush's visit to India and Pakistan in the first week of March 2006. India, it seems, is pursuing multiple option to fulfil its steadily growing energy requirements and nuclear energy (through the cooperation of the US) is part of that component in the long term. While explaining the rational for the nuclear deal with the US, Dr. Manmohan Singh urged the members of the parliament to look at it through the larger perspective of energy security. [17] The nuclear deal with the US and statement made by Bush in Delhi regarding the regime change in Iran and other countries has created anxiety and concern.

Responding to the Left parties' concern in this respect, Dr. Singh told Rajya Sabha (Upper House of the Indian Parliament): "I have no hesitation in saying that India is not part of any international effort to regime change in any part of our region." [18] The prospect for this vital project has further brightened following Bush's statement in Pakistan that US has no objection to the said pipeline project. [19] Though India's growing relationship with the US and some recent foreign policy postures of India such as its stand on the Iran nuclear programme has created doubts about its commitment to the IPI project, however, if we closely examine the whole gamut of its actions it becomes clear that India is trying to create wider options of energy security.

Conclusion

The project, which is very vital and has great potential, is bound to be subject of the controversy. However, it is hoped that all the three countries involved in the project would not allow the extraneous consideration to impact upon the project. Since overwhelming stakes spanning from energy, trade to security issues are involved, it is therefore imperative for Iran and India to resist the US pressure and successfully accomplish the completion of the project. This would create interdependence and inter-linkages among the countries of the region and would contribute greatly towards the economic development and prosperity of the region. The project is very significant as a factor to improve Indo-Iran relation. Given the potential and vitality of the project, it is hoped that both the countries would make every possible efforts to implement the project.

End Notes

1. See the Joint Press Statement issued after (SJWG) meeting in New Delhi on 29th December, 2005.
2. Sir John Brown, "The State of the Gas Industry", Middle East Economic Survey, Vol. 43, No. 11, 13th March, 2000, D1-3.
3. Tata Energy Research Institute (TERI), *"India's Energy Sector"*, October 2000.
4. Anthony H. Cordesman, *Energy Developments in the Middle East,* Praeger, Westport, 2004, pp. 187-95; for oil and gas reserves of Iran and also its policy to exploit and develop this resource, see S.D. Muni and Girijesh Pant, *India's Search for Energy Security: Prospects for Cooperation with Extended Neighbourhood*, Rupa & Co. Delhi, 2005, pp. 208-264; Manouchehr Takin, "OPEC and the Expansion of Iran's Oil Production Capacity" *Middle East Economic Survey,* 24th November, 2003, pp. D1-9; Iran: Country Analysis EIA November 2003, on the site, http://www.eia.doe.gov/emu/cabs/iran.html. And also Mehr News Agency, iranexpert.com, 4th January, 2004, on the site: http://www.iranexpert.com/.
5. Muni and Pant, op.cit., pp. 265-267.
6. Muni and Pant, op.cit., pp. 266-278.
7. The price at which the gas is likely to make available is estimated to be at US$ 1.80 per million metric British thermal units (mm Btu) delivered to the Indian border. This is almost half the price of imported natural gas, for which specific projects in India are currently in hand. See R.K. Pachauri. "The pipeline of Peace - What could also flow through the India-Iran pipeline: improved Indo-Pak Relations" *Indian Express*, New Delhi, 21st

January, 2003.

8. Mani Shanker Aiyar, former Indian Petroleum and Natural Gas Minister, proposed the formation of an Asian Grid. He favoured a synergy and cooperation in place of contention among Asian buyers and producers of Energy.
9. *The Hindu*, 11th February, 2005.
10. *The Hindu*, 17th March, 2005.
11. *The Hindu*, 6th December, 2005.
12. For the geopolitics of the oil, see Edward L. Morse and James Richard, "The Battle for Energy Dominance", *Foreign Affairs*, March/April 2002, pp. 16-13; John V. Mitchel, "Oil and the Wars", *The World Today,* Vol. 58, No. 1, January 2002, pp. 5-6 and Talmiz Ahmad, "Geopolitics of Oil", Seminar, 555, November 2005, pp. 19-55.
13. George W. Bush, State of the Union Address, 29th January 2002, see ww.whitehouse.gov/new/releases/2002/01/2002129/11/html.
14. Though differences have cropped up between New Delhi and Tehran over India's vote against Iran at Veinna and even there was speculation over the US$ 21 billion LNG deal being called off but both sides tried to contain the fall out from this. Ali Larijani, Secretary of the Supreme national Security Council (SNSC) of Iran is reported to have said: "we did not expect India to do so. [but] I believe the friends should not be judged by a single action. Iran enjoys friendly relations with India". See the Press Release issued by the Embassy of the Islamic Republic of Iran in New Delhi *in the Hindu,* 29th September 2005. K. Natwar Singh then India's Foreign Minister paid a visit to Tehran to smoothen the ties.
15. *The Hindu*, 16th August, 2005.
16. The Joint Press Statement issued after the meeting between Amanullah Khan Jadoon, Minister of Petroleum and Natural Resources, Pakistan and Murli Deora, Minister of Petroleum and Natural Gas, India in New Delhi on 17-18 February 2005.
17. *The Asian Age*, 8th March, 2006.
18. *The Asian Age*, 7th March, 2006; *The Hindu*, 7th March, 2006.
19. *The Hindu*, 5th March, 2006 His nod for the IPI project should seen in the context that while singing the civilian nuclear deal with India, he refused to extend same benefit to Pakistan.

4

Non-resident Indian Entrepreneurs in Gulf Countries

Prakash C. Jain

This paper seeks to present a sociological profile of non-resident Indian (NRI) entrepreneurs in the Gulf region, particularly in the United Arab Emirates, Bahrain, Oman and Kuwait. It focuses on the socio-cultural and regional background of such entrepreneurs, their business profiles, their motivations for migration to the Gulf countries, and more importantly, their role in India's development programme.

India has had trade and cultural relations with the Persian Gulf region since antiquity. However, there is evidence of Indian settlement in the region only since the sixteenth century. Small communities of Indian traders called *Baniyas* existed in present-day Iraq, Oman, Yemen and Saudi Arabia in the seventeenth and eighteenth centuries. When the region came under British influence in the nineteenth century, Indian merchant communities flourished in a number of towns in the Gulf countries. Indians served as bankers, importers and exporters, customs farmers, agents for local merchants, government contractors, financiers, etc.

All these merchant communities however dwindled after the Second World War and more decisively after the independence of the Gulf countries. At the same time, the emergence of the Gulf countries as oil-producing and exporting economies and the consequent demand for labour changed the size and complexion of the Indian and other expatriate communities in the region. With the increase in oil prices in the mid-seventies, Indians began to migrate in large numbers into the Gulf countries for a variety of jobs, and the upward trend has continued since then.

Whereas we know reasonably well about three million or so expatriate Indian labourers working in the Gulf countries [1], who mostly originate from Kerala and other South Indian states and are mostly employed as skilled and semi-skilled workers in construction industry and utility, maintenance, office and paramedical services, our knowledge of the Indian entrepreneurs living and working in the Gulf countries is only superficial. We do not know for sure what is their social, economic ethnic and regional background, what kinds of business and profession they are engaged in, what is their social life like, what perceptions they have of India, and what they wish to do for its. It is to seek answers to some of these questions that the present study is proposed.

Extensive literature review done by this author in connection with his research work on Overseas Indians suggest that there is a definite lack of any systematic study on Indian migrants in West Asia. Books on the colonial West Asian history generally refer to the Indian traders' presence and their commercial activities in the region but no detailed studies have been done on them. More or less similar is the fate in this respect of the contemporary non-resident Indian entrepreneurs in the Gulf area. Hence, this brief exploratory study.

A Methodological Note

The article is based on secondary sources newspaper, and magazine inputs, website information etc. As would be evident from the references given at the end of the piece this article would not have been possible without the special issue of *The Khaleej Times* in which about a dozen prominent non-resident Indian entrepreneurs were profiled by various journalists. I am thankful to Mr. B.N. Sarkar and his wife in Abu Dhabi who were kind enough to share a copy of the newsmagazine with me. Another source of information on NRIs in Gulf countries is *International Indians,* a glossy magazine published from

Dubai. It must be pointed out here that due to the diversity of sources there is no uniformity in quality as well as the size of the database regarding the NRI entrepreneurs.

Conceptual Framework

The above mentioned research objectives need to be viewed in the wider perspective of Indian emigration and settlement abroad. In this context five major historical patters of Indian emigration can be pointed out. There are: (i) indentured labour emigration to Guyana, Trinidad, Surinam, Surinam, South Africa, Mauritius and Fiji; (ii) *Kangani or Maistry* emigration of Burma, Malaysia and Sri Lanka; (iii) free or passage emigration of trading castes and classes to East Central and Southern African countries; (iv) Brain drain or emigration of highly trained manpower to Europe, North America, Oceania and other parts of the world; and (v) labour emigration to West Asia, including the Persian Gulf countries whereas the first three patterns of emigration were the results of British colonialism in India, the last two patterns represent the post-colonial development in India.[2]

One important feature of India emigration since the late nineteenth century has been the migration of traders and entrepreneurs to various parts of the world. At times they emigrated on their own as in the case of Eastern and Southern African countries, but mostly they followed or accompanied the emigrating Indian labourers and others. The Gulf countries are no exception. Studies suggest that entrepreneurship among overseas Indians is as much caste and/or community-bound phenomenon as in India itself. It is likely that hereditary occupational specialization which is one of the central features of the traditional Indian caste system greatly helps in acquiring and using the entrepreneurial skills. As such perhaps the family plays an important role in these matters.

Bahrain

Among the most successful Indian entrepreneurs in

Bahrain two names figure prominently: a toy seller turned hotel baron Mohammed Dadabhai and an international banker Iqbal Mamdani. Their success stories are briefly narrated below.

Mohammed Dadabhai: Mohammed Dadabhai and his Dadabhai group of companies epitomize the Indian success story. Mohammad Dadabhai, 61 who migrated to Bahrain at the age of 4 and whose father Ahmedali Dadabhai migrated to Bahrain in 1925 from the princely State of Dungarpur in Rajasthan. Senior Dadabhai initially hawked *samosas* and later owned a small toy shop in Manama. As a young man Mohammed sold toys after school on the pavement outside his father's shop subsequently he got into construction and tourism business. By 1998, the Dadabhai Group owned six blocks of service apartments with 275 luxury flats and two four-star hotels, with a third under construction. Apart from these, Dadabhai Group also ran the Hawar Island retreat of the Amir. [3] Dadabhai Group employs about 900 workers. With an initial investment of over two million dollars the group has set up an institute for training Bahrainis in hotel management and catering. Dadabhais hold Bahraini passports. Mohammed Dadabhai is married to a Japanese with three sons and a grandson. [4]

Iqbal Mamdani: An international banker, Iqbal Mamdani is the founder of Bahrain-based TAIB Bank. Currently, he is vice-chairman and CEO; Mandani comes from a family of entrepreneurs that immigrated to East Africa in the early twentieth century. He studied Economics and Japanese language at Tokyo University and earned his masters degree from the University of California at Berkeley. After a brief stint at the United Nations Development Programme he joined his family business in Uganda. The expulsion of about 150,000 Indians from Uganda by Idi Amin forced the mandanis to move to the US where Iqbal Mamdani joined the American Express bank as head of its Japanese division in New York. [5]

In 1974, Iqbal Mamdani was sent to Bahrain to head

American Express Bank's Middle East operations. In 1979, he founded the TAIB Bank with an initial capital of US$ 10 million. Today, the Bank's worth is more than US$ 100 million. It has operations in India, Kazakhstan, Turkey, Kenya, Uganda, Tanzania, the UK and the US.

Kuwait

Lalit K. Malhotra: Mr. Lalit K. Malhotra is one of the few Indians who consider Kuwait as their first home. His father went to Kuwait in 1946, started a popular restaurant, diversified into wholesale and distribution Mr. Malhotra's entire family lives in Kuwait. His brothers run a ₹ 100 crore family business in Kuwait, representing leading multinationals such as SmithKline Beecham, Brook Bond and Indian companies like Dabur. They are the single largest importers of Indian tea into Kuwait, enjoying nearly 60 percent of market share. Mr. Malhotra has himself spent 20 years in Kuwait, till he came back to India in the year 1984. Now Mr. Malhotra owns and runs the Hotel Best Western Surya in South Delhi and Hotel Mela Plaza in Ghaziabad. But he returns home to Kuwait very often, to visit his family and friends. [6]

In the Iraqi invasion of Kuwait in 1990, the Malhotra's godowns were looted by the Iraqi army in which he lost more than three-four million Dnars worth of stocks, that translates to at least ₹ 50 crore? During the Gulf War and the Iraqi occupation, he pressed his hotels into service for what he calls duty? In New Delhi, he organized the Kuwait Non-Resident Forum which took out protest marches against the invasion and in support of Kuwait.

Oman

Khimji Ramdas: Established in 1870, Khimji Ramdas is a name synonymous with a wide range of products and services in Oman. The group holds services for many internationally known companies dealing in household goods, foodstuff, electrical and engineering equipments, building materials, furniture and shipping, sports and leisure goods. Besides these, Khimji Ramdas has also diversified into manufacturing paints and processing selective consumer products. [7]

Kanaksi Gokaldas Khimji: The doyen of business houses in Oman, Kanaksi Gokaldas Khimji is a descendant of Thackeersey and Ramdas who started trading foodstuff between India and Oman some 300 years ago and also of Khimji who had settled in Oman over 160 years back. Son of Rai Bahalur Gokaldas Khimji, Kanasksi not only presides over a group of companies with diverse business but also is a great philanthropist. He was instrumental in revitalising the Hindu Mahajan Association, acquiring land for a temple complex and founding an Indian Schools at Mattrah and its branch at Sohar. Kanakshi Khimji was the founder president of the Oman Cricket Association which presently has more than 50 teams as its members. Thanks to him, Republic Day Cricket Match held on 26th January every year is a much awaited event in Oman.

Through Khimji Ramdas Trust and Gokuldas Khimji Trust, a girls school and a hostel, an auditorium and a well-equipped hospital are run by the family at Mandavi, Gujarat. During the droughts of late 1970s and again at the time of recent earth quack in Gujarat Khimji family did their utmost to help relieve the suffering of the people in India. A citizen of Oman, he was bestowed with the honorary title of the Sheikh of the Indian Hindu Community by the Government of Oman, perhaps the first person to get such an honour anywhere in the Gulf. [8] Kanaksi Khimji was also the first Gulf NRI to have been awarded the Prawasi Bhartiya Samman by the Government of India in January 2003.

United Arab Emirates

There are hundred of Indian entrepreneurs in the UAE. However, only about a dozen case studies of well-known ones are presented here. The main consideration has been the availability of documented information about them. The listing of Indian entrepreneurs is done here in alphabetical order.

Yousaf Ali: EMKE Group, established in 1966, is a group of concerns with diversified activities manly in the consumer line focusing on the department store and supermarket business, with import, export and re-export of all kinds of garments, computer software and jewellery. The EMKE group globally employs more than 6,000 workers. With its corporate office based in Abu Dhabi, the group is headed by its managing director Yousaf Ali, a Business Management graduate. The Group has nine supermarkets and department stores throughout the Emirates.

The group has a garment division with two large-scale manufacturing factories one in the United Arab Emirates and the other situated at Mombassa in Kenya, employing more than 1,200 skilled workers. This division with its head office in Abu Dhabi, manufactures and exports all type of garments including high fashion designs. With its own quality control and buying houses in Barcelona, Nachang, China, and Jakarta, these offices also facilitate sourcing of garments and other consumer items for the department store chain.

Yousaf Ali was instrumental in realizing the dream of building the Cochin International Airport in May 1999, which was dedicated to the nation by the then President of India K.R. Narayanan. ₹ 3.25 billion project, the Cochin International Airport at Nedumbassery was initiated in 1999 with the formation of a company spearheaded by Yousaf Ali and a dedicated band of non-resident Keralites (NRKs) to back him in the Odyssey Contributions from Indians Overseas, mainly NRKs from as many as 27 countries have gone into building the airport [9] Yousaf Ali is a member of the Board of Directors of the CIAL.

Joy Alukkas: The Alukkas have a family business in Kerala. The first venture of internationtising it begun in 1987 resulting in the Alukkas gold empire within less than a decade. Joy Alukkas presently own about a dozen gold jewellery outlets in the UAE and one each in Bahrain, Doha and Muscat. An exclusive diamond jewellery shop in Dubai is also on the cards. [10] Now Alukkas is also a well-known name in India.

Bhatia Brothers: The Bhatia family has been in the Gulf region for over five generations. The Bhatia Group which started doing business in the early 1950s is spread over in the fields of engineering services and supplies, hotels and tourism, and general trading and services. Ajay Bhatia who was born and brought up in Dubai is the Chairman of the Bhatia Brothers Group. He is also the president of the Indian Association Dubai, perhaps one of the most active socio-culture organizations in the Gulf countries. [11]

Ram Buxani: A Prominent businessman and champion of NRI causes, Mr. Ram Buxani has made Dubai his home for over 40 years. He is the director of ITL Cosmos and since 1987 founder and chairman of the Overseas Indians Economic Forum (OIEF). OIEF has been an important platform for highlighting the grievances of the NRIs. Mr. Buxani believes in providing strong legal and diplomatic support and protection to PIOs and NRIs. He favours privatization of higher education in India and its professional management. The quality Indian education, he believes, is not only a prerequisite of economic liberalization but would also meet the needs of Gulf NRI children, who have to go to Europe and America for getting higher education.

Among his other important suggestions mention must be made of expanding the PIO card facilities to the Gulf NRIs, elimination or reduction of airport tax in the case of Gulf going Indians (about 70 percent of whom are blue or white collar workers), creation of free port in Goa and parliamentary representation to NRIs. [12] Ram Buxani also founded *Asian Sindhi*, a cultural group that has brought in a Sindhi Renaissance in India itself. He is also the author of memoirs which had been weekly serialized in the Sharjah-based newspaper *The Gulf Today*. These memoirs have recently been published as a book under the title *Taking the High Road*.

Manu and Vidya Chhabria: Founder and former Chairman of the Dubai based Jumbo Electronics, late Manohar

(Manu) Chhabria was perhaps the most successful NRI businessman around the world. Founded in 1974, the company today is worth over US$ 20 billion and is located in Alsalam Towers in Dubai. Apart from Jumbo Electronics, his group-Jumbo International Holdings Limited, comprises a host of companies maintaining their presence across the globe employing more than twenty thousand people. These include the Supra Corporation based in Tokyo, Shaw Wallace and company limited, and Dunlop India. Jumbo Electronics represent twenty top international brands in the UAE including Sony, Supra, Motorola, Brother, Casio, Electrolux, Ricoh, Oki and others. In 1999, there were 16 outlets of the Jumbo in the UAE with a planned addition of a dozen more in the near future. Expansion work was also on the cards in other Gulf countries. [13]

Following Manu Chhabria's death in April 2002, his wife Vidya Chhabria has been successfully looking after the business of tyre retreading under the company, Bandag. In 1997, they put up another plant at the cost of US$ 5 million for manufacturing automobile batteries. There is also a joint venture with Exide of USA known as Exide Al Dobowi. This plant is also located in Jebel Ali free zone. They also own a three star hotel in Vijayawada and an automotive battery manufacturing plant in Ahmedabad. [14]

Khimchand N. Khiara: Shri K.N. Khiara (known as Chacha) was born on February 2, 1925 at Thatta (Sind). After completing his secondary school education he moved to D.J. Sind College in Karachi to get Arts education. Shri Khiara is one of the old timers Thattai in Dubai, having completed 47 years. He came to Dubai at the age of 19 years to join the family firm M/s Narsingdas Naraindas dealing in textiles, foodstuffs, building materials and also acting as a confirming house.

Chacha has seen a lot of changes in Dubai from sandy roas, donkey and camel as the main mode of transport between Dubai and Sharjah, in those days, to a most modern city today with all kinds of comforts.

In addition to concentrating on his business activities, Shri K.N. Khiara has also contributed his time toward several social activities as shown below:

- Remained Chairman of the Indian Association, Dubai for two terms.
- Served the Indian Merchants Community Dubai for three years in the capacity of Honorary Chairman.
- Remained the Honorary Secretary of the Indian High School, Dubai for 18 years and later on the Honorary Chairman for a period of 4 years. [15]

Thumbay Moideen: Thumbay Moideen is the President and founder of the Gulf Medical College in Ajman which was opened in 1998 with the backing and support of the ruling family of Ajman and the cooperation of the Ministry of Higher Education in the UAE. The college caters to the need of about 100 students annually of which about 60 percent students are nationals and Arabs, mainly girls. The college functions within the parameters of Islamic environment with separate facilities for practicals and segregation in the lecture halls.

A graduate from Mangalore, Moideen hails from a business family which is involved in timber, logging, manufacture and health care apart from education including a medical college. Moideen and his family also own Mohiddeen Wood Works and a steel mill Emirates Technocast in the UAE. [16]

K. Muraleedharan: A graduate in Commerce from Kerala University, Mr. K. Muraleedharan joined K.M. Brothers, Dubai as an accountant in 1975 at the beginning of his carrier overseas. Subsequently, he was responsible for opening a branch in Muscat and later on another in Abu Dhabi. The stupendous success of the Abu Dhabi Branch operation led the K.M. Brothers management to induct him as managing partner of the Company in 1992—a role he successfully played until 2002. [17]

Meanwhile, Mr. Murleedharan had set up an industrial

institutional catering establishment *Southern Food and Catering Services* as an independent venture in 1986. SFCS (as this operation is now called, caters to several large oil field industrial and construction camps. Each day, SFCS caters to more than 3,500 people and serves around 10,000 meals per day, across 14 locations. SFCF was awarded he coveted ISO 9001 certification in 1999. The Group today employs more than 1,000 employees.

Foreseeing the opportunity in the hospitality industry and quick service restaurants (QSR) a Master Franchise Agreement was entered into, with Fast Food Systems (UK), to set up a chain of Southern Fried Chicken outlets, in 1978. Today, SFC Group has 20 Southern Fried Chicken outlets over the length and breath of the UAE and in India. Abu Dhabi-based *49ers The God Rush,* a themed wild-west night-club and steak-house spread over an area of 6,500 sq. ft. and opened in 1996 is another *success* story of the Group. This prompted the Group to start an up-market Indian restaurant—*The India Palace Restaurant* in Abu Dhabi in 1997 and another in Dubai in 2001 that caters to the affluent local and expatriate population.

Realizing the need of Information Technology to support the Groups expanding operations, Oceanic Technologies was set-up in 2000, to cater to the internal needs of the Group and also provide software and hardware service to other organisations. As part of the diversification plan of the Group into restaurant, leisure and hotels, the Group had purchased a 4-star hotel property building on Al Riqqa Street in the heart of Dubai. The hotel property consist of 130 rooms, suites, 4 F&B outlets with bar and entertainment facilities, swimming pool etc.

In spite of the hectic pace of progress, Mr. Murleedharan has not overlooked India. *Southern Fun City,* a leisure and theme park in Tiruvananthaouram (Kerala), set up in association with the Department of Tourism, Government of Kerala, has all unique features and sophisticated facilities of a most modern theme park. He also owns the *Mid East Couriers* in Kerala that provides a link with Emirates Postal services. Mr. Murleedharan holds directorships in Kerala Institute of Medical Sciences (KIMS), Great India Aviation Service, and Companie De B.M.R. He also owns and manages two educational institutions: N.S.V. Vocational Higher Secondary School, and Chaitnya Nursery and Primary School. Mr. Murleedharan is the author Trustee, Founder Chairman and current Chairman of *Vidya International Charitable Trust* established in 2000. With over 1,000 non-resident Indians trustees, VIDYA was established with a view to bring quality education in the emerging fields of science, technology and the other related areas. The vision of this unique trust is to provide a state of the art, higher education opportunity to the younger generation in India, with special focus on financial backward students. Under the Trust, a world class I.T. Institute and Vidya Academy of Science and Technology (VAST), an A.I.C.T.E. approved Engineering College had started functioning in 2003.

Maganmal J. Pancholia: Maganmal J. Pancholia is a leading Indian businessman of Dubai and chairman of the Arabian Trading Agency, an apex multinational company that has been into a wide variety of business such as textile, gold, electronics, watches, banking and currency exchange etc. Residing in Dubai for over six decades now, Mr. Pancholia has seen the Emirate grow and prosper from a tiny village to a cosmopolitan city in which has own contribution is quite significant. A Gandhian by nature he has also been deeply involved in the community affairs of the Indian expatriates in general and the Sindhi in particular.

Mr. Pancholias achievements are legion. He was nominated by the former rulers of Dubai, Sheikh Rashid bin Saeed Al Maktoum as the first Indian member of the Dubai Chamber of Commerce (1965-80); he founded the Indian High School of Dubai (1961); he was named on the Al Maktoum Hospital Board by British Political Agent as a representative of the Indian community (1965-80); he was twice President of the

Indian Association (1960-68 and 1988-92); he introduced electricity to Dubai (1957) even before the government started its own four years later and is a founder trustee and life member of the Indian Sports Club since 1965.

Bharathkumar J. Shah: Mr. Bharatkumar J. Shah is the Chairman of Al Mustaneer Trading Co. LLC, Dubai, UAE with business associates in Saudi Arabia and Yemen. The business activities cover a wide spectrum including international trade especially in sanitary ware, building materials, exiles, sundries and building maintenance.

Mr. Shah, an NRI for over 55 year, has got a very vast experience. Sine 1948, he was in Aden and then migrated to Saudi Arabia in 1971. Later in 1983, he shifted his headquarters in Dubai, the re-export hub of the Middle East. Because of his vast experience and business contacts, he has been able to introduce quite a member of Indian companies and products thereof in this part of the world. Mr. Shah has authentic knowledge on exports from India to the Middle East. He is the living encyclopaedia on export trade.

Having lived for so many years in Yemen and Saudi Arabia, Mr. Shah has very deep understanding of Arab culture. Also Mr. Shah and Mrs. Shah have very strong command on Arabic language and speaks Arabic like the children of the soil.

Mr. Shah is the founder member of the executive committee of the Overseas Indians Economics Forum, Dubai. He is also the Chairman of NRI Forum for Indian Business Council (IBC), Dubai. He is the founder of *Gujarati Samaj* in Dubai and also a Vice-President (International) of *Gujarati Vishwa Samaj* being operated from Ahmedabad under the patronage of Chief Minister of Gujarat State.

Mr. Shah is the most out-spoken and vocal speaker on NRI matters and Indian community in Dubai. In the capacity as chief of the various committees on NRI matters, he has taken up number of difficult and important issues pertaining to overseas Indians with the Government of India and have been successful in getting positive results on many issues. He has also attended and/or addressed many Seminars on NRI matters as well as export trade from India to the West Asia.

Mr. and Mrs. Shah are social workers of Gandhian style and spend most of their time in the social service. His friends often address to him as Father Theresa of the Middle East. [18]

B.R. Shetty: A pioneer in providing modern medical services and supplies to the Gulf region, NRI entrepreneur and businessman, B.R. Shetty is the vice chairman and managing director of the New Medical Centre Group of Companies. Besides the flagship New Medical Centre Hospital, providing state-of the art, comprehensive medical facilities under one roof, the group today his diversified into numerous other business such as trading in pharmaceuticals, consumer cosmetics, medical and scientific equipment, foodstuff, electronics and telecommunication, heavy earth moving equipment and advertising and public relations.

The financial division of the group UAE Exchange Centre is the largest exchange house in West Asia with nine branches in the Emirates and two associate companies in Oman and Kuwait. The centre has draft drawing arrangements with over 40 correspondent banks all over the world. It is also a member of SWIFT, an electronic money transfer network.

The cause of India and non-resident Indians has always been close to his heart. He is the chairman of the Board of Governors of the Abu Dhabi Indian School and the founder-patron of the *Karnataka Sangha* in Abu Dhabi which regularly meets to celebrate festive days in Karnataka. He is also the founder-president of the Indian Pharmacists Association. He has assisted the Indian Ladies Association and the Special Care Centre that it runs. He has hosted several charitable projects in India, including school organizations, centres for handicapped and religious institutions. Mr. Shetty's generosity has won considerable appreciation. A case in point is the praise he received from the Pakistani community when he offered a sum of half a million rupees to cricketer Imran Khan's fund-raising campaign to build the cancer hospital. [19]

Sunny Varkey: UAE-based Sunny Varkey is an educational entrepreneur par excellence. Currently chairman of the Varkey Group, he started his career as a banker in Dubai in the 1970s and since 1980 has turned his parents run Our Own English High School venture into a multi-million dollar international enterprise. From just 720 students in 1980, the Varkey Group today has eighteen schools, with more than 30,000 students from around sixty nationalities and employs over 3,000 people. More schools are slated to open in the UAE, Middle East, USA, Africa and the UK in the next few years [20] Quality and excellence are the twin philosophies of the Varkey Group.

Besides education, Varkey Group is also involved in health care. A very well-equipped 120-bed Welcare Hospital in Dubai is another major enterprise of the Group in this field, besides the Emirates Diagnostic Centre at Satwa which treats more than 20,000 patients every year. [21]

In India, the Varkey Group runs the Centre for Help Trust which supports housing projects and provides education for the underprivileged in the southern state of Kerala, from where the Varkey family hails. Cheshire home for handicapped, Oxfam Relief Organisation and the late Mother Teresa Missionaries of Charities, all represent areas of humanitarian interest of the Varkey Group [22]

Abdul Wahab P.V.: A prominent NRI industrialist of over three decades standing with business establishments under the Bridgewary banner in the Middle East, Mr. Abdul Wahab is currently a Member of Group of Companies with operations across South rooms across the land and seas did not deter Mr. Wahab from addressing the common mans problems at large. As Chairman, Advisory Committee KMCC UAE Chapter, he has day-to-day involvement with the largest grass root organization of India expatriates in the Middle East.

As a man with clear perception of life and understanding the importance of value based quality education in grooming tomorrows global citizens, Mr. Wahab founded Peevees Public

School and Peevees Model School at Nilambur, which are non-profit institutions of paramount concern. The Kerala Legislative Assembly elected him unopposed as a Member of Parliament (Rajya Sabha) in 2004 a fitting recognition of the contributions Mr. Wahab has made to the Keralite society at large and NRIs in particular. God fearing and caringly possessive about his dear and near, Mr. Wahab is married to Ms. Yasmine and has four sons. In Kerala, Mr. Wahab is involved in a wide variety of social welfare activities. He has received numerous awards including the one in 2003 for outstanding business achievements by an Overseas Keralite at the House of Commons, England. [23]

Conclusion

The case studies presented here amply highlight the entrepreneurial spirit and skills of the Gulf NRIs. Our findings suggest that the United Arab Emirates and particularly Dubai hosts the largest number of Indian entrepreneurs. Most of them are Sindhis, Gujaratis or Keralites; some of them are settled in the Gulf for over 50 years and have diversified businesses. Many of them are actively involved in the socio-cultural life of the diaspora community. Most of them have made significant contributions in the developmental and welfare programmes in provinces of their origin in India. Theoretically speaking, two major hypotheses appear to be validated from our preliminary study: (i) Indian entrepreneurship in the Gulf countries is largely a caste and/or community-bound phenomenon mainly a transplant of the traditional entrepreneurship from India, and (ii) Diaspora-motherland linkage is strong among the Gulf-based Indian entrepreneurs.

End Notes

1. Prakash C. Jain, "An Incipient Diaspora: Indians in the Persian Gulf Region", in Bhikhu Parekh et al. (eds.) *Culture and Economy in the Indian Diaspora,* Routledge, London, 2003. See also Prakash C. Jain, *Indians in Oman*, working paper Gulf Studies Programme, JNU, New Delhi, 2003 and *Indians in the*

United Arab Emirates, working paper, Gulf Studies Programme, JNU, New Delhi, 2004.

2. Prakash C. Jan, "Indians Abroad: A Current Population Estimate", *Economic and Political Weekly,* 1982, Vol. 17, No. 8, pp. 299-304. Also Prakash C. Jain, "Emigration and Settle of Indians Abroad", *Sociological Bulletin*, 1989, Vol. 31, No. 1, pp. 155-68 and Prakash C. Jain, "Indian Diaspora: An Overview", *Think India,* 2003, Vol. 6, No. 1, pp. 8-17.
3. Mohini Kent, "Little India in the Gulf", *The Express Magazine*, New Delhi, 25th January, 1998. See also Archie D. Cruz, *How Toy Seller Turned Hotel Baron.*
4. Isa Mubarak, *Indian Family Builds top Business Group in Bahrain.*
5. Ibid.
6. *Kuwait News,* 1(2), 1993, p. 6.
7. Advertisement on the back cover of the Souvenir Magazine published on the occasion of the *Golden Jubilee Celebrations of the Indian School at Muttrah and Sohar,* Hindu Mahajan Association, Muscat, November 1991.
8. Anonymous, "Shri Kanaksi Gokaldas Khimji: Man of Many Accomplishments", *Souvenir Magazine,* Ibid.
9. N. Srinivasan, "Yousaf Ali: Flying High", *Khaleej Times Special Report,* 15th August, 1999, p. 12.
10. Leena Mathew, "Joy Alukkas: All that Glitters", *Khaleej Times Special Report,* 15th August 1999, p. 19.
11. Kay Khanna, "What is the Lure of the Arabian Gulf", *The International Indian* (Dubai), 1998, p. 12.
12. Kum Kum Ramchandani, "Ram Buxani: Mr. NRI", *Khaleej Times Special Report,* 15th August 1999, p. 10.
13. Issac John, "Manu Chhabria: Jumbo Heights", *Khaleej Times Special Report,* 15th August 1999, p. 8.
14. Ali Ishrati, "Surendra Singh Kanhari: Treading New Ground", *Khaleej Times Special Report,* 15th August 1999, p. 22.
15. Reproduced with minor changes from *The Mercantile Hindu Community of Thatta (Sind), Dubai News Letter,* 28th March, 1991.
16. Sudha Chandran, "Setting Standards in Education", *The Gulf Today,* Sharjah, 15-21 December, 2000, pp. 5-53; See also Sudha Chandran, "A Quiet Gentleman", Ibid, pp. 54-55.
17. The information about Mr. Murleedharan and his entrepreneurial

activities is based on a personal interview with him in Abu Dhabi and his bio-data.

18. This is Mr. Shahs' profile given to me in Dubai on 1st May, 2001. It is reproduced here with minor editing.
19. "New Medical Centre Group: Sterling Performance at the Turn of the Century", *Khaleej Times Special Report,* 15th August 1977, p. 147; see also Rajeev Nair, "B.R. Shetty: India Shaped his Values; the UAE Festered his Dreams", *The International Indian* (Dubai), November-December 2000, pp. 30-34.
20. Leena Mathew, "Sunny Varkey: Educational Entrepreneur", *Khaleej Times Special Report,* 15th August, 1999, p. 18.
21. Rajeev Nair, "Welcare: Ethical Medicine and Uncompromising Standards", *The International Indian,* 1998, Vol. 6, No. 3, pp. 22-26.
22. Ibid., p. 22.
23. The information about Mr. Abdul Wahab is based on personal interview with him in Delhi and his website profile.

5

Economic and Social Consequences of Indian Emigration to West Asia

Anisur Rahman

The main aim of this paper is to assess the economic and social consequences of Indian emigration to West Asia, especially the Gulf region. To fully understand these two dimensions, an effort is made to trace the historical presence of the Indian community in West Asian region which has always been strategically significant for India for a variety of reasons. An attempt is also made to examine the annual trends of Indian labour outflow as well as the volume of Indian emigrants present in this region during the last three decades. How has it affected the place of origins as well as the place of destinations will be dealt within this paper? In what way remittances are benefiting to India will also to be discussed. What is the overall impact of the Gulf migration will be given due attention in this paper. Finally, the working and living conditions of emigrant workers in the host countries will also be examined with emigrant's demands and expectations from India government. What could be the possible solutions on the parts of Indian government? Some suggestions are given in this regard.

Although, India has had trade and cultural relations with West Asian region especially to the Gulf since ancient times, but Indian settlement in this region is established only since the sixteenth century. Small communities of Indian traders namely Baniyans were present in contemporary Iraq, Iran, Oman, Yemen and Saudi Arabia in the seventeenth and eighteenth centuries. When the region came under British influence in the nineteenth century, Indian merchant communities flourished in a number of towns in these countries. Indians served as bankers, importers and exporters, customs, farmers, agents for local merchants, government contractors, and financiers, etc.

The Indians settled in this region also imported Indian good and redistributed them throughout the Arabian Peninsula. Before 1970, there were 3,000 Indian merchant families in Dubai which was the major trade centre in the region. Bahrain and Oman had some special Indian connections during the British rule in India. They were made British protectorates and were controlled by the Government of India. During that period, Indian merchants were also settled in Bahrain who imported rice, tea, sugar, etc. Indians also began to migrate to work as clerks, technicians and nurses during the 1930s with the development of the Bahrain Petroleum Company. The Indian merchant community had also dominated the economy of Oman even during the nineteenth century.

All these merchant communities however, dwindled after the Second World War and more decisively after the independence of the Gulf countries. But the emergence of the Gulf countries as oil-producing and exporting economies and the consequent demand for labour changed the size and complexion of the Indians and other expatriate communities in the region. With the increase in oil prices in the mid-seventies, Indians began to migrate in large numbers into the Gulf countries for a variety of jobs, and the upward trend has continued since then with some variations. Let us now examine these trends and patterns of Indian emigration.

Trends of Annual Emigration

It was found in 1950s and 1960s that the destination of Indian workers was mainly the United States of America, United Kingdom, Canada and other developed countries. During the mid-seventies, the oil boom in West Asia especially the Gulf countries vastly changed the complexion of emigration. The steep hike in oil prices during 1973-74 and thereafter led to a considerable in crease in the revenue of the oil producing and exporting countries in West Asia region. As a result, development programmes including construction of roads, creation of amenities like schools, hospitals, houses, airports, office and commercial complexes etc. were taken up in a big way. This resulted in spurt in demand for not only highly skilled technical experts but also semi-skilled and unskilled workers. India was well placed to meet these emerging demands.

It was found that out-migration from India was only 4,200 in 1976 and it had increased at a phenomenal rate throughout the late 1970s and it reached a peak level of a more than 2,76,000 in 1981. But it went down slowly until 1984, declined sharply in the mid 1980s and picked up somewhat thereafter and increased steeply in the 1990s, though it started declining once again in the late 1990s This is primarily due to the determined efforts of the Gulf countries to provide job to local population, maintenance of ethnic balance and completion of several projects. It is interesting to point out that the average rate of outflow was almost a quarter of a million workers per annum between 1980 and 1983. This is considered to be the peak period for out migration. It is also found that 1.8 million workers were added to West Asia from India during 1976-87. During 1988-99, about 3.7 million more workers from India were added to the oil exporting countries. It is further observed that about 1.8 million Indian emigrants were further added to the workforce in this region during 2000-2004.

Recent Emigration of Indians

As we know that the maximum Indian emigrants are going to West Asia especially, the Gulf countries like Saudi Arabia, United Arab Emirates, Oman, Kuwait, Bahrain, and Qatar. Out of these, Saudi Arabia, UAE and Kuwait are the major countries in terms of importing maximum migrants from India. Saudi Arabia was at the top followed by the UAE till 2002 but

Saudi Arabia was replaced by the UAE in 2003. It is also noted that more than 50 percent Indian migrants were exported to these two countries. We further observe that there are new destinations that have come into picture at the end of the 20th century. Indians began to migrate to South Asian countries like Singapore from 1998 and Malaysia from 1999. In 2002, about 35,000 Indians migrated to this region (South East Asia). Singapore and Malaysia combined together imported more than 10 percent Indians in 2003 which is not shown in the table. Malaysia alone imported 6.06 percent Indian emigrants in 2004. We now conclude by saying that the places of destinations for Indian migrants are widening day by day. India must make a policy which promotes manpower export not only to the Gulf region but also to other countries which need manpower for their development and growth.

Changing Profile of Emigrants

It was found that majority of the Indian migrants were semi-skilled or unskilled workers. Given the skill composition of migrant workers in West Asia, the contribution of the different labour exporting countries to various categories of migrants were different. In case of India and Pakistan, unskilled workers were 65 percent and 80 percent respectively. As between the three major labour exporting countries of South Asia, there had been a remarkable difference between India on the one hand and Pakistan and Bangladesh on the other. The proportion of the completely unskilled workers was significantly high in case of migrants from India, while Pakistanis and Bangladeshis had, to some extent, possessed some manual skill. Even the state of Kerala, which has the highest literacy rate in the South Asia, sent more unskilled workers to West Asia than those of Pakistan and Bangladesh.

There are, however, some reasons to believe that since 1975 the average skill level of Indian migrants has improved. The unskilled workers are either construction workers or farm labourers and household workers. The category of semi-skilled workers in the construction sector comprises carpenters, masons, steel-fixers, fabricators, fitters, equipment-operators, welders, painters, pluck smothers and bar tenders. Semi-skilled workers in other activities and services include drivers, cleaners, electricians, plumbers, mechanics, air-conditioning mechanics, denters, blacksmiths, tanners, shoemakers, goldsmiths, fishermen, tailors and waiters. The category of white collar workers comprises storekeepers, clerks, typists, salesmen, accountants, secretaries, cashiers and office attendants. The highly skilled personnel are largely of nurses, and it also includes radiologists and laboratory technicians. The category of technical and supervisory personnel includes engineers (with diplomas rather than degree), technical surveyors, computer operators, draftsmen foreman and supervisors.

It was found that in the mid-1980s, unskilled workers comprised about 40 percent of the total labour outflow from India to the West Asian countries, skilled workers accounted for less than 50 percent, while white-collar workers and highly skilled workers made up a little less than 5 percent of them. The outflow of workers engaged in construction activities, when the skilled and unskilled are taken together, declined not only in absolute terms, but also as a proportion of the total out-migration the outflow of skilled workers engaged in non-construction activities also declined in absolute terms but increased relatively because of the greater contraction in total outflow.

In contrast, the absolute levels of labour outflow were sustained for white-collar workers as well as for the high-skilled workers and registered an increase among unskilled workers in non-construction activities, so that the share of each for these categories in total out-migration rose. It is observed that large proportion of the out migration was made up of workers employed in the service sector, so much so that proportion employed in the manufacturing sector was small while that in the agricultural sector was negligible. Since emigration to the West Asian countries is temporary, it would appear to provide an example of international trade in services. Today, the profile of demand for workforce has changed.

It is now less for unskilled and semi-skilled and more for skilled and highly qualified professionals. India must be prepared accordingly as we know that there is no dearth of such manpower in India.

Shift in Originating Regions of Emigrants

It is found that Indian migrants have started going to different parts of the World from every nook and corner of the country. Gulf emigrants are found from almost all Indian states and some states like Kerala, Tamil Nadu, Andhra Pradesh, Maharashtra, Rajasthan Punjab, Uttar Pradesh and Bihar dominate in the process of migration.

These are the states that send a considerable number of migrants abroad every year. Out of these, Kerala, Tamil Nadu and Andhra Pradesh send more than fifty percent migrants from these states.

It was found that in 1970s and 1980s, migration was dominated by Kerala which sent about 50 percent migrants from its state alone. At present, its share has declined to less than 14 percent due to the entry of other Indian states in this arena. Tamil Nadu is now at the top is sending maximum migrants abroad followed by Andhra Pradesh and then Kerala. It is observed that south Indian states are still far ahead in terms of sending more migrants outside the country. It is also observed that significant number of migrants from Northern Indian state like Punjab, U.P. and Bihar are going to this region. U.P. and Bihar together send more than 10 percent of the total Indian emigrants. Thus it was Kerala—now there are many other states.

We now conclude by saying that there are about 4 million Indian expatriates in the Gulf Cooperation Council (GCC) countries. Indians constitute about one-third of the total expatriate population and 10 percent of the total GCC population. The largest number of Indians live in Saudi Arabia followed by the UAE, Oman and Kuwait, There are about 1,00,000 Indians in Yemen who are permanently settled there. Israel has the other permanently settled Indian community in West Asia. Following the creation of Israel in 1948, over 25,000 Indians Jews migrated to Israel until 1948 well settled in their new homeland, Jews of Indian origin today number around 50,000.

Keralites constitute the major group followed by Punjab among Indian immigrant in West Asia. There are about 18 lakh Keralites working in the Gulf countries. The skill composition of the migrant workforce is still dominated by unskilled and semi-skilled workers followed by administrative staff and skilled workers. Currently, the Gulf migrants are a major source of remittances and foreign exchange to India. This is realised by Indian government.

Economic Consequence of Emigration

Apart from Gulf remittances, various incentives schemes for investment in India for the non-resident Indians (NRIs) and the permission to bring gold while returning to the country are the contributing factors responsible for increase in the amount of remittances. The employment of Indian labour workers abroad helps to earn foreign exchange and thereby adds to the foreign exchange reserves in India. There has been an increase in the remittance of foreign exchange resulting in increase in the foreign exchange reserves.

The Gulf money has also improved the income level of the migrant households considerably. This rising income level has directly affected the consumption and investment and saving patterns in migrating areas.

In this situation, the inflow of remittance played a significant role. The benefit of remittance seemed to be distributed in favour of the districts of the state which ranked low with respect to per capita domestic product and the growth of population.

Consumption: Information is available to us about three high migration districts of Kerala, namely, Alleppey, Trichur and Malappuram. All these three districts had a per capita domestic product lower than the state average and Trichur went above the state average in terms of the capita income. It is also found that consumption level was better in the two districts as compared to the average level of per capita consumption for the state as a whole. Malappuram, the third district whose per capita consumption was 9 percent below the state average, was better than that reflected in Mallapuram's per capita domestic product which was 19 percent lower than the state average.

Savings: It is found that Gulf remittances are the major attraction of employment in the Gulf countries which has the possibility of saving a substantial proportion of annual income. This is so because the migrant workers are not seriously affected by the prevailing high cost of living since they are generally entitled to get free housing, food, transportation and medical facilities. The absence of costly items of entertainment such as bars and gambling house and low cost of petrol and several items of consumer durable are also factors which enable migrants to save a substantial proportion of their earnings.

The incentive to save is great particularly among those in the middle and low level occupations since most of them must have bought employment at formidable prices, incurring debt at home, or selling out property and jewellery. Moreover, every Indian migrant worker is well aware of the fact that his employment in the Gulf countries is purely of a temporary nature and his work permit may be cancelled any moment. Above all, an average migrant worker looks for the employment in the Gulf countries as perhaps his only chance to accumulate enough money to purchase lands and construction house, educate his children, marry away his sisters and daughter.

It is generally felt in India, especially among the

government authorities and banking circles that foreign remittances have been increasing at an unprecedented rate. This increase, has however, resulted mainly because of the remittances from the Gulf countries. Since Indians living in other parts of the World remit only a tiny proportion of their savings, the Gulf remittance has affected the income of the migrants' families considerably. Hence, Gulf migration has positive effects.

It is also found that emigrant workers become more skilled while working in this region. They work there with highly sophisticated machine and instrument. There is no brain-drain in case of migration to the Gulf. It may be rather called brain bank because the migrant workers acquire more skills while working in the Gulf. Even after returning from the Gulf, they are the assets to the nation because their services could be utilised for developmental activities in India. It cannot however, be denied that there is an acute shortage of labour at migrating areas due to outflow of labour from there. As a result, agriculture is badly affected. Moreover, it is also observed that there is a price rise due to the inflow of the gold remittance in migrating villages. All people who reside there are adversely affected on account of Gulf money coming into this region. There is a conspicuous consumption amongst emigrants families that too has affected adversely the non-migrants' families.

Social Consequences of Emigration

Gulf Migration has also brought social and psychological effects on migrants' families. A visible change may be noticed in their attitude towards education. There is rising demand for educational facilities by the migrants. An increasingly large proportion of children, particularly the girls are now going to schools and colleges. A large proportion of young men are turning up to training centres for different technical skills. Social mobility has also taken place rapidly. A family which was looked down in the past is now welcomed in social functions. Poverty stricken and desolated villages are suddenly becoming prosperous. A sizable proportion of houseless population is now having own houses. Demand for more schools, health centre and domestic electrification, sanitation and transport facilities are rising at the places of migrants' origin.

Moreover, changes are taking place in the attitude of the Gulf migrants' families towards their customs, habits and life style also. The rise in their social and economic status is gradually resulting in the deprivation of the privileges and power, of certain sections of the society which they had been holding in the past for many decades. This is really a positive development towards the balance of power and social justice. On the other hand, social and psychological implications of migration cannot however be ignored.

The major factors responsible for the social and psychological problems of the migrants are job insecurity, discrimination in wage/salary, isolation from the social function in the countries of employment, lack of opportunities and avenues for entertainment, inabilities on the part of the majority of Indian workers to bring their wives and children to the countries of employment, poor accommodation facilities, unfavourable climatic conditions, restrictions on seeking alternative employment opportunities. It is also said that the new generation of educated Arabs treat the Indians and other Asian migrants with arrogance and contempt. In sum, the problem is of being total outsiders, facing a future full of uncertainties.

It is also found that members of the migrants' families left back home also live in tension ridden lives for a variety of reasons. The problem arises for brothers of migrants left back home because of increasing disparity in income between them. This leads to frustration for left back home brothers. There is a long separation between husbands and wives due to migration and consequently wives suffer from separation of anxieties.

Psychiatrists in Kerala report that the Gulf boom has taken

toll on mental health of the people of emigrant families. Marriages for Gulf migrants are another factor for concern. Workers in Gulf coming on leave, marry in haste, have a quick and short honeymoon and leave their wives with their (husband's) parents for long intervals. The sharing of remittances between their parents and wives becomes another bone of contention. Psychologists also point out that prolonged post-marital separation has led to deviant sexual behaviour by both partners, ending in guilt and tensions. Separation has also fuelled suspicions about the partner's fidelity and several marriages have broken down consequently.

Another psychological problem relates to the children of the migrating families. Mothers are unable to take full control of the children in the absence of their fathers. Psychologists have coined the term "Gulf Syndrome" for all these problems. The Gulf money has brought about drastic change on the demand patterns for consumer goods as well. Cotton clothes are discarded for synthetics, private cars in place of the public conveyance are used for travelling, ready-made food is used instead of kitchen made foods and other extravagance is becoming the status symbol. Thus, the Gulf migration has both positive as well as negative effects.

Emigrants' Conditions in the Host Countries

It is said that the working and living conditions of emigrants are not much satisfactory in the host countries. It is also reported that they are discriminated in many ways. As a result, the rules and regulations for the recruitment of workers in the Gulf region were laid down by the Government of India. The policy of the Indian Government regarding the recruitment of highly qualified experts in such recruitment should be on a government-to-government basis. Semi-skilled and unskilled workers were found to be discriminated in terms of wages and salaries, working conditions, work, security and welfare facilities.

The Indian government also got information about the

miserable working conditions especially from those migrant workers who were recruited by unauthorized agencies that used false passports, visa and work permits. There were also many complaints about high fees charged by these unauthorised agents. In response to these problems, the labour Ministry prepared a draft model agreement for use by migrants and recruiting agents. Foreign employers are required to provide free roundtrip passage, free furnished accommodation commensurate with the category of work, free medical care, free transportation and other benefits. The employment contracts also contain provisions for over time wages, hours of work terminal benefits, compensation for accidents, etc.

In spite of these requirements and provisions however, malpractices and contract violations are continued. After reaching the Gulf, the migrants are found themselves to be discriminated against, despite all these measures taken by the Government of India. It is also reported that a Westerner is paid double the salary of an Asian, even though the Asian is employed in the same capacity. A British reporter employed in the UAE was paid twice the salary of an Indian reporter. The work contract between employers and emigrants are often violated by employers. Persons who were promised the job of an electrician are put to the work of an ordinary unskilled labourer. According to a report published on 25th May, 1983, the Government of India received 274 complaints pertaining to wide variety of subjects including cheating by recruiting agents, repatriation of contracts and poor working and living conditions.

Although the migrants working in the Gulf region are a part of its economy but do not enjoy rights of political or social participation. They live in their own enclaves and cannot obtain citizenship, even property or join trade unions. They have thus restricted social benefits and excluded from participation in the political system. Since labour legislation and social security institutions are not yet fully developed in many countries of the Gulf region, the employment contract, to some extent, depend on honesty and integrity on the part of employers in respect of the terms and conditions of the agreements. Moreover, wage and salary are not determined by the force of demand and supply. The host countries' government can dictate how migrants are to be admitted, what qualifications they must have, how long they can stay, what wage should be paid, what rights and benefits should be provided, and whether they should be exported from Arab countries or not. For all practical purposes, the power to regulate is primarily in the hands of the labour importing countries not of labour exporting countries.

Despite all these limitations and restrictions, Indian migrants rush to the Gulf countries for getting lucrative job and they receive wages which are several times higher than what they might receive in India for similar work in addition to free housing facilities, food and medical care. Workers are able to save large part of their wages income. Since in the Gulf region, opportunities for costly entertainments such as bars and gambling-houses are non-existent. The prices of consumer durables are much lower in the Gulf than in India. Moreover, Indian migrants know that their employment is purely of temporary nature and they are also aware of the constraints of the Indian Government regarding their protection against in the host countries.

Emigrants' Demands and Expectations

It is fully realized that Gulf emigrants are assets to the nation. They are contributing significantly in terms of remittances for economic development of this country. They are also our cultural messengers who carry Indian culture with them in the Gulf countries. While working in the Gulf, they face a number of difficulties to which they expect from Indian Government to sort out their problems. They demand from Indian Government to evolve appropriate policies in order to safeguard their interests. The following measures should be taken in this direction to resolve their problems.

1. First of all, effective measures should be formulated by the Ministry of Labour to prevent exploitation by recruiting agents. There are several unscrupulous agents who exploit the aspiring innocent migrants.
2. It is suggested that there must be an appropriate agency to rightly advise Indian workers about their rights and obligation in the countries where they are working.
3. It is also demanded that Indian Government should set-up a standard labour export agreement in consultation with the Gulf countries regarding minimum wage, fare housing, health care, a weekly day off, a limit on daily working hours, over time allowances rates, return air tickets and compensation in case of death or injury.
4. Frequent visit to labour camps by the Indian consular officers in the Gulf countries must be in routine work in order to understand the difficulties faced by emigrants.
5. Since the tenure of employment is uncertain in the Gulf countries, workers should therefore be given alternative option in case of termination of their jobs in the Gulf.
6. Indian women also migrate to work in the Gulf as cooks, housemaids, governesses for children, etc. Since the local labour laws do not apply in their case, hence they, sometimes become victims of physical violence, molestation and even sexual abuse. In this regard, Indian Government should devise some measures to protect them from this kind of humiliation.

Thus, it is noted that the catalogue of demands of the Gulf emigrants is rather long, but there are some demands which are quite reasonable. Their genuine demands and expectation must be considered by Indian Government in order to motivate them to earn more money and send it back to India.

Conclusion

We conclude by saying that the Gulf has been one of the most important destinations for a large number of Indian emigrants, especially semi-skilled and unskilled manpower.

This population mobility has had positive impact on India's employment, balance of payments, commodity export, business profits and government earnings. The inflow of the Gulf remittances is playing a major role in this direction. The Indian business and government have been benefited in many ways. The manpower migration has particularly helped to boost commodity exports from India to the Gulf markets which have shown a spectacular increase in several countries. This migration has also provided additional revenues to provide services through airlines, hotels, travel agencies, banks, medical clinics, recruiting agencies, training institutions, translation services and ISD phone services.

The development impact of remittances is also observed in terms of physical assets, financial investment, human capital investment etc. Many studies reveal that a good proportion of remittances are kept in the form of financial assets after spending a major proportion of it in the acquisition and construction of physical assets. Some proportion of remittances is also kept in banks as fixed deposit. It is also found that some proportion of expenditure also increased on education and medicines as a result of the receipt of Gulf remittances. There is, however, no doubt that some proportion of remittances is used for unproductive purposes such as construction of houses and consumption, expenses on marriages and purchases of jewellery and ornaments, etc. Despite all, we can definitely say that the net benefit of Indian migrants in West Asia is positive for India.

References

Birks, J.S. and C.A. Sinclair (1980), *International Migration and Development in the Arab Region,* Geneva: ILO.

Calvin, Allen Jr. (1991), "The Indian Merchant Community of Masqat", *Bulletin of the School of Oriental and African Studies,* Vol. 44, No. 1, pp. 39-53.

Chengappa, Raj (1982), "The Mental Gulf", *India Today,* 15th September.

Commerce Research Bureau (1978), *Emigration, Inward*

Remittances and Economic Growth of Kerala: Report of a Survey, Bombay.

Davis, K. (1951), *Population of India and Pakistan,* Princeton University Press, Princeton, New Jersey.

Ecevit, Zafer and K.C. Zackariah (1978), "International Labour Migration", *Finance and Development,* Vol. 15, No. 4, p. 34.

Government of India (2002), Report of the High Level Committee on the Indian Diaspora, New Delhi.

Gulati, I.S. and Ashok Mody (1983), Remittances of Indian Migrants to the Middle East: An Assessment with Special References to Migrants from Kerala State, Working Paper No. 182, Trivandrum: CDS.

Gulati, Leela (1993), In the Absence of Their Men: The Impact of Male Migration on Women, Sage Publications, New Delhi.

Hindustan Times, "Indians in the Middle East", 1st June, 2004.

Indian Express, "Migrant Workers Complain of III-Treatment", 25th May, 1983.

International Organisation of Migration, *World Migration report: 2000.*

Jain, Prakash C. (1989), "Emigration and Settlement of Indians Abroad", *Sociological Bulletin,* Vol. 38, No. 1, March.

Mathew, E.T. and P.R.G. Nair (1978), "Socio-economic Characteristics of Emigrants' Households: A Case Study of Two Villages", *Economic and Political Weekly,* 16th July.

Naaz, Farah (2005), West Asia and India: Changing Perspective, Shipra Publication, New Delhi.

Nair, P.R.G. (1983), Asian Emigration to the Middle East: Emigration from India, Trivandrum: Centre for Development Studies.

Nangia, Parveen and Usha Saha, "Profile of Emigrants from India: A Comparative Study of Kerala and Punjab", http://www. iussp.org/Brazil2001/s20/S27_01nangia.pdf.

Nayyar, Deepak (1994), Migration, Remittances and Capital Flows: The Indian Experience, Oxford University Press, New Delhi.

Prakash, B.A. (1978), "Impact of Foreign Remittances: A Case Study of Chavakkad Village in Kerala", *Economic and Political Weekly,* 8 July.

Radhakrishnan, C. and P. Ibrahim (1981), "Emigration, Inward Remittances and Economic Development", *Manpower Journal,* New Delhi, January-March.

Rahman, Anisur (1999), "Migration of Indian Labour to West Asia: Trends and Effects", *Manpower Journal*, July-September, IAMR, New Delhi.

Rajghatta, Chidanand, "India Gets US$ 21.7 Billion from NRIs in 2005", *Hindustan Times,* 18th November 2005.

Weiner, Myron (1982), "International Migration and Development" *Population and Development Review*, Vol. 8, No. 1, March.

Part II
India's Palestine Policy

6

India's Palestine Policy: A Historical Review

Shamir Hasan

Our natural tendency to assume that what exists today has always been, can only afford us psychic solace, at the terrible cost of denying reality. The tendency to deny historical reality on our part would perhaps destroy our capacity to understand and react meaningfully to the present.

Therefore, in this paper dealing with 'India's Palestine Policy', an attempt has been made to briefly review and analyse India's stance towards Palestine question in historical perspective with a precise survey of overall India-West Asia relations as an introduction for the sake of perspective.

West Asia occupies a very significant position in the world politics, particularly since the second half of the 20th century. In ancient times, India had experiences of contact with West Asian region. For a long time, Indian and Arab civilizations have interacted with each other and have drawn inspiration from each other. History is shown with the evidences of mutually advantageous relations between the two regions. For example, it was the Indian Muslim, which the Egyptians used to wrap the mummies. Similarly, it was the Arab craftsmanship, which is believed to have produced figurines for the Indian temples and buildings. [1]

Several evidences have been found from historical records that India had close relationship with West Asia in general and Ancient Palestine in particular in various fields such as culture, commerce, religion, medicines and politics. During the time of King Solomon, son of King David, a port of Etzion Gter was built at the head of the Gulf of Aqaba. It seems that from there he carried out trade with Arabia, Africa and India. [2] Solomon also made voyage to the east every three years. The destination of his expedition was called Ophir, which was identified as Sopora near Bombay from where they brought gold, precious stones, peacocks and Almond Trees. [3] His fleet was built by Hiram of Lebanon. [4] The arguments have been strengthened by testifying some Hebrew words which are to be of Indian origin, like Koph monkey (Sanskrit Kopi) and Twkki peacock (Tamil togai). [5]

Christian tradition also holds that St. Thomas, one of the twelve disciples of Jesus, came to India and preached the gospel to the Indians before he died a martyr's death at the hands of a King, called in Christian tradition, Misdeos. This could be possible because travelling from Palestine to India was not totally unknown. [6] Christian faith from Palestine found a way to India, which is still evident today.

With the rise of Islam, Palestine came under the Muslim Arabs and the inhabitants embraced Islam. By the 7th century A.D., the whole of Palestine became a Muslim majority Land. [7] The Arab conquest still expanded eastward and by 712 A.D. they reached Sind.

They captured both sea and land routes and the Mediterranean Sea virtually became an Arab Lake. They carried on trade with India for some eight hundred years until the Europeans ousted them [8] In the North India, the Arabs came as conquerors, but in south India they came as travellers and merchants. This made their relations with their Indian rulers peaceful and cordial. [9]

Though the Palestine did not occupy the hub of civilization in the Arab world, its importance could not be ruled out. The growth of the European maritime presence after 16th century adversely affected these contacts. The British East India Company came to India as merchants in the 17th century and became the rulers of the country. During this time, Palestine was under the Ottoman rule and remained so as neglected

Sanjak of the empire.

With the coming of the 20th century, a new relationship developed between India and the countries of West Asia. The West Asian countries placed under the mandatory control of the Western imperialists were fighting for independence. Nationalist India looked upon them as brothers-in-bondage. Indian National Congress rallied to the support of these countries under European bandage. [10]

Indian National Congress and Zionist Congress

While Indian National Congress came into existence in 1885, elsewhere in Basle, Switzerland, the Zionist Congress was found under the leadership of Theodore Herzl in 1897 which aimed at the creation of a homeland for the Jewish people in Palestine. [11] These two organizations were diametrically opposite to each other in their aims and objectives. The Indian National Congress was anti-colonial and directed against the Western Colonial powers, the Zionist Congress was colonial in nature and sought the protection of the European colonial powers. The INC struggled against the colonial rule while the later constantly remained a movement of cooperation with the same powers for the creation of a state for Jews in Asia. [12]

The objective of the Indian National Movement at the behest of INC was to expel alien rulers from their land while the Zionists were attempting to gain a foothold in another country from which the local inhabitants by force or persuasion would have to be evicted. In this aim, Zionists succeeded and Palestine, which under the Ottoman and British authority was an Arab majority area, was now being converted into a Jewish majority and an Arab majority area under the auspices of British mandatory power with whom Zionists had been colluding.

Indian National Congress and the Palestine Question

The Congress looked at the whole issue as a struggle

between nationalist Arabs and Zionist colonization where the Zionists had the support of the British imperial power. The fact placed them on the side of the Arabs. This was in consonance with their views way back in 1922, when the Congress supported the Turks because of its policy against the imperial forces. [13] The Congress though expressed its sympathy to the Jews, deplored the way the Zionists were joining hands with the imperial powers. Therefore in 1936, the Congress Working Committee sent its greetings to the Palestinian Arabs and observed September 27, 1936 as a Palestine day in order to show their solidarity with the Palestinian people. [14]

There were many other organizations, which expressed sympathy towards the Arabs in Palestine. The Sind Congress Socialist Conference held at Karachi on July 18, 1936 sent its greetings to the Arabs in Palestine. In the 1930, the Congress expressed its sympathy and support for the Palestinians in their struggle for independence against the British and applauded the bravery shown by the Arabs in their fights against the British. The Committee also noted the Arabs and Jews should not fight each other but join their hands to have direct cooperation in establishing a democratic state in Palestine. [15]

Congress in its Resolution stated [16], "while sympathizing with the plight of the Jews in Europe and elsewhere, the Committee deplores that in Palestine the Jews have relied on British armed forces to advance their claims and thus aligned themselves on the side of British imperialism. The Committee trusts that Arabs and Jews will endeavour to find basis for direct cooperation with a view to establish a free democratic state in Palestine with adequate protection of Jewish right". The Indian National Congress sympathized with the Arabs and hailed them as nationalists. But it was not out rightly anti-Jews but anti-Zionist. India and its nationalist leaders resolutely opposed the Zionist ideology as a matter of principle.

Their antipathy towards Zionism was reflected in the official statements of the Indian National Congress and after Independence in the attitude of the Government of India. There were some who believed that Indian National Congress's reaction against Zionism was due to the pressure from the Muslim leader like Abul Kalam Azad. It would be a gross mistake to presume that this policy of Indian National Congress was formulated to ingratiate the Indian Muslims or to appease the Arabs. The Indian National Movement led by Mahatma Gandhi and his disciple Jawaharlal Nehru cherished certain principles which are still close to the heart of every conscious Indian. One of them was separation of religion from the realms of nationalism. The foundations of a secular India are laid on this principle.

Gandhi and the Palestine Question

During his 21 years stay in South Africa, Gandhi came very close to two prominent Jews—Henry S.L. Polak, a journalist and Hermann Kallenback, a prominent wealthy man. These two men tried to entice Gandhi towards Zionism. However, they did not succeed and Gandhi remained anti-Zionist throughout his life. [17]

Gandhi remained firm on his idea. He said, [18] "my sympathies are all with the Jews. I have known them intimately in South Africa. Some of them became life along companions. Through these friends I came to learn much of their age long persecutions. But my sympathy does not blind me to the requirements of justice. The cry for the national home of the Jews does not make much appeal to me. The sanction for it is sought in the Bible and the tenacity with which the Jews have hankered after their return to Palestine. Why should they, not like other people of the earth, make that country their home where they earn their livelihood? Palestine belongs to Arabs in the same sense that England belongs to the English or France to the French. It is wrong and inhuman to impose the Jews on the Arabs. Surely it would be a crime against the humanity to reduce the proud Arabs so that Palestine can be restored to the Jews partly or wholly as their national home.

Mahatma Gandhi's rejection of Zionist ideology was categorical since he refused to accept it as a basis of nation state. On the eve of Palestine tragedy, he was more convinced of the grievous wrong done to the Arabs and wrote in August 1947 in *Harijan* expressing his moral support to the helpless Palestinians who were being uprooted from their homes and fields. "The Jews", he wrote, [19], *"have erred grievously in seeking to impose themselves on Palestine with the aid of America and Britain and now with the aid of naked terrorism.* Why should they depend on American money or British arms forcing themselves on an unwelcome land?" Gandhi was hurt when he was told that the Zionist lobby has given a new twist to his convictions against the Zionist antics. The international Zionist magnets especially in Britain and the United States came out with a starting clarification of his pronouncements.

They often replaced the argument that Gandhi was opposing the Zionist moves because he wanted to please the Indian Muslims some of whom are his close associates. Gandhi after knowing such perceptions of the Zionists came out with a stronger statement. "I have said often", he wrote, and "that would not sell truth for the sake of India's deliverance. Much less would I do so for winning Muslim friendship" [20]

The inherent danger in the Zionist Movement for which Gandhi rejected the Zionist doctrine, is that the foundations of the Zionist enclave were laid on the assumption that the Jews the world over constitute a "nation" and that by virtue of their religion alone they are the prospective inheritors of Israel. Like Indians, the Arabs are also the victims of an unpardonable conspiracy of division of their land on the basis of race and religion.

Jawaharlal Nehru and the Palestine Issue

Jawaharlal Nehru had a similar view as Gandhi on Palestine question. His knowledge of the Jewish history and their persecution did not have much influence on his judgement of the issue. Indian nationalist leader Gandhi had categorically rejected the idea of a Jewish national home. [21] Like him, Nehru too was against the demand for Jewish national homeland. Jawaharlal wrote and spoke strongly about the deteriorating situation in Palestine. He firmly held that the Palestinian Arabs were struggling against a colonial power and its machinations.

"To the Jewish victims of Fascist terror and brutality", he wrote, [22] "we must extend all sympathy and help, but that does not and cannot mean that Arab interests in their country of Palestine can be ignored. Palestine is an Arab country and Arab interests must prevail there".

Nehru remarked that the happenings in Palestine since the Balfour Declaration of 1917 represented a gross betrayal of the Arabs by British imperialism. He argued that the Jews had a right to look to Jerusalem as their holy land and to have free access to it, but pointed out that the Balfour Declaration went much beyond that and had envisaged the creation of a Jewish state within an Arab community. He also pointed out that certain number of Jews could go and settle in Palestine in an atmosphere of peace and good will, but when they went with the objective of dominating the country, they could hardly expect to be welcomed by the Arabs. He considered the problem of Palestine as a nationalist one. It was a pity; therefore, that the Jews of Palestine instead of aligning themselves with that struggle, had thought fit to take the side of British imperialism and to seek its protection against inhabitants of the country. [23]

India's Stand at the UN

At the UN, India along with Yugoslavia and Iran had submitted minority report as a member of UNSCOP. India did not want that outsiders should take part in solving a problem of a nation. Nehru argued that "Palestine is essentially an Arab country and no decision can be made without the consent of the Arabs". [24]

Sir Abdur Rahman, the representative of India and the

member of UNSCOP in a special note observed, [25]

"...There is no escape from the conclusion that independence should be granted to Palestinian forthwith subject to such intern arrangements for the transfer of power as may seem to be desirable. The people of Palestine have now admittedly reached a stage where their recognition as an independent nation can no longer be delayed. They are in no way less advanced than the people of the other free and independent Asian countries.

Nehru on December 4, 1947 explained India's position in the constituent Assembly in reply to a cut motion, [26] "we suggested a federal state with naturally an Arab majority in charge of federal state but with autonomy for the other regions —the Jewish regions. After a great deal of thought we decided that this was not only a fair and equitable solution of the problem, but the only real solution of the problem. Any other solution would have meant fighting and conflict.

The negative voting of India against Israel's admission to the United Nations at best be interpreted as a continuation of India's policy on the issue that it did not support the occupation of Palestine by the Zionists. As stated earlier, India's leaning towards the Palestinian cause was a matter of principle, which she was fighting for. It was not absolutely due to her uncompromising attitude towards Zionism, but India was more motivated by her desire to demonstrate publicly to the world that standing by the Palestinian cause was principled and human".

The Present Phase

India was called the leader and a major force in NAM and a bulwark against imperialism. Much has changed since then. Imperialism is perhaps stronger than ever but the world is muddier and more confused and the Indian government under NDA clearly abandoned every effort to project itself an anti-imperialist in any way. In the past few years, NDA government systematically dismantled the entire edifice of the independent foreign policy based on non-alignment which was created in the post-Independent period. [27]

Politically, India has already signalled its wilful acceptance of the US's world leadership based on its hegemonistic military power and a right wing "free market" agenda. It has also unconditionally embraced what may be called the new "Bush Doctrine" on terrorism; America's "anti-terrorist" war (you are with us or against us) and elevates blind revenge to the level of a "rational strategic response". [28]

Charting course for a new foreign policy, the NDA government announced its unconditional support for the "Bush Doctrine". No one has applied the "Bush Doctrine" to such devastating effect as Israel's Ariel Sharon and his disciple Olmert. Killing large number of innocent people bears testimony to this. Having unconditionally welcomed the "Bush Doctrine", how can India condemn its application in Israel?

National Security Advisor Brijesh Mishra's visit to the US was an abashed bid to cajole the Bush administration. Mishra announced that Washington, Tel Aviv and New Delhi share common democratic values and face the same dangers. Stronger Indo-US relations and Indo-Israel relations have a natural logic. [29] L.K. Advani and Jaswant Singh expressed similar views.

The new UPA government has continued absolutely the same policy. The common minimum programme (CMP) of the UPA government includes the historical commitment of India to the Palestine cause. But this is just a paper commitment. The left parties have been firm in their demand for a change in the government's policies towards Israel but to no effect. Many non-aligned members have called for partial sanctions against Israel until it starts implementing the accord it has signed and allows Palestinians to form an independent and viable state. [30] This too has drawn no response from India.

Thus, the present government seems intent on persisting with special relationship with Israel. It has been appalling to hear Natwar Singh, speaking to the media after the funeral of Yasser Arafat, "Good relations with Israel should not come in the way of expressing sympathy and our support to the Palestinian people". What is the worth of "sympathy" with a victim if one subsidies the assassin at the same time!

End Notes

1. Khataybeh, Syed Zaki Hamid, *India's Foreign Policy and Arab World*, Jaipur, p. 4.
2. Allen, Richard, *Imperialism and Nationalism in the Fertile Crescent*, New York, 1974.
3. Ahmad Maqbool, *Indo-Arab Relations*, New Delhi, 1969, p. 67.
4. Hitti Philip K., *A Short History of Lebanon*, New York, 1965, p. 29.
5. Basham, A.L., *The Wonder that was India*, New Delhi, 1989, p. 232.
6. Ibid., p. 345.
7. Nashif, Taysir N., *The Palestine Arab and Jewish Political Leadership*, Bombay, 1979, p. 1.
8. Allen, Richard, *Imperialism and Nationalism in the Fertile Crescent*, New York, 1974, p. 22.
9. Besham A.K., No. 7, p. 232.
10. S.P. Singh, *Indo-Arab Relations in the Light of Palestine Problem (1930 to 1945)*, in proceedings of the Indian History Congress, 65th Session, Bareilly, 2004, p. 1025.
11. David Vital, *Zionism: The Formative Years*, Oxford, 1982, pp. 3-4.
12. Ahmad Maqbool, No. 5, p. 6.
13. Zaidi A.G. and Zaidi S.G., *The Encyclopaedia of the Indian National Congress*, Vol. VIII, New Delhi, May 15, 1966.
14. Prasad Bimla, *The Origin of Indian Foreign Policy: The INC and World Affairs, 1885-1947*, Calcutta, 1962, p. 131. See also Resolution, Congress Working Committee Wardha, 1936.
15. Zaidi, A.G. and Zaidi S.G., No. 16, Vol. XI, pp. 153-487.
16. *Arabs in Palestine*, The Encyclopaedia of the INC, Vol. I-III, 1936-38.
17. Schectman, Joseph B., "India and Israel" in Grover, Verinder (ed.) *International Relations and Foreign Policy of India*, Vol. 04, New Delhi, 1922, p. 469.
18. Gandhi, M.K., "The Jews in Palestine 1938" in Khalidi Walid (ed.) *From Haven to Conquest*, Beirut, 1971, p. 367. Also *Harijan*, 11th November, 1938.

19. Jansen, G.H., The Statesman, New Delhi, 5th April, 1966.
20. Ibid.
21. Ibid.
22. Patriot, New Delhi, 5th May, 1966.
23. Nehru, Jawaharlal, 'Eighteen Months in India: 1936-37', *Essays and Printings,* Allahabad, 1938, pp. 133-137.
24. Jansen, G.H., No. 19; pp. 191-193.
25. UNSCOP, Report to the General Assembly Record, Session of the General Assembly, Supplement no. 1; Vol. II UN Document A/364, Add 1, 9th September, 1947, p. 24.
26. Constituent Assembly of India (Legislative) debates, Official Report, Vol. 11, No. 5, 4th December 1947, pp. 12-61.
27. Jayati Ghosh, "The Dubious New Alliance", www.hind *wonnet.com.* Also, *Frontline,* Vol. 20, Issue 12, June 7-20, 2003.
28. John Cherian, "Sharon's War", *Frontline*, January 4, 2002, p. 53.
29. Seema Sisohi, "Lost Tribes, Rewnited", *Outlook*, 26th May, 2003.
30. John Cherian, A Breach of Trust, *Frontline*, 17th December, 2004.

7

Mahatma Gandhi, Jawahar Lal Nehru and the Palestine Issue

Mohammad Gulrez

Writing on the history of the Holocaust of Jews by the Nazis, the Israeli occupation of Palestine and the origin of the bloody conflict and the Gaza carnage, Dilip Simon expresses his anguish in *Hard News* that despite many calls from Human Right Watch and Amnesty International to the UN Security Council to set up a commission of inquiry over a wide area of Israeli military incursions in Gaza which constitutes *"prima facie evidence of war crimes* and for "massive intervention by the international community", asking the world to *"condemn and not become an accomplice in Israeli's crimes"*, the West continues to give carte-blanches to Israel, and equates the colonised people of Palestine with a rampaging army which has always blocked all attempts to stop its expansionism. In extreme situations, the issue is treated as if it were one of two equal parties, one of whom—the Palestinians—are for no rhyme or reason, launching terrorist attacks upon the other, Israel, which we are repeatedly told, has *"the right to defend itself.*

The question one can ask therefore is, whether the Palestinians too have a right to defend themselves or whether they must passively accept forced dispossession, encroachment and perpetual humiliation.

The purpose of writing this article is to present a factual picture before questioning as to why Palestinians in the face of overwhelming odds 'what they rightly regard as an unwarrantable encroachment upon their country', renounce violent means to end the occupation. During the Arab revolt in the 1930s, Gandhi asserted that "according to the accepted canons of right and wrong, nothing can be said against the Arab resistance in the face of overwhelming odds."

This study is largely based on Gandhi's political viewpoint on the formation of Israel for he firmly believed that what is going on in Palestine today cannot be justified by any moral code of conduct. The mandates have no sanction but that of the last war. Surely it would be a crime against humanity to reduce the proud Arabs so that Palestine can be restored to the Jews partly or wholly as their national home.

Analytically, it is difficult to fix a specific date for the inception of Palestinian ethnic nationalism as we now know it, as it developed over time simultaneously with other ideologies of identity, including Arab Nationalism, the nationalisms of the individual Arab states and various versions of political Islam.

Palestinians are regarded as national ethnic people with a strong sense of national identity, dispersed among the multitude of countries with politically active segments using the criteria of the 'Minority at Risk Project' in Jordan, Israel Lebanon, as well as the West Bank and Gaza. Israel has granted citizenship to Palestinians in Israel, but has given them unequal treatment. Arab countries, except for Jordan, have not offered the mass of Palestinian refugees citizenship (there have been relatively rare exceptions), nor have the Palestinians desired assimilation.

Palestine during the British mandate period (1919-1947) was a relatively well-settled, agriculturally productive land. Religiously based communal identity was nevertheless fragmented, pitting Sunni oligarchies against landless peasants, Christian Arabs against Muslim Arabs, Jews against Muslims, and Shiites against Sunnis etc. In general, ethnic solidarity tends to increase as a result of adversity. When competition for land became part of the Arab political experience in the twentieth century, Palestinians were denied to secure a territorial base for their political aspirations. The Jewish Diaspora, combined with external intervention by former colonialists and later by the super powers (the United States and the Soviet Union), systematically prevented them to have a territorial compromise of their legitimate right for a statehood (Gurr, R. Ted., 1993: 221).

One can explain to this injustice done to Palestinians by referring to UN Partition Plan of 1948. The UN Plan for the Partition of Palestine in 1948 (supported by the USSR, but opposed by India and many Third World countries) awarded 56 percent of Palestine to Israel and 44 percent to Palestine's original inhabitants. When Palestine was first provisionally recognised at the end of World War I, it encompassed all of what is presently recognised as the State of Israel, as well as the West Bank and the Gaza trip. Its population, according to the 1922 census, was 87.4 percent Arab-Muslim and Christians and 11 percent Jewish.

In 1947, the UN established a committee to evaluate the situation in Palestine and make recommendations regarding the future of the territory. In August, a majority of the Committee recommended a partition plan that divided Palestine into three territories—an Arab state, a Jewish state, and an internationally administered enclave around Jerusalem as follows:

- A Jewish state converting 56.47 percent of mandatory Palestine (excluding Jerusalem) with a population of 498,000 Jews and 325,000 Arabs.
- An Arab state covering 43.53 of Palestine, with 8,07,000 Arab inhabitants and 10,000 Jewish inhabitants.
- An international trusteeship regime in Jerusalem, where the population was 10,000 Jews and 105,000 Arabs.

The Partition Plan, however, never came into effect. Although after some initial hesitation, the Israelis declared their willingness to accept the recommendations, the Palestinian Arabs rejected them out of hand, arguing that the United Nations had no right to allocate the majority of their territory to the Zionists, who, in March 1947, claimed possession of less than seven percent of the land in Palestine and ownership of only 5.66 percent and represented less than a third of the territory's population. The United Nations General Assembly nevertheless endorsed the partition resolution on November 29, 1947. In May 1948, Israel declared itself independent, establishing control over all of the territory allocated to the Jewish state (and over some allocated to the Arab State), a provisional Zionist National Council announced the establishment of the State of Israel on the portion of Palestine allocated land by the Partition Plan to form the Jewish State. After a cease fire and UN mediation, Jordan controlled the rest of the area called the West Bank and Egypt controlled Gaza.

Most Palestinians particularly those who live in the occupied territories recognize that they cannot recover all of Palestine. What they seek is that part in which many still live: the West Bank, East Jerusalem, and Gaza; a state formed from these territories, many believe, need not be a place of residence for all Palestinians. For some, it is believed, under UN General Assembly Resolution 194 III (1948), Palestinian would seek compensation for their property rather than return. For others, the main issue is attainment of a political identity. But a Palestinian's right to return, most argue, must be no less than that accorded to Jews under Israel's law of return, which provides every Jews a right to immigrate to Israel. Absorption, they believe, if it is a problem should be one for the Palestinians to solve (Segal, 1989:9).

The argument leading to the conclusion that the Palestinians need a state of their own begins with a premise that the creation of a Palestinian state (which would be consistent of their legitimate right to self determination) would simply rectify previous injustices and restore Palestinian dignity.

The present crisis in West Bank and Gaza, on should realize therefore is not a *'Muslim'* concern. Sadly, this is how the mainstream media insists on seeing it. The Palestine issue is an outcome of colonial occupation and settlement. As already noted, reacting on the Arab Revolt in the 1930s, Gandhi asserted that Palestinians are not obliged to acquiesce in assaults on their human dignity; quite the contrary, they have a responsibility to defend their dignity against such assaults, non-violently if they can, violently if they must. It might also be recalled that for Gandhi "no greater evil can befall a country than that it should lose its independence".

The Indian media these days is obsessed with Israel's "war against terror". The media persons must remember what the Mahatma had to say on the subject of Zionism and on the formation of Israel despite his close friendship with Jewish intellectuals and Zionists.

Its origins, though, are complex, yet Gandhi and Nehru were clear that the Zionist project was misconceived and essentially colonial. Despite their western education and European experience, Gandhi and Nehru were not willing to endorse Zionist aspirations in Palestine. Although Gandhi believed that Jews were treated worse than the untouchables in India, (CW, v68, 1958: 37) but his personal sympathy towards Jews did not influence his views on Palestine question. He firmly believed that "by no canons of ethics or war...can Palestine be given to Jews" (Young India in CW, v19: 472).

Gandhi also expressed his dislike for partition during the late 1930s in response to the topic of the partition of Palestine to create Israel. He stated very clearly his views in *Harijan* on 26th October 1938:

"Several letters have been received by me asking me to declare my views about the Arab-Jew question in Palestine and persecution of Jews in Germany. It is not without hesitation that I venture to offer my views on this very difficult question. My sympathies are all with the Jews. I have known them intimately in South Africa. Some of them became life-long companions. Through these friends I came to learn much of their age-long persecution. They have been the untouchables of Christianity. But my sympathy does not blind me to the requirements of justice. The cry for the national home for the Jews does not make much appeal to me. The sanction for it is sought in the Bible and the tenacity with which the Jews have hankered after return to Palestine. Whey should they not, like other peoples of the earth, make that country their home where they are born and where they earn their livelihood? Palestine belongs to the Arabs in the same sense that England belongs to the English or France to the French. It is wrong and inhuman to impose the Jews on the Arabs. What is going on in Palestine today cannot be justified by any moral code of conduct".

At about the same time in 1938, Gandhi wrote in *Harijan* about his sympathies with the Jews, and said: "...If I were a Jew and were born in Germany and earned my livelihood there, I would claim Germany as my home even as the tallest Gentile German might, and challenge him to shoot me or cast me in the dungeon; I would refuse to be expelled or to submit to discriminating treatment. And for doing this I should not wait for the fellow Jews to join me in civil resistance, but would have confidence that in the end the rest were bound to follow my example".

One can note in the same reference that in the late 1920s, the Indian National Congress passed a number of Resolutions of sympathy with the people of Egypt, Syria, Palestine, and Iraq in their struggle against imperialism and for independence. The Congress passed a resolution in October 1937, stating that the Congress emphatically protests again the reign of terror as well as the partition proposal relating to Palestine and assures the Arabs of the solidarity of the Indian people with them in their struggle for national freedom.

(D.G. Tendulkar, cited in Leonard, A.G., 1975, Summer-Autumn, JSS: P222).

In 1939, the Indian National Congress (INC) sent a communication to Aminul Husseini, the Mufti of Palestine, wishing the Arab Higher Committee "complete success in the attainment of their objective" against the Zionists (Joseph B. Schechtman, (1922: 471).

Nehru argued that Palestine "is essentially an Arab country and no decision can be made without the consent of the Arabs" (Nehru's speech to the Asian Relations Conference in March 1947, cited in Malik, Tauqir A.K., 'Palestine Question and India's Israel Policy', Journal of Research).

By the time the issue of Palestine was taken up by the UN, the Indian attitude toward Israel was fixed. The Zionists were viewed by the Indians as a European people, who with backing of the imperialist powers, were setting up a theocratic state in Middle East at the expense of the Arabs. India was appointed to a special UN committee with the charge to consider appropriate solution for Palestine.

The United Nations Special Committee on Palestine's (UNSCOP) partition plan was opposed by India and it stood for Federal State of Palestine.

Detailing Indian position, the Indian representative on UNSCOP submitted a special note to the Committee disputing validity of Balfour Declaration and questioning the rationale of Zionism (UNSCOP Report to the General Assembly, cited in Malik, Tauqir A.K.).

While explaining India's position on Palestine question, Mrs. Vijaya Lakshmi Pandit maintained in Ad hoc Committee of 11th October 1947 that "peace in Palestine and Middle East was of vital significance to India because of its geographical proximity to the region".

She also categorically mentioned that Palestine was predominantly Arab country and the predominance should not be altered to the disadvantage of the Arabs and that, once Palestine became independent, Jews could be given wider autonomy in areas where they were in majority (United Nations General Assembly, Ad hoc Committee on Palestine Question, 25th September-25th November 1947, Summary Record of the meeting, p. 62).

To Gandhi, the world was essentially a moral landscape and religious quests should be interior ones that individuals and even people should carry out wherever on the earth they happened to be born. Gandhi did not give credence to Jewish nationalism associated with a particular territory. He did not recognize the legitimacy of such a movement. The ancient Jewish presence in Palestine and the modern fervour for the recreation of a Jewish state have never evoked any sympathetic response from Indian nationalists struggling in their own way for the recapture of their homeland. How could Gandhi reconcile his opposition to Jewish nationalism on the grounds of inappropriately mingling religion and politics and his own activity of mixing Hinduism and Indian nationalism? Gandhi maintained that Indian nationalism was a non-sectarian or all-sectarian movement, i.e., it was for all Indians regardless of their religion (Joan V. Bondurant, The Conquest of Violence, Berkely, 1965, rev. (ed.), Chapter 4).

Nehru's postures about Jews were same as that of Mr. Gandhi. He was sensitive to their problems but opposed creation of Jewish national home. He believed that "Palestine was not a wilderness or an empty uninhabited place. It was already somebody else's home. So that this generous gesture of the British government was really at the expense of the people, including Arabs, non-Arabs, Muslims, Christians, and, in fact, everybody who was not a Jew protested vigorously at the Declaration" (Jawaharlal Nehru Memorial Fund, 1987:763).

Nehru believed that Balfour Declaration was "made to win the good will of International Jewry, and this was important from the money point of view..." (Jawaharlal Nehru Memorial Fund, 1987: 763).

In several essays written during 1936, Nehru outlined his views on the Palestine question. In one he wrote, In Palestine the problem seems to be one of Arabs and Jews...That is a wrong and misleading outlook. It is a problem of a growing nationalism desiring freedom and being suppressed by imperialism. In this process, British imperialism, as in India, has tried to play off one community against another and set the Jews against the Arabs. Like our own communal problem, they have sought to produce a communal problem in Palestine. It is true that at present there is ill will and conflict between the Arabs and Jews in Palestine...Their [the Jews'] future in Palestine lies in cooperation with the Arabs and in recognition of the fact that Palestine is and must continue to be essentially an Arab country. For the moment the immediate issue is the fresh determination of British imperialism to crush the Arab movement. Large additional British armies are being sent to Palestine almost to conquer the country afresh...The crushing of their movement is a blow to our nationalist strength as well as to theirs. We hang together in this world struggle for freedom (Jawaharlal Nehru, cited in Leonard, A.G., 1975, Summer-Autumn: 225).

Like Gandhi, Nehru also spoke about his sympathy for the Jews: I approach this question...with every sympathy for the Jews. So far as I am concerned the racial or religious issue does not affect my opinion (cited in Leonard, A.G., 1975, Summer-Autumn: 225).

He also said that the Jews had some claim to Palestine because of their ancient connection but the Arabs, he maintained, had a stronger one; For thirteen hundred years or more they had lived there....Palestine was not an empty land fit for colonization by outsiders. It was a well populated and full land with little room for large numbers of colonists from abroad. (cited in Leonard, A.G., 1975, Summer-Autumn: 226). The land, and the Middle East generally, belonged, Nehru thought, to the Arabs. The Jews were entitled to access to their holy places, but had no right to move for the establishment of a state there. No other nationalism in that area of the world was legitimate. Therefore the Jews, in demanding autonomous territory there, were seen by him as an intrusive force sponsored by British imperialism and paid for by outside money (Nehru, Eighteen Months, 127).

Many Indian leaders in the nationalist period up to 1947 felt that they shared certain historical experiences with the Arab nationalists in the West Asia. The most important of these was oppression by the common foe: British Imperialists. Jawaharlal Nehru simplified the forces of world politics into two: Western Imperialism and Afro-Asian nationalism. In this scheme there was no room for intrusive peoples like the Jews in Palestine. Mahatma Gandhi knew, that the Jews had ancient roots in Palestine, but he saw the Jews as Europeans. The Jews are not organic to the Middle East, but rather a group used and manipulated by western imperial powers for their own ends in the area.

The only people organic to the Middle East and specifically to Palestine, in this view, are the Arabs. This territory belongs to them for they have lived there continuously for more than one thousand years. The Jews did have a connection in antiquity but when they moved on the Europe and became citizens of European communities and their connection to Palestine lapsed. To Gandhi and Nehru, the Jews are essentially a European religious group that has suddenly developed national pretensions and wants to re-establish itself in a territory with which it was once identified. To secure this end, the Jews first gained the assistance of the major imperial power of the pre-World War II generation, Great Britain. The Jews now continue in the area with the massive aid of the major imperial power of the post World War II generation, the United States (Leonard, A.G., Jewish Social Studies, 1975, Summer-Autumn: 233-234).

The situation in the present is no more different as it existed during the time of Gandhi and Nehru. In fact, the Palestinians' collective disadvantages vis-à-vis Israelis are very high and are likely to remain high until a viable political settlement can be reached.

If Israel continues to persist rejecting the demands of Palestinian self determination, whether by repression or eviction, the foundation of Israeli society will only be eroded by resulting hostility.

Presently, India has managed a comfort level with Israel which signifies the substantive recession in India's interest on the

Palestine question. Indian vocal posturing on Palestine issue during pre-independence and post-independence Nehruvian period has virtually ceased after the end of cold war with official pronouncements leaning more towards the restoration of peace in the region than an active call for recognizing Palestinian rights. With these policy pronouncements whether India retains any leverage at all in pressing the Israelis to make an amicable settlement with Palestine is open to question.

References

Collected Works of Gandhi (1958), Vol. 68, Ministry of Information and Broadcasting, Government of India.

Collected Works of Gandhi, Vol. 59, Ministry of Information and Broadcasting, Government of India cited in Finkelstein-http://www.normanfinkelstein.com/resolving_the_israel_palestine_conflict_what-we-can-learn-from-gandhi/)

D.G. Tendulkar (1961), *Mahatama,* cited in Leonard, A.G., Jewish Social Studies, Summer-Autumn.

Gurr, R. Ted (1993), *Minorities at Risk,* Washington, DC, United States Institute of Peace Press, 1993.

Jawaharlal Nehru (1938), *Spain and Palestine' Eighteen Months in India,* Allahabad, cited in Leonard, A.G., Summer-Autumn, 'Indian Nationalist Ideas about Palestine and Israel', Jewish Social Studies. Jawaharlal Nehru Memorial Fund, 1987:763, Glimpses of World History, New Delhi.

Joan, V. Bondurant, The Conquest of Violence, Berkeley, 1965, rev. (ed.).

Joseph, B. Schechtman, (1922), "India and Israel" in *International Relations and Foreign Policy of India,* (ed.), V. Grover, New Delhi, Deep and Deep Publications.

Nehru's speech to the Asian Relations Conference in March 1947, Asian Relations: Report of the Proceedings and Documentation of the First Asian Relations: Report of the Proceedings and Documentation of the First Asian Relations Conference, New Delhi, March-April 1947 (New Delhi: Asian Relations Organization, 1948), 70. cited in Malik, Tauqir A.K., 'Palestine Question and India's Israel Policy', Journal of Research (Humanities) 2007, Vol. 27.

Segal, Jerome M. (1989) *Creating the Palestinian State,* Chicago:

Lawrence Hill Books.
UNSCOP Report to the General Assembly, Second Session, Ad hoc Committee on Palestine Question, 25th September-25th November 1947, Summery Record of the Meetings, p. 62.
Young India (1921) in Collected Works of Gandhi, Vol. 19, Ministry of Information and Broadcasting, Government of India.

8

Palestine as a Factor in Indo-Israeli Relations

Jawaid Iqbal

The roots of India's policy towards West Asia in general and Palestine issue in particular can be traced back to the mid-1930s. Palestine which was then a British Mandate was in the process of becoming the focal point of bitter Arab-Jewish conflict. European Jews, facing persecution in their countries of residence were emigrating to Palestine in large numbers with a view to establishing a Jewish state there. The Palestinian Arabs strongly resented the influx of Jews from Europe and by early 1930s began to resist often violently, the pro-Jewish policies of the mandatory authorities. Nationalist leaders in India who were leading India's struggle for independence from British colonial rule evinced a keen interest in the Palestine problem and the ongoing Arab-Jewish struggle in the Holy Land. Both Mahatma Gandhi and Jawaharlal Nehru had strong views about Zionism and the proposed Jewish state in Palestine. Though Mahatma Gandhi was very sympathetic to the plight of Jews in Europe, he was very much opposed to the idea of creating a Jewish state in Palestine. For Gandhi, the Zionist movement's territorial ambitions in Palestine constituted a crime against humanity and Zionism's dependence on British assistance was deplorable. He stated:

"Palestine belongs to the Arabs in the same sense the England belongs to the English or France to the French. It is wrong and inhuman to impose the Jews on the Arabs. What is going on in Palestine today cannot be justified by any moral code of conduct". [1]

Nehru's view regarding Palestine was akin to that of Gandhi. He sympathized with the Jewish diaspora and the suffering of the Jews in Europe. He writes:

"They (the Jews) had no home or nation, and everywhere they went they were treated as unwelcome and undesirable strangers. They were humiliated, reviled, tortured and massacred; the very word "Jew" became a word of abuse, synonym for a miser and a grasping money-lender; These people without home or country...have never ceased to dream of Jerusalem which appears to their imaginations greater and more significant than it ever was". [2]

Notwithstanding Nehru's sympathetic attitude towards the Jews, he was resolutely opposed to the creation of a Jewish National Home at the expense of Palestinian Arabs because as he said, "Palestine was not wilderness or any empty, uninhabited place. It was already somebody else's home". [3] India's policy towards the Palestine problem and the Arab-Jewish conflict was thus guided by the basic outlines as laid down by Gandhi and Nehru. India's opposition to a Jewish State in Palestine was therefore a foregone conclusion when the state of Israel came into existence in May 1948 by partitioning Palestine the Jewish state had been created in the midst of intense opposition first form the indigenous population, the Palestinian Arabs and later on by the Arab states who came out in support of the Palestinians. [4] In February 1947, the British government as the Mandatory Power over Palestine had placed the issue before the United Nations (UN). In May 1947, the UN set up an eleven member fact-finding committee known as the United Nations Special Committee on Palestine (UNSCOP) which was asked to submit its report by September that year. India was a member of the UNSCOP. The UNSCOP submitted its report of 1st September.

A seven member majority consisting of Canada, Czechoslovakia, Guatemala, Netherlands, Peru, Sweden and Uruguay were in favour of partitioning Palestine into an Arab and Jewish state, an economic union between them and a an international status for Jerusalem. India, Iran and Yugoslavia put forwards a Federal Plan as a solution to the Palestine problem. The Indian stand was nothing new. The Indian National Congress (INC) had consistently supported the cause of the Palestinian Arabs and as early as 1938. Jawaharlal Nehru had pointed out that the Palestine problem was a creation of the British who wanted a Jewish state in the region for political and strategic reasons. Nehru had warned that portion of Palestine would increase instability in the region for several years to come. [5]

After the submission of the UNSCOP report there was a debate in the UN General Assembly and on 25th November 1947, the ad hoc committee of the General Assembly approved the partition plan by a margin of twenty five votes to thirteen with nineteen abstentions. Four days later, the UN General Assembly adopted Resolution 181(II) recommending portion of Palestine with thirty three votes in favour, twelve against and ten abstentions. India in keeping with its earlier stand voted against partition both in the ad hoc committee and the General Assembly. Israel emerged as an independent state on 14 may 1948, and in the first Arab-Israeli war that followed increased its territory by forty-five percent in excess of that authorized by the UN resolution through military conquest. The following year Israel was admitted into the UN as its fifty-ninth member. India voted against Israel's admission and the Indian delegate to the UN declared that India "could not recognize an Israel which had been achieved through the force of arms and not through negotiations. [6]

Recognition of Israel

The Indian government continued with its refusal to recognize the Jewish state for the next one year despite repeated requests from the latter. It was only in September 1950, twenty eight months after the state of Israel had been created that India formally recognized Israel. By this time,

Israel had already become a fait accompli and was recognized by large number of countries including three Islamic states-Turkey, Iran and Indonesia. Moreover, India was genuinely interested in mediating in the Arab-Israeli conflict in the overall interest of regional peace and security. Non recognition would have severely limited India's role as a possible peacemaker between the Arab and Israelis. Despite India's lack of interest in the Jewish state, the Israeli's were keen to establish close ties between the tow countries. Soon after recognition, Nehru ruled out any diplomatic exchange citing financial and other reasons.

The cold Indian response, however, did not deter the Israelis who kept their pressure on Nehru through numerous ways. Tel Aviv at first proposed to open a legation in New Delhi without insisting on reciprocity but India turned down the proposal. A little while later Israel suggested that the Indian ambassador in Turkey be concurrently accredited to Israel but this suggestion was also turned down by the Indian government. In early 1952, the Director General of Israeli Foreign Ministry came on a week long official visit to India. During his visit, he met several top Indian leaders including Prime Minister Nehru and tried to convince them of the need to improve relations between the tow courtiers. It was a sequel to this visit that Nehru relented partially and allowed an Israeli consul to function in Bombay but India refused to set up one in Israel. Some attempts to improve relation between the two countries were made but these were quickly overshadowed by the Suez Crisis of 1956 following which relations remained virtually frozen for the next six years.

In the wake of the 1962 Chinese aggression against India, Nehru appealed to several world leaders for assistance including the then Israeli Prime Minister David Ben Gurion. Seizing this opportunity to bring about a thaw in relations Israel responded positively and supplied India with a substantial quantity of small arms. [7] Bilateral cooperation between India and Israel which had started with the Sino-

Indian war raised hopes in many quarters that soon it would lead to the normalization of relations between the two. However, such hopes were belied with the passing away of Nehru in May 1964 and India under Prime Minister Lal Bahadur Shastri who succeeded Nehru, reverted back to its anti-Israeli stance of pre-1962.

The first Arab Summit meeting in 1964 marks an important turning point in the history o the Arab-Israeli conflict. Since the establishment of the state of Israel all matters relating to Palestine had been handled by the Arab League in which the Palestinians had no direct representation. The summit meet decided to establish a Palestine Liberation Organization (PLO) which would serve as the official representative of the Palestine national interest. In November 1964, India extended an official invitation to the newly formed PLO. [8] The invitation extended to the PLO marked a new phase in India's policy towards Israel and the Palestine issue. Till then, while generally endorsing the Arab, particularly Egyptian stand on the Palestine issue, India had left the detail undefined. From 1964 onward, the PLO became an important factor as far as Indo-Israeli relations were concerned.

Relations between India and Israel deteriorated further in the wake of June 1967 Arab-Israeli war and the Israeli occupation of West Bank, Gaza and the Golan Heights. India condemned Israel in unequivocal terms and stood firmly on the Arab side. [9] The aftermath of the June 1967 War saw the popularity of Palestinian guerrilla organizations, particularly Fath led by Yasser Arafat and Popular Front for the Liberation of Palestine (PFLP) led by George Habash, rising among Arab masses and Palestinians.

The sweeping Israeli victory completely discredited the Arab regimes as well as the PLO whose Chief Ahmed Shuquari had to resign in December 1967. Shuquari's successor Yahya Hamouda asserted that the PLO would have to associate the guerrilla organizations if it was to survive. In July 1968, an agreement was reached between the PLO, Fath and PFLP according them representation in the Palestine National Council. During that year, the guerrillas, particularly Fath, became very influential within the PLO and in February 1969 they established control electing Arafat as Chairman of the PLO executive committee. [10] In September 1969, a three member Fath delegation arrived in India at the invitation of the Indian Association for Afro-Asian Solidarity and met several politicians and government officials in a bid to consolidate indo-Palestinian ties.

The Indo-Pakistan war of 1971 revived hopes of a thaw in Indo-Israeli relations. Israel offered humanitarian aid in the form of medical supplies and indirect military assistance by withholding eighty of Pakistan Air Force F-86 Sabre Jet fighters that has been sent to Tel Aviv for depot level maintenance at US insistence. [11] These goodwill gestures on the part of Israel did not lead to any fruitful dialogue or meaningful interaction. On the contrary, after 1971, India under the leadership of Indira Gandhi began to champion the Palestinian cause with greater vigour and utmost commitment. Anti-imperialism, anti-colonialism and decolonization were the principal motivating factors behind India's staunch support for the Palestinian liberation struggle. There was, however, an element of realism too behind the Indian policy. The Kashmir problem propelled Indian not to establish relations with the Jewish state as that would have provided Pakistan with an opportunity to undermine India's influence and cordial relations with the Arabs. [12]

Recognition of the PLO

The October 1973 Arab-Israeli war is an important watershed in the struggle to liberate Palestine. In the War's aftermath, the American Secretary of State Henry Kissinger initiated peace negotiations between the frontline Arab Sates and Israel. Kissinger's diplomatic initiative better known as the step-by-step approach was based on the following guiding principles: (a) to avoid the Palestinian problem and the question of their involvement in the peace process even though it was the central problem in the Arab-Israeli conflict, (b) to deal with each Arab state separately and step-by-step thus avoiding confrontation with a collective Arab position, and (c) to avoid linking initial diplomatic steps with the nature of the final peace agreement. [13] From the very beginning of the peace negotiations, therefore, Kissinger assiduously side-tracked the Palestinian problem and avoided the PLO participation in the negotiation process trying instead to bring about a series of bilateral agreements between Israel and the frontline Arab states. The Egyptian-Israeli disengagement agreements were in keeping with this approach.

Kissinger's step-by-step diplomacy was quite an alarming development for the PLO. In order to assert their presence and to maintain their cause as a focal point of attention, the PLO launched a vigorous diplomatic campaign aimed at counteracting Kissinger's efforts to bypass the Palestinians. The PLO's diplomatic initiative met with resounding success when the seventh Arab Summit conference held at Rabat in October 1974 declared the PLO to be the only legitimate representative of the Palestine people.

The conference was dominated by a dispute between Jordan and PLO as to which of them should be the legitimate representative of the Palestinian people in the Israeli occupied West Bank. After a protracted debate the conference resulted in a political victory for the PLO whose rights was recognized not only to be the "sole and legitimate" representative of the Palestinians but also to lead them in establishing "national Palestinian authority" on any part of liberated Palestine. [14] The Rabat Summit decision was a severe setback for Kissinger who was trying to restore sovereignty over the West Bank to Jordan. As the PLO was now the sole representative of West Bank Palestinians, this effectively debarred Jordan from arriving at any understanding with Israel with regard to the fate of the West Bank.

The Rabat Summit was soon followed by another major Palestinian milestone with considerable international impact.

In November 1974, the UN General Assembly adopted two resolutions with regard to the Palestine problem. The first one declared "the inalienable right of the Palestinians to return to their homes and property from which they had been displaced and uprooted". It further declared the Palestinian "right to self-determination without external interference" and to "national independence and sovereignty". [15] The second resolution granted the PLO a permanent observer status at the UN General Assembly and at other international conferences sponsored by the UN. These major political and public relations gains not only enhanced the prestige of the PLO but made its participation practically indispensable in any overall peace settlement.

At around this time support for the Palestine cause also began to grow steadily within India. In December 1974, a group of thirty Members of Parliament demanded that the government accord diplomatic status of the PLO. [16] In early January 1975, the Indian government recognized the PLO and permitted it to open an independent office in the Indian capital, thus becoming the first non-Arab country to take this step. [17] The following year the PLO with Indian support entered the on-Aligned Movement as a full member at the Colombo Summit. A little while earlier, in November 1975, India backed the highly controversial Arab-sponsored UN resolution equating Zionism with racism and racial discrimination. [18]

In 1977, the Congress party was defeated at the polls and the Janata Party headed by Morarji Desai came to power. One of the constituents of the Janata Party was the Jan Sangh a right wing nationalist group which had always been a consistent supporter of Israel. Atal Bihari Vajpayee a former leader of the Jan Sangh was made the foreign minister in the Desai government and this raised hopes in many quarters that Indo-Israeli relations would certainly improved after having touched a low under Indira Gandhi. However, this was not to be as the Desai government lasted only two years. There was hardly any breakthrough in Indo-Israeli relations and the only significant development during the two years of Janata rule was the secret visit of the then Israeli Foreign Minister Moshe Dayan to New Delhi in August 1977. [19]

In January 1980, when Mrs. Gandhi returned to power, she immediately accorded the PLO, diplomatic recognition and upgraded its office to that of a full-fledged embassy. Indo-Israeli relations touched a new low in June 1982 when the Israeli consul Yosses Haseen gave a provocative interview to Sunday Observer published from Bombay. Haseen accused Indian politicians of being afraid of the Arabs and this was interpreted as a personal attack on Prime Minister Indira Gandhi. The Indian government reacted quite sharply. Haseen was asked to leave within forty eight hours and Israel's official representation in Bombay was demoted to the rank of Vice-Consul. [20]

With the tragic assassination of Indira Gandhi in 1984, her son Rajiv Gandhi became India's Prime Minister. Rajiv Gandhi while continuing with India's policy of unconditional support for the Arabs and the Palestinians cause sought to bring about some degree of balance in Indo-Israeli relations. In March 1988, reports began circulating in the Indian press of a joint Indo-Israeli attack on Pakistan nuclear facility at Kahuta. [21] Israel wants the destruction of Kahuta because it sees in it a threat to its own hegemony of West Asia, a sphere of influence that has been carefully carved out for it by the WS which finds in Israel an able proxy to control the region. In order to preserve its hegemony, Israel attacked and destroyed the Iraqi Osirak reactor outside Baghdad out of fear that a nuclear weapon in Arab hands would negate the advantages of its own nuclear weapons and its superior conventional military might. [22]

Its desire to bomb Kahuta too is based on the calculation that Pakistan will hand over the bomb to one of its Arab friends and thereby pose a threat to Israel. [23] Indian and Israeli diplomats had several rounds of secret meeting in Paris to discuss Tel Aviv's proposal but India ultimately decided against cooperating with Israel. The reason uppermost in the minds of Indian military experts was the fear that India's own nuclear research centre at Bombay would become vulnerable to a Pakistani counter-strike. Having declined the Israeli offer, the best that India could offer Tel Aviv was an exchange of intelligence data.

The very fact that Indian and Israeli diplomats had started talking and that too on defence and security issues was pointer to the growing ties between the tow countries. There were some minor setbacks to bilateral ties [24] but these did not deter the two countries from continuing their dialogue. That Rajiv Gandhi was indeed serious about improving relations between India and Israel become apparent when in June 1988 while on a visit to the US, Morris Abrams and held wide ranging talks with the latter on Indo-Israeli relations, [25] Shortly after this meeting, the then Israeli Foreign Minister Shimon Peres declared that India had pledged to upgrade ties with Israel. [26]

As a sequel to this meeting, the following month the Government of India announced that it was upgrading Israeli official representation in Bombay to that of Consul six years after is was demoted to vice-Consul rank. [27] Before any further progress could made in the direction of improving Indo-Israeli relations, the Rajiv government got mired in a multi-million dollar bribery scandal and the Congress Party was defeated in the November 1989 general elections.

Consolidating Indo-Israeli Ties

The early 1990s was a period of great uncertainty and political turmoil both at home and abroad. At home, two successive Prime Minister V.P. Singh and Chandrashekhar failed to provide stable government and India had to go for mid-term elections in mid-1991. At the international level, the policies of glasnost and perestroika introduced by Mikhail Gorbachev, promised to radically alter the system and structures of governments across much of Eastern Europe and the Soviet domain.

With the fall of the Berlin wall in November 1989 and the subsequent disintegration of the Soviet Union two years later, the US became the sole super power. The old bi-polar structure which had dominated global politics for the previous forty five years crumbled without any stable alternative to take its place, allowing historical animosities to resurface and causing an increase of crises in developing countries. In early 1990, a need was felt to bring about a suitable reorientation in Indian foreign policy in order to cope with the fast changing international political scenario. As a result of this, there was considerable improvement in Indo-US relations and lessening dependence on the Soviet Union which was going through a period of internal political and economic turmoil.

It was precisely during this phase of international political uncertainty that in August 1990, Iraq invaded and occupied Kuwait. Shortly after the Iraqi invasion, US troops backed by forces from various countries were quickly dispatched to Saudi Arabia in an attempt to shield the Kingdom from Iraqi assault and to pressurize Saddam Hussain of Iraq that he should withdraw from Kuwait. Though India did not condemn the Iraqi invasion, it called for Iraq's withdrawal and went along with the US at the UN. The fact that the government of V.P. Singh and then Chandrashekhar were minority governments made it easier for the US to influence India. The Chandrashekhar government in particular repeatedly called for unconditional withdrawal of Iraqi troops from Kuwait and provided refuelling facilities to US military aircrafts. It was only after nation wide protests that Chandrashekhar announced that the refuelling facilities were being withdrawn. [28]

Soon after the second Gulf War was over, UP President George Bush stressed in a major speech to joint session of the Congress that he regarded the drive for a settlement of the Arab-Israeli conflict as one of his administration's top priorities in the post war era. The regional realignment during the war, he contended, had meant Arab states and Israel standing together against a common aggressor Iraq. This, he said, had brought the prospect of peace in the area closer the than ever before. In June 1991, Bush wrote letters to a number of West Asian leaders in an attempt to advance moves towards convening a peace conference and the first phase of the West Asian peace talks were held in Madrid in October that year. [29]

The holding of peace talks in Madrid cleared the decks for normalization of Indo-Israeli relations. In the post-Gulf War scenario India saw no compelling reason why it should not normalize relation with Israel. The first indication of a change in India's policy was apparent when in December 1991 India voted in favour of UN Resolution 46/86 which sought to repeal in 1975 UN General Assembly resolution equating Zionism with racism. [30]

After the UN vote, there was a rapid movement towards normalization of relations. In early January 1992, official level talks were held between the Israeli Foreign Ministry Director General Yosef Hadass and India's Deputy Chief of Mission Lalit Mansingh at the Indian embassy in Washington D.C. Within a few days, on 29 January 1992, the Indian Foreign Secretary J.N. Dixit announced India's decision to establish normal and full diplomatic relationship with Israel.

The establishment of full diplomatic relations was followed by a spate of reciprocal high-level official visits. The Indian Foreign Secretary visited Israel in March 1993 to discuss the overall framework of the Indo-Israeli cooperation. In May 1993, Maharashtra's Chief Minister Sharad Pawar visited Israel for participating in the Israeli AGRITEC exhibition during which wide ranging discussions on bilateral issues were also held. [31] In May the same year, Israeli Deputy Prime Minister and Foreign Minister, Shimon Peres arrived in News Delhi. The most significant aspect of Peres' visit was that it underlined the growing convergence of strategic perception between New Delhi and Tel Aviv under the changed international and regional setting. Peres unequivocally supported India's unity and territorial integrity. While taking a stand on the Kashmir issue, he assured India that Israel supported the Simla Accord as the basis for resolving the issue bilaterally. While expressing grave consent about the twin threats of terrorism and Islamic fundamentalism which affected both India and Israel, Peres offered his county's help in combating the menace.

This was internal security by fighting the Pakistani-aided terror in the border states of Punjab and Jammu and Kashmir. The convergence of views on security related issues has raised the hopes of many in India that the powerful Jewish lobby in Washington will come to India's rescue should the US waver in its support to the Indian stand on Kashmir. It is also hoped that the Jewish lobby may facilitate a better understanding of India by the Clinton administration on the issue of signing the Nuclear Non-Proliferation Treaty (NPT) as Israel shares some of New Delhi's reservations on the NPT. [32]

Indo-Israeli relations got a further boost when the Israeli President Ezer Weizmann came on a week long visit to India in Later December 1996. During his visit, both countries explored the possibility of enhancing economic cooperation, particularly in fields of agriculture, energy, health, science and technology. The most significant aspect of Weizmann's visit was that it underlined the growi9ng cooperation between New Delhi and Tel Aviv which stretch over a vast and multi-dimensional landscape. The most important of all is in the field of defence. Indian defence experts had identified areas where Israel's technology and expertise could be useful. These include medium and high defence technology both in the lethal and non-lethal sectors in which Israel has praiseworthy achievements. The lethal areas cover weapon systems while the non-lethal ones include support and logistic equipments like radar, electronic warfare equipments and a rage of engineering goods used in border fencing.

The advantage of seeking defence cooperation with Israel is that the latter technology is largely indigenous which facilitates technology transfer with no end user problems. In view of our resource crunch, India could benefit from Israel by upgrading its existing armaments and acquiring force-multipliers. Furthermore, Israel has vast experience of fighting in stony as well as sand dune waste areas. Since India has similar desert terrain a regular interaction between defence forces of the two countries will be quite useful. [33] India is also considering drawing upon Tel Aviv's expertise in dealing with terrorism. The National Security Guards (NSG) are seeking Israeli help to train sky marshals who like trained Israeli commandos would travel aboard aircraft to discourage hijackers. During Weizman's visit, Israel offered to India its latest Kfir fighter aircrafts and multi-mode maritime surveillance radar ELM2022A to counter Pakistan's Orion P-3c. It is evident that there is immense scope for defence cooperation and in the coming months Israeli is likely to emerge as India's key defence and strategic partner. [34]

In the field of trade and economic relations there was little direct trade between India and Israel before 1992 apart from trade mainly carried on through Indian diamond merchants based in India. With the normalization of relations direct trade has increased by an average of 50 percent every year crossing the half billion US dollar mark in 1994, the balance of trade is in Israel's favour, primarily due to large scale imports by India of two items rough diamonds and chemicals. The major items of exports from India are polished diamonds and cotton yarn. Israel can act as a springboard to the European and American markets for India's textile industry due to its free trade agreements with both markets. Indian textile industry which is feeling stifled with quotas can take its products to Israel for re-export with a 35 percent value addition, following the footstep of some of the far-eastern countries. Taking advantage of this situation an Indian promoter has set up a textile unit in Beersheva which will import cotton yarn and gray cloth from India and produce garments for the American market. [35]

Since 1992, government to government interaction

between India and Israel has concentrated on establishing the legal framework of trade and economic cooperation. In December 1994, an agreement on trade and economic cooperation was signed which granted Most Favoured Nation (MFN) status to both countries and allowed for the import of Indian goods into Israel without import permit except where such permits are required from all countries under Israeli custom regulation. Other important agreements signed in the filed of economic cooperation are: Agreement on Customs Cooperation (1996), Industrial Research and Development Co-operation Agreement (1996) and Agreement of Double Taxation and Bilateral Investment Protection (1996). Transport links which are an important part in bilateral trade have also developed extensively during the past five years. El Al began its flight to India in 1993 and Air India inaugurated its Bombay-Tel Aviv-Bombay flights in February 1996. Since 1994, Haifa port has been included in the list of stopovers by the Shipping Corporation of India and Zim Israel Navigation introduced direct shipping services in 1996. [36]

Israel has been active for many years in assisting developing countries set up an agricultural infrastructure. The application of drip irrigation technology is considered one of Israel's most significant contributions to modern agriculture the world over. Apart from drip irrigation, Israeli farmers have employed advanced water management technologies such as re-use of water for irrigation and the utilization of recycled marginal water for irrigating industrial crops such as cotton. Israel has offered its latest drip irrigation and other water conservation technologies to India. Besides this, India has much to gain from the Israeli experience in the filed of arid zone farming and agricultural innovation. A number of agreements in the filed of agriculture have been signed between the two countries.

For instance, the Rajasthan Agricultural University and Ben Gurion University in the Negev have entered into a collaboration to further improve water conservation techniques. During

Weizmann's visit, a memorandum of intent on a joint high-tech agricultural research-cum-demonstration farm was signed between the two countries. Under this, the Centre for Agricultural, Technological Assessment and Transfer (CATAT) was set up in New Delhi. [37] Besides agriculture, horticulture and animal husbandry are other areas which are of interest to India. One of Israel's outstanding achievements has been the breeding of cows which can tolerate extreme desert temperature and at the same time give every high milk yields. The introduction of such high yielding variety cows suited to Indian climatic conditions could give a much needed boost to India's white revolution.

From the foregoing analysis, it is apparent that there is great potential in bilateral cooperation between India and Israel. Indo-Israeli commercial and economic relations are still in their infancy. Much still depends on the West Asian peace process so that stability and security prevails in the conflict ridden region. The frequent setback to the peace process could cast its shadow on Indo-Israeli relations because India still wholeheartedly supports the Palestinian demand for statehood. A comprehensive and lasting peace would certainly go a long way in consolidating Indo-Israeli ties in the new millennium.

Conclusion

India recognized the State of Israel in 1960 but recognition was not followed by the establishment of normal diplomatic relations. During the Cold War years, India's policy towards Israel operated within the framework of the Cold War bi-polar politics. Israel was viewed as an outpost of Western imperialism in the strategic West Asian region. As a result, in the struggle between Arab nationalism, epitomized by the Palestinian struggle, and Zionism, India sided with the former. Many top Israeli leaders tried to persuade Nehru to establish diplomatic relations but the maximum he was prepared was to allow Israel to open an Israeli Consulate in Bombay.

During Indira Gandhi's tenure as Prime Minister, India's

opposition to Israel became stronger. This was manifest many a times in the UN voting pattern on issues concerning the Israel-Palestinian conflict. India always stood on the side of the Arabs. At the same time, India became one of the foremost champions of the Palestinian cause. In 1975, the Indian government recognized the PLO and permitted it to open an independent office in New Delhi, thus becoming the first non-Arab country to do so. Rajiv Gandhi who assumed office in 1984 while continuing the pro-Palestinian and pro-Arab policies of Nehru and Indira Gandhi, sought simultaneously to bring about some improvement in Indo-Israeli relations. Rajiv Gandhi however, had to quit office in 1989 before he could bring about meaningful changes in Indo-Israeli ties.

The end of the Cold War changed the entire landscape of international politics. A little before the dissolution of Soviet Union, the latter resumed diplomatic relations with Israel after a gap of twenty four years. Later, the People's Republic of China too established relations with Israel. The second Gulf War of 1991 witnessed a major realignment of forces in West Asia. The leading Arab countries including radical Syria joined hands with the US in waging a devastating war against a fellow Arab country, Iraq. In the War's aftermath, they all started talking face to face with the Israelis at the Madrid peace conference. Two years after Madrid, Israel and PLO recognized each other and started negotiations for a final settlement.

Under the changed international scenario, when the Arabs and Israelis were talking to each other, India decided that the time had come to establish diplomatic relations with Israel, which it did in early 1991. Since then, bilateral cooperation between the two countries has expanded rapidly. The most important area of cooperation is defence where there is a growing convergence of strategic perceptions between New Delhi and Tel Aviv. There has also been a boom in direct trade which has increased by an average of 50 percent every year since 1992. The prospects of peace in the religion have brightened after Ehud Barak became the new Israeli Prime Minister in mid-1999. A comprehensive and lasting peace in the region will certainly give a tremendous boost to Indo-Israeli relations in the years ahead.

End Notes

1. M.S. Agwani (1983), "India and Palestine", *Man and Development*, Chandigarh, Vol. 5, No.3 September, p. 33.
2. Jawaharlal Nehru (1987), Glimpses of World History, New Delhi, pp. 762-763.
3. Ibid., pp. 764-765.
4. For the historical background to the creation of Israel see *inter alia* Christopher Sykes, Crossroads to Israel: Palestine from Balfour to Bevin (London, 1965); Nevill Barbour, Nisi Dominus: A Survey of the Palestine Controversy (Beirut 1969); and Howard M. Sachar, A History of Israel: From the Rise of Zionism to out Time, Oxford, 1977.
5. A.K. Pasha (1993), "India's West Asia Policy: Continuity and Change", *Strategic Analysis,* New Delhi, Vol. 16, No. 6, September 1993, pp. 789-790.
6. Richard J. Kozicki (1997), "Indian Policy towards the Middle East", *Orbis* (Philadelphia), Vol. 11, No. 3, Fall.
7. Negille, Maxwell, "India's China War", Bombay, 1970, p. 385 and Mohammaed H. Heikal, The Cairo Documents: The Inside Story of Nasser and his Relationship with World Leaders, Rebels and Statement, New York, 1973, p. 297.
8. William Korey (1967), "India and Israel: Unmasking a Neutral", *New Leader,* New York, Vol. 50, No.15, 17th July, p. 8.
9. K.R. Singh (1967), "Indian and the Crisis", in M.S. Agwani (ed.), The West Asian Crisis, Meerut, 1968, pp. 74-88. See also M.D. Japhet and P.K. Rajiv, The Arab Israeli Conflict: An Indian Viewpoint, Bombay.
10. Helena Cobban (1984), The Palestinian Liberation Organization: People Power and Politics, Cambridge, pp. 42-44.
11. Moonis Ahmar (1996), "Pakistan and Israel: Distant Adversaries or Neighbours", *Journal of South Asian and Middle Eastern Studies*, Villanova, Vol. 20, No.1, Fall, pp.43-44.
12. Pasha, n. 2, p. 270.
13. Mohammed K. Shahid (1981), The United States and the

Palestinians, London, p. 100.

14. Keesings (1974), Contemporary Archives (Bristol), Vol. 20, 1-24 November, p. 26813.
15. Ibid., Vol. 20, 16-22 December, 1974, p. 26862.
16. Hindustan Times, New Delhi, 23rd December, 1974.
17. Asian Recorder, New Delhi, Vol. 21 March 5-11, 1975, p. 12475.
18. Bernard Lewis (1976), "The Anti-Zionist Resolution", *Foreign Affairs,* New York, Vol. 55, No. 1, October, pp. 54-64.
19. Moshe, Dayan (1981), Breakthrough: A Personal Account of the Egypt-Israel Peace Negotiations, New Delhi, p. 26.
20. Farah Naaz, "Indo-Israeli Relations: An Evolutionary Perspective", *Strategic Analysis,* Vol. 23, No. 2, May 1999, pp. 245-246.
21. Times of India, New Delhi, 28th March 1988; Patriot, New Delhi, 28th March 1988; Hindu, Madras 28th March 1988; and Indian Express, New Delhi, 28th March 1988.
22. Amos Perlmutter, Michael Handel and Uri Bar-Joseph, Two Minutes Over Baghdad, London, 1982.
23. Reports have indicated that President Muammar al-Gaddafi of Libya has financed the Pakistani bomb and even helped divert nuclear fuel from Niger to Pakistan.
24. For instance, the Indian government refused to allow an Indian team to play against Israel in a tennis match to he held in Tel Aviv in the Second week of April 1988. The assassination of PLO leader Khalil al Wazir in Tunis in April 1988 by the Israelis was strongly condemned by a number of Indian Members of Parliament and there were even demands for closing down the Israeli consulate in Bombay.
25. Hindustan Times, 12th July 1988.
26. Statesmen, New Delhi, 11th June 1988.
27. Times of India, 14th July, 1988 and Statesman 18th July, 1988.
28. P.S. Jayaramu, "India and the Gulf Crisis", in A.K. Pasha (ed.), The Gulf in Turmoil, New Delhi, 1992, p. 157.
29. International Herald Tribune, Paris, 7th March, 1991.
30. Times of India, 17th December, 1991.
31. Ibid, 7th May, 1993.
32. Bansidhar, Pradhan, "Indo-Israeli Ties after the Peres visit", *Link,* New Delhi, Vol. 35, No. 41, 23rd May, 1993, p. 21.
33. A.K. Pasha, "Indian and Israel: Great Leap forward", *Third Concept,* New Delhi, Vol. 10, No. 120, February 1997 p. 12.

34. This is evident from the fact that dialogue on defence related matters between the tow countries has been going on at a steady peace. Frequent visit by top defence officials to each others country is now routine. The Israeli Air Chief and the Navy Chief have visited India and from the Indian side A.P.J. Abdul Kalam, Secretary, Defence Research and Development Organization (DRDO) and Chief of Air Staff S.K. Sareen have visited Israel. The latest in these rounds of mutual consultation is the visit of Brajesh Mishra National Security Advisor in September 1999. Mishra held extensive talks with Israeli leaders including Prime Minister Ehud Brak on matters of mutual concern and various regional and international issues. The visit has led to considerable concern in the Arab World. The Deputy Secretary General of the Arab League recently declared that India-Israel nexus will in the long run help India's nuclear programme. Mishra's visit to Tel Aviv is a pointer in that direction. See Times of India, 3rd September, 1999 and Hindustan Times, 8th September, 1999.
35. News from Israel, Bombay, May 1993, pp. 12-13.
36. Business and Management, New Delhi, January-February 1994, pp. 13-14.
37. Pasha, n. 33, p. 12.

9

Cultural Relations between India and Israel: Role of Indian Jews

Khurshid Imam

That this world is a multi-cultural place is a fundamental fact of international relations. When two nations are motivated to strengthen their economic relations their leaders underline the historical and cultural association between the two people from time immemorial. In this era of globalization, with its concomitant revolution in communications, communities around the world can exchange views and influence one another even when the governments of the two countries are not on friendly terms. The nature of communications, capable in being carried through even over the heads of governments, challenges the traditional and the most important concepts of sovereignty and national territorial boundaries in international politics. Such communications have not only strengthened relations between the nations but remain quite productive in eliminating many of the misunderstandings and stereotypes that are the result of these very concepts.

The present paper attempts to analyze the channels of communication that exist apart from the *official* state-to-state diplomatic relations between India and Israel. In contemporary world, politicians and academicians alike have realized the importance of non-official channels like people-to people interaction, which in diplomatic parlance is known as Track II diplomacy. The diaspora of population and the non-residential citizens, for obvious reasons, have gradually attracted the attention as they play important diplomatic roles in their own right. India and Israel have maintained a steady relationship long before the formal diplomatic relations was established in 1992. The consulate in Mumbai facilitated the trade and mobilized the immigration of the Indian Jewish communities to Israel. The immigration of the Indian Jewish community to Israel was due partly to religious conviction and also in search of greener pasture. [1]

The study of the role of this Jewish community in building a people-to-people contact between two nations deserves attention. The Jewish community in Israel has, to great extent, been successful in introducing the panorama of Indian culture in Israel. Indian entertainment industry, Indian cuisine in chain of Indian restaurants, India as a destination of spirituality, Vedic wisdom and knowledge, alternate therapies are some of the areas which have attracted interest among the Israelis. The result of this inquisitiveness has made India a favourite tourism spot for young Israelis. The widening interest of Israelis in India owe a lot to the Indian Jewish community both historically as a diasporic Jewish community in India and their presence in Israeli society after they made *Aliya* (immigration to Israel).

Israel is the only Jewish country in the world inhibited by 6.5 million people of which some 60,000 are Jews of Indian origin. [2] According to available data, the major waves of Indian Jews migrated to Israel soon after the establishment of the state of Israel in 1948. The Indian Jews migrated to Israel primarily for religious and economic reasons for they never faced discrimination in India contrary to what their contemporaries in Europe had to pass through. The migrants from India belonged essentially from three groups: the *Bene-Israel* of Maharashtra; the Cochini Jews (comprising *of Pardesis and Malabarees* Jews); and the Baghdadi Jews. [3] Of these, the *Bene-Israeli* and the Cochini Jews had lived in India for thousands of years and were thoroughly Indian in the sense that they adopted the local language namely Marathi and Malayalam respectively, food habits and other cultural traits. The *Baghdadi* Jews had a comparatively shorter stay starting from 19th century and they retained many elements *of* the Iraqi Jewish culture. However, they were considered Jews *of* Indian origin in Israel. Apart from these three major groups there are others like the *Bnei Menashe of* Mizoram and the Telugu speaking Jews who claim their Jewish linkages and some of them have already migrated to Israel. [4] The *Bnei Menashe* are generally accepted as the lost tribe of Israel.

After immigration to Israel the Indian Jews had to adjust in a system established and run by *Ashkenazi* Jews from Europe. Many *of* the Indian migrants had difficult time adjusting and assimilating as they lacked adequate economic and social support systems. They had to struggle in small development towns and agricultural settlements to establish themselves in Israel. To this day they have not recovered fully and still feel the pinch in their socio-economic status. The community has a good reputation for being law abiding and modest. They belong by and large to the middle class. A large proportion of the *Bene-Israel* population lives in small towns and works or is employed in firms and government agencies. Few among them have become business executives, while some, own small business. Many of the Cochinis took to agriculture (in contrast to their professions while in India) and have succeeded.

The Cochini Jews is a socially marginalized community in Israel with minimal interaction with the mainstream Ashkenazim community. The European Jews considered Indian Jews as underdeveloped and primitive. They were often being alluded to in a derogative term as "chocolate kiddies". [5] The Cochini Jews often faced uncomfortable questions with regard to their Jewishness or Jewish identity. For nearly three decades the intra-ethnic marriages was widely prevalent among the Cochinis due to the lack of social interaction with other Jewish groups in Israel. In spite of the immigration to Israel, the animosity among *Pardesis* and *Malabarees* continues, although not in an explicit manner. The Cochini Jews were a highly orthodox community with various diaspora rituals and rites. Upon their arrival, the Cochinis continued their tradition for some time but they later realized the disadvantages of these traditions when there was a great uproar against the *Bene Israelis* of Bombay from the orthodox Rabbi alleging that they were not Jews. In addition, the *Paradesi* Jews of Cochin never accepted the *Malabaree* Cochini Jews and branded them as impure due to the influence of Hindu traditions.

The tales of saints and tombs as holy places and sources of miracles were quite familiar and deep-rooted within the Oriental Jewish communities. For the Cochini Jews, the 25th day of the Hebrew month *Kislev* which also is the first day of *Hanukah* was celebrated as Choruda as the memorial day of Rabbi Nahamia Motta. Rabbi Motta, a Yemenite by origin, was a great Jewish poet who settled and died in Cochin. It is believed that he performed many miracles and his grave is described as "a Mecca not only for Jews but also for Hindus and Christians". [6]

The memorial ceremony of Nahamia Motta was called *Choruda* or Oath (in English). Till mid-1970s, the Cochinis did not observe this festival explicitly fearing that they will be socially marginalized. However, by late 1970s, the tomb worships and cult festivals have re-emerged in Israel like Hilluloth of Moroccans and Mimonuah of Iranians. The Cochini Jewry has more than five ethnic organizations and they conduct various activities and congregate regularly. Moreover, the amount of Cochinis visiting India is increasing rapidly—even some are planning to buy lands in Kerala to build houses and settle back in India. It seems today the Cochinis are trying to revive their heritage and culture which they had once ignored to attain the status and acceptance in the Israeli society.

Jewish Community in Indian Diaspora

The Indian Jewish community has long history which for our purpose can be studied in two distinct phases. The first phase starts with their coming to India and settling there until their immigration to Israel. The period was smooth in which they made contribution in various fields with distinction. The second phase starts with their immigration to Israel, their dream land, where they restarted a new life which had its own difficulties particularly when the Ashkenazim were at the helm of affairs. This paper would delve into this dual process of Jewish life in India and its evolution in Israel in a chronological order moving back in history.

Jewish Entrepreneurship in India

The archival material of the European companies in India and the different archives of India still need to be examined for materials pertaining to Indian Jewish community. Their prominence in the economic and public arena and their role as merchants, agents, negotiators, diplomats, and pioneers in the expansion of trade and commerce have found place in the documents of these companies.

Imbued with an enterprising and pioneering spirit, in search of new economic prospects and promises, and in some cases also in search of great religious freedom, many of these Jewish immigrants made their mark in the economic life, contributing greatly to the expansion of trade and commerce in Asia as well as constituting a link between India and Europe. Wherever they settled, whether it was Cochin, Surat, Madras, or other trading-posts, they turned their attention to new commercial adventures, penetrated into new territories, and opened hitherto untouched markets. The Jewish merchants in Surat and Madras had close commercial connections with Manila, Burma (Pegu), Siam, China, Sumatra, Mocca, the Persian Gulf and Muscat. [7]

There are a number of Jewish individuals who made it big from the initial days of their arrival in India. They became influential and thus were in a position to save and serve the interest of their community in their own right. The first individual Jews who appeared on the scene of India (1498) with the coming of the Portuguese, was the famous Gaspar da Gama, originally of Posen (Poland), who served as Shabandar of the Muslim ruler of Bijapur in Goa whose spectacular role as interpreter and agent of the Portuguese viceroy, up to 1510, is well documented. The other prominent individual Jew recorded in documents of European sources in the archives of Lisbon in Garcia d'Orta, the author of the "Coloquis" and the famous scientist and physician who lived in Goa from 1534 to 1569. Their entrepreneurship is reflected by the fact that many had a monopoly of certain commodities such as pepper, timber, amber, cotton goods, diamonds and precious stones, spices, indigo and so on.

Others were engaged as contractors, gun powder manufacturers, cocoanut planters, wood-cutters, and shipbuilders. Many of them were ship owners and Jewish ships with Jewish captains and crew were plying the Indian Ocean, the Arabian Sea, the Gulf of Bengal and the Persian Gulf. Some of the ships owned by Jewish merchants in India were given Biblical names such as Daniel, Isaac, Rachel and others. Some of the prominent merchants were Ezekiel Rahabi, Ephraim Cohen, Isaac Surgun, J.G. Febos. [8]

The Indian trade was a source of great wealth for the Jewish merchants and the staggering amounts of investments in their commercial expeditions to Europe as well as to Asia, including China, indicate their successful enterprises. Their financial resources were often in demand by the chiefs of the various East India Companies and the loans given by Jewish merchants with large amounts and a high percentage of interest have been registered. The economic activities of these Jewish merchants were greatly facilitated by the favourable political and legal status they enjoyed. The protection granted by the European company was particularly important if and when conflicts arose with native rulers—whether a Hindu Raja, a Muslim Mughal Nawab, representative of Mughal emperor, or any of the innumerable chieftains and potentates on the Malabar Coast.

Jews' Participation in Diplomatic Arena

The Jewish merchants in India by virtue of their linguistic

abilities and influences among the various native Rajas, sultans and potentates were given political and diplomatic assignments of the highest order. Thus there were court Jews, negotiators, interpreters, linguists, agents, and ambassadors in the service of the East India Companies. The service of the 'Court Jews' was put to use in times of tension, conflict and war to bring about peace and accord among the rival parties. In the Anglo-Mughal conflict during the rule of Emperor Aurangzeb (1690), the Anglo-Portuguese Jew Abraham Navarro, on behalf of the English East India Company, was sent as their accredited envoy and ambassador to the Mughal ruler to negotiate a peace treaty. [9]

In the Anglo-Mysore and the Dutch-Mysore wars, Isaac Surgun was assigned as linguist and spokesman for the Dutch Company to the Muslim rulers Haidar Ali Khan and Tipu Sultan. Ezekiet Rahabi and his sons were repeatedly called upon diplomatic missions to help resolve the conflict of the Dutch with the Zamorin of Calicut and the rulers of Tranvancore. In Surat, the Dutch-Portuguese Jew, Pedro Pereria, was closely connected with the diplomatic mission of Sir William Norris to the Moghul court. In Bengal (Calcutta and Benares), Pellegrino Treves, a member of the famous London Sephardic Jewish family, who had entered the civil service of the East India Company in 1785, successively moved up to such positions as Acting-Resident of Benares, Judge, Custom collector, and Post-Master General in Calcutta, and after a very checkered career, died in Lucknow in 1825. [10]

The influence on the local ruler was such that the Raja of Cochin refused to fight a battle on Saturday because n that day his Jewish soldiers would not fight; and they were the best warriors he had raised. The Jews could not have survived under Portuguese rule (1502-1663) had it not been for Parumal. He appointed a hereditary mudaliar [11] (chief) from among the Jews and invested the position with special privileges and jurisdiction in all internal matters in the Jewish community. This office continued in force under subsequent Rajas and even under Dutch and British rule. The Hallegua family, which still holds the title, continues to be influential in Cochin.

Cultural Presence of Jewish Community in India

The Jews of India are not one singular community. Among themselves they are divided into different communities. Each community has its own culture, background and origin. Each community claims its arrival in India in different ways and it is not always clear how they really came to India. The three main Jewish communities of India have a distinct history. The *Bene Israel* Jews of greater Bombay arrived, they claim, some 1600 years ago. They believe themselves to be the descendants of the original settlers who came to India. Cochini Jews of southern India, who were centered in Kerala, arrived as early as the first century; and the Iraqi Jews, called Baghdadis, who began settling in India at the end of the 18th century, mainly in Bombay and Calcutta (Kolkata). They were Ashkenazi Israeli origin, speculated to be one of the lost tribes, and called themselves *Bnei Menashe*. Each group has active synagogues. Synagogues are the cultural representation of the Jews in India

The most sacred place for Jews is the Synagogue. In the Diasporic times, these synagogues were made whenever the native ruler provided Jews with land, copper plates indicating special privileges and assisted them in building synagogues. The Jews after immigration to Israel have left behind a rich legacy of synagogues and public institutions. The Jews have adopted many Indian customs and cultures, a fact amply reflected in the architecture and decoration of the synagogues. The Jews have adopted and modified many of their host country's customs. In consonance with Hindu tradition, colourful oil lamps hang from synagogue ceilings, all synagogues are entered barefoot and four hardala flowers are sniffed and then tucked into a pocket, signifying Shabbat's end.

Although the Jews are outside the rigid structure of India's caste system, they have gradually developed a strict code of their own which for centuries dictated that the three communities and their subgroups could not live together, socialize or intermarry. The divisions between Jews began to break down after 1948, when large scale immigration forced everyone together. The majority of Jewish marriages are still arranged and married couples and their children live with the husband's parents. Jewish women now wear bindis, the small marks in the middle of their foreheads that at one time signified a woman's marital status but are now merely a fashion statement.

The Paradesi Synagogue

Built on land given to the Cranganore exiles by Raja Perumal and reconstructed after the Portuguese bombardment in 1662, the Paradesi is the oldest surviving synagogue in India. It is a National Heritage and a protected monument. White-walled and tile-roofed, with an inner courtyard lined with ancient Hebrew-inscribed gravestones, it was embellished in the mid eighteenth century by Ezekiel Rahabi. He was the Dutch East India Company's principal merchant and diplomat in malabar, who built a Dutch style clock tower with three faces: Hebrew numerals facing the synagogue, Roman numerals facing the place and Indian numerals facing the harbour. Rahabi also had the floor paved with hand painted porcelain tiles, each with a different weeping willow pattern, brought from Canton. The synagogue shares a wall with the Raja's temple.

The synagogue also contains silver and gold decorated Torah scrolls; an oriental carpet in front of the Ark (a gift from Ethiopian Emperor Haile Selassie), two brass columns commemorating pillars that stood in the Temple, two bimot (one in the women's section, a feature unique to the Jews of Kerala) and Torah crown of solid gold set with gems given to the Cochini Jews by neighbouring Rajas.

The most striking feature, however, is the forest of lights hanging from the ceiling-silver, brass and glass oil burning lamps and Belgian crystal chandeliers. In addition, the Paradesi houses

10 paintings which depict the history of the Jews of Kerala, as well as the 1,600-year-old copper plates—deposited in an iron box called a pandeal and carefully guarded by the elders—which are shown to visitors on request. The Paradesi celebrated its four hundredth anniversary in 1968; Prime Minister Indira Gandhi attended the festivities and the Indian government issued a commemorative postage stamp for the occasion.

Thekumbagum and the Kadavumbagham Synagogues

Across the harbour from Cochin is Emakulam, which once had a thriving Jewish community. The Thekumbagum synagogue [12], on Jew Street (Market Road), was built in 1580. Today, the building is empty but it is eerily beautiful as it awaits dismantling and shipping to Israel. The Kadavumbagham synagogue, also on Jew Street a short distance away, is reputed to have been built in 1200. Rebuilt in 1554, it was closed in 1972, when its Torah scrolls were sent to the Cochini synagogue near Beersheba. Today the building, which still has an intact ark and Hindu-style ceiling lamps, houses a plant nursery.

The first *Bene Israel* synagogue was built by Samuel Divekar in 1796. Divekar with other *Bene Israelis* served as a soldier of the British in India. In one of the wars against the kingdom of Mysore in south India, he along with other British Indian soldiers was captured. After being spared by Tipu Sultan, Samuel Divekar decided to thank the Lord by building a synagogue. Later on, more synagogues were build by the Bene Israelis in India. There was even a Reform Jewish synagogue built in 1925. Among the synagogues, the synagogue in the town of Panvel (near Mumbai) is considered special and sacred where, it is believed, the prayers are fulfilled.

The synagogues built by the Baghdadis still survive. David Sassoon built the Magen David Synagogue in 1861 in Byculla, where the family first lived. This was then the best location in Bombay before other areas were developed. The large synagogue was set in extensive grounds, which were to prove very valuable. Built in the spacious style of Victorian architecture, it was fronted by pillars and a clock tower. David Sassoon also built an elementary school on one side in the same compound to provide an education for the community's children in Torah and proper behaviour. This was later expanded into a high school by his grandson Jacob Sassoon, and renamed "The Sir Jacob Sassoon Free High School". The synagogue and school grounds became in effect a community centre for the Jewish community of Byculla, where young and old would meet together in the evenings.

The Ohel-David Synagogue was built by David Sassoon in 1863 in Pune, where he had his resort home. The synagogue is a well-known landmark in Pune, of impressive architecture in spacious grounds in a central location in Pune cantonment. David Sassoon, much mourned by Jews and Indians alike, died in 1864 in his Pune home which is across the street from the synagogue. His sons buried him in the synagogue grounds in a fine mausoleum. The synagogue and mausoleum were visited by the President of India, Dr. Zakir Hussein, at a special Memorial Service on 10th December 1968, on the occasion of the Centenary celebrations of the Sassoon General Hospitals in Pune established by the Sassoons. David Sassoon's grandson, Jacob Sassoon, Built the Kneseth Eliyahoo Synagogue in the Fort in 1884, in memory of his father Eliyahoo Sassoon (founder of E.D. Sassoon and Company). While very few Baghdadis now remain in Mumbai and Pune, the synagogue buildings are well maintained and services continue to be held.

Today, only a few Kolkata Jews remain in the bustling city. Of the five synagogues, only two remain open for a population of about 60 Jews. Neveh Shalome Synagogue established in 1825, the first Synagogue in Calcutta was rebuilt in 1911, and the Magen David Synagogue, built by Elias David Joseph Ezra to perpetuate the memory of his father, David Joseph Ezra who died in 1882. This is the largest Synagogue in the East and is magnificent in architecture and design. Each week on every Shabbat, prayer services are held, alternating between the Synagogues.

The Jews of India saw several phases including the Portuguese, Dutch and the British periods. [13] The Portuguese period was a dark phase for the Cochni Jews. In 1662, the Dutch attacked Cochin but were driven out. The Jews were severely punished by the Portuguese for allegedly aiding the Dutch. In 1663, the Dutch returned and defeated the Portuguese. The Jews were treated more tolerantly by the Dutch rulers. The Cochini Jews re-established their links with European Jews.

The Dutch period was the Golden era for Cochini Jews. They provided services for the Cochin rulers and the Dutch East India Company and dominated the export trade. Eskiel Rahabbi was one such trader based in Mattancherri. He had close links with other local communities and European countries. He was also interested in science and mathematics. He reprinted in Amsterdam many of the books destroyed earlier by the Portuguese.

The British period starting in 1795 was also favourable for the Cochini Jews. In 1832, a visiting rabbi David Beth published from Madras "Travels of Rabbi Beth Hillel". [14] This book gives a clear picture of India in the 19th century. The British established a school to teach English and Hebrew in 1835. When the Jews learned that the English had religious conversion in mind they withdrew their children from the school. The Cochin government took over the school later. A Hebrew Malayalam press was established in 1877. The first British viceroy who visited the Jewish synagogue in Cochin was Lord Karson (Curzon) in 1900.

Expansion of the Diaspora Role in Agency Affairs

The socio-economic condition of the Indian Jewish community in Israel can be understood in the larger paradigm of Israel-Diaspora relationship since the beginning of the Zionist movement. For the Zionist pioneers who primarily were Ashkenazim, European powers and the US were the main source for their ideological and financial support. [15] Fund raising was in important binding factor which decided the level of state and Diaspora interaction. American Jewry had a prominent place in this regard whereas India was towards the other end because of the small number of Jews in India, poor fund raising capability and geographical distance. Not the least was this important fact that India itself was struggling for independence during this period.

This issue is considerably more complex when it comes to the participation of each centre in the affairs of the other. Israel has been notably reluctant to encourage diaspora involvement in policies affecting it directly, even where diaspora money is involved. Until the mid-1970s, diaspora Jews were reluctant to press matters. For example, where Israel has demanded Jewish mobilization in the United States on its behalf, diaspora Jewry has been content to follow the Israeli lead on the grounds that Israel's vital interests are those most immediately affected. Similarly, American Jewry has strongly resisted Israeli attempts to intervene in its communal affairs for many of the same reasons. Though from time to time Israel has shown more interest in doing so, it generally has respected American Jewish wishes and pulled back when asked to do so. In matters affecting world Jewry, because they are the major centres of Jewish life, both feel free to act for the resolution of world Jewish problems or the defence of world Jewish interests.

During the first-generation of statehood, contact between Israel and the Diaspora was like contact between two pyramids that touched at their tips. No more than a handful of leaders on each side had regular and meaningful contact with one another. In Israel, the prime minister, a few of his ministerial colleagues, the chairman of the executive of the Jewish Agency, and a few of his departmental colleagues handled almost all the regular contacts with a handful of diaspora leaders. The latter were drawn from the very top echelons of the fund raising organizations or, in a few instances, from the community relations bodies.

After the six-day War in 1967, the ties began to stretch

further down the pyramid. Project Renewal transformed the two pyramids into a single matrix. Not only were the ties between the top leadership intensified, but ties were developed between the second and third echelon leaders and then between ordinary Jewish activists and their Israeli counterparts through Project Renewal committees and volunteer programs. This helped in the integration of the Jewish people into a single entity. Interaction at different levels between Israel and Diaspora began which made the potential immigrants comfortable and paved the way for their final immigration. The implications of this integration are yet to be fully realized. The Indian Jewish community too was mobilized in phased manner and the Jews with controversial lineage like the *Bnei Menashe* were the last to be touched.

Precisely because Diaspora leaders are not directly engaged in the internal Israeli politics and are not inside its society—the very things that make them diaspora leaders, namely, being in the diaspora and being inside other Jewish societies means that their ability to use their access is limited. By the very nature of the situation, there is no remedy for this predicament. Perhaps there are a few people who can be sufficiently inside both Israel and some Diaspora Jewish society to have influence in both but it is likely to be a modest influence, because of the time and location factors involved.

As Charles Liebman has pointed out, the degree of influence by the leaders or groups from one centre on the internal life and activities of the other depends on three conditions: [16] (i) how serious the desire for influence is, (ii) how focused the effort is to bring influence to bear and perhaps how persistent the effort is, and (iii) whether the particular group has strong allies in the other centre. Thus, Orthodox Jews have had more influence on religious issues in Israel than any other Diaspora group because they best meet the three conditions. The issue is of extreme importance to them and they are willing to make focused and persistent efforts to exert their influence. Moreover, they have strong allies in Israel.

On the pyramid, Indians fell on the lower echelons and thus were weaker in influencing the leaders in Israel. The absence of this link put them on the periphery. Similarly, the concern of Conservative and Reform Jews to gain official recognition in Israel has been stymied in the sense that only recently has any of the "heavyweights" in their movements threw their weight behind the effort. The effort has been sporadic and diffused and those leading it had no strong allies within Israel. Nevertheless, when changes were proposed in the laws defining "Who is a Jew?" which could substantially affect Conservative and Reform conversions, the two groups did get together and made a serious and focused attempt for which they found allies in Israel and succeeded in tabling the matter whenever it has been raised. A number of Israeli Rabbis made visits to India to sort out the controversies of the Jewishness of some of the Jewish community in India and only then their migration to Israel was made possible.

Fund raising is another very important and serious issue for Israel. For a very long time, the Diaspora community had strong allies in Israel and the importance of the community was dependent on the share of fund raising amount. The Sephardic Jews in general and the Indian community in particular were very weak on this front.

Indian Jewish Community in Israel

The Indian community in Israel maintained the cultural heritage they had carried with them from India, however, their long stay and with the subsequent new generations getting more and more involved in the community affairs they are losing the 'Indian ness'. The younger generations born in Israel are conversant in Hebrew as it is required in all walks of life there and the knowledge of Marathi and Malayalam is diminishing among them. Yet, there is considerable interest among them in maintaining cultural links with India. Israelis of Indian origin have participated in gatherings of Marathi speakers from all over the world and a session of the World

Marathi Conference was held in Israel. The most evident cultural link today, however, comes through the popular culture, particularly Hindi films and dance forms associated with the film world. This is popular with many young people in the Indian Jewish communities and even other Jews, irrespective of whether or not they understand the language.

Many prominent movies have been made with Hebrew subtitled [17] and some of the movies have become big success in Israel. Israelis of Indian origin have limited economic involvement with India. Their political status in the country of their adoption is very modest. There are a number of 'Indian Jewish' and *'Gene-Israel'* associations in small towns, along with a loosely structured umbrella organization, the Central Council for Indian Jews in Israel. But the community does not have a high degree of political mobilization at the national level and consequently have little bargaining power in the intensively competitive Israeli political system. There is only one person of Indian origin in the Knesset-Eli Ben Manachim-Labour (One Israel) MK who was born in Mumbai in a Gaghdadi family. A few others have been successful in local politics in areas with sizable Indian Jew population. *Yesod Hamala,* a small town in northern Israel, had a Cochini Jew as the council president and a group of Indian Jews have started a movement (Hodaya) to mobilize the community for political action. They had marginal impact in the 1999 election, but are seeking to continue their organizational activity.

There is a small group of Non-resident Indians in Israel. They are mostly Gujaratis engaged in the diamond business. There are about 20 families mainly from Palanpur and some of their employees are resident in Israel with employment permits. They play important part in the diamond trade which constitute about half of overall India-Israel trade. Till August 2005, Israeli export to India was US$ 818 million and import from India was US$ 895 million and about half the trade each way was in diamond. [18] The Gujarati community is socially active and by and large well respected in Israel. It has set up an informal association called the Gujarati Indian Association that celebrates major cultural festivals.

The Indian community has formed several associations and tries to remain alive by performing cultural and other activities. The Central Organization of Indian Jews is the main association of Jews of Indian origin in Israel. It conducts meetings of all Indian Jews once in a year and organizes cultural events, especially popular Hindi and Marathi song and dance performances. The Central Organization of Indian Jews also publishes a quarterly journal. The Indo-Israel Cultural Association organizes a variety of cultural events in Israel including lectures on India and artistic performances. The Centre of Jewish Heritage, located in Moshav Nevatim in Israel, is broadly the main organization of the Cochini Jews in Israel and administers the Museum on Jewish Heritage in India. The Gujarati Indian Association revolves mostly the diamond merchants in Israel. [19]

The Jewish community in Israel has great hopes from India. The older generation of the Israeli community of Indian origin has notions about India that are largely nostalgia for the irretrievable past. Members of the second generation have high expectations from India, derived from what it heard from the older generation. They expect things in India to conform to standards in Europe and Israel, and get a cultural shock when they visit India and find that this is not so. With liberalization and Indian government's proposal to allow dual citizenship, the hope is reignited in the Indian community.

Emerging to Prominence: A Long Task

Despite all the odds of language, relocation in a new society, profession shift, the Indian Jewish community in Israel has started emerging in prominence and asserting itself in the socio-political setup. It is not only that the new setup in Israel provided space for men to emerge out successfully. Women too climbed the ladders of success; Rina Pushkarna, an entrepreneur in food and catering services, has a chain of Indian restaurants. Rinat Dokerker, an Israeli beauty queen of Indian origin, is just another name in the list. She was the second runner up at the Miss Israel beauty contest in the year 2003. She also represented her country at the Miss Europe contest, where she said that she was not only representing this country [Israel] but also the vast Indian community here. She has a fascination about India and aspires to break into the Indian modelling scene in time to come.

It is interesting to note the strong Indian connection which this community underlines either through Indian cuisine or their public statements in pageant contest. This connection was further strengthened when Dikerker along with eight other youngsters participated in the internship program for Diaspora youth as part of the fourth 'Pravasi Bhartiya Diwas' celebrations in India in 2003. Rinat Dikerker said participation in the Pravasi Bhartiya Diwas would enable her to "connect" to her roots. To quote her: "My Indianness gives me a distinct identity and this program will enable me to connect to my roots." [20] Sharon Binyamin, Deputy Director of Social Services of Jerusalem Municipality, who was born in Delhi and immigrated to Israel at the age of 19, says she would have the Indian citizenship for ideological reasons, to have her bond renewed. It is difficult to erase 19 years of one's existence. Noah Massil, the president of the Central Organisation of Indian Jews (COIJ) and editor of 'Maiboli' [21] (Marathi quarterly in Israel) expresses satisfaction for the lack of anti-Semitism in India and says we brought the message of peace and non-violence from India so vital for this region. Roley Horowitz (earlier name Savitri), president of the Indo-Israel Cultural Association, who still retains her Indian passport twenty years after she cam to Israel as a tourist and converted to Judaism.

Brigadier (retired) Isaac Samuel, the highest-ranking Indian Jew in the Israel Army, died in November 2005. In Israeli politics, Mumbai-born Eli Ben Manachem, was the deputy speaker of the Knesset, the Israeli parliament. Noar Gudker, secretary of the Israel Cricket Association, whose family immigrated from Mumbai when he was only five years old, says that this extension of goodwill towards people of Indian origin would hopefully compel him to pay at least one visit to the place he was born. David Nagani, a bus driver in Jerusalem, enthrals his passengers with Indian music every day. The common thread of "Indianess" runs through all these successful entrepreneurs who represent India in their own fashion. Their success further strengthens their attachment with India.

Indians and Israeli Scholars Study Sanskrit Poetry

Under the cultural exchange programme between the two governments young scholars as well as distinguished scholars from both the countries are visiting the other country thus generating knowledge as well as curiosity. The Hebrew university of Jerusalem as well as Tel Aviv University conduct regular courses on Indian and Sanskrit studies. 14 renowned Sanskrit scholars from the US, Britain, France, Germany, Netherlands and Indonesia are working on a project coordinated by Yigael D. Bronner of the Department of East Asian Studies at Tel Aviv University and Professor David Shulman from the department of Indian studies at the Hebrew University of Jerusalem. [22]

Two Indian experts are part of the project. Professor H.V. Nagaraja Rao of the International Sanskrit Research Centre at Mysore University is a Sanskrit grammar expert and is a visiting research fellow at the Hebrew University's Institute for Advanced Studies in Jerusalem. The aim of the project is to map the crucial social milieu of historic moments when innovative literary fashions were created, or when poets deviated from their predecessors to break new paths in 'kavya' (Poetry). The study concentrates on key moments of shift and innovation to expose the hidden tensions within an evolving poetic praxis, naturally focusing on revolutionary changes of

Sanskrit prosody, syntax, diction, theme, style, figuration and structural integration," says Bronner.

Until the Twentieth century, the *Bene Israelis* referred themselves as *Bene Israelis* or simply Israelis and not as Jews. In the twentieth century, they slowly began to refer themselves as Jews but normally they used to define themselves as *Bene Israelis* or Jews from Arab countries who settled in India (Baghdadi Jews) came to be known as 'Yehudi. [23] In some of the birth certificates and other legal documents of the early twentieth century their religion was specified as 'Bene 'Israel' and not Jew.

Cochini Jews were known as 'white' (pardesis or foreigners) and 'black' (Malabarees). [24] This division is perhaps contrary to Jewish rules which state that children born to a Jewish mother will always be Jewish irrespective of skin colour. In their rituals Kala could not be offered wine for kiddush untill all Gora had drunk theirs. The Goras were preferred in holding the 'Book' or to blow the 'Shofar'. These two groups used to pray together but they didn't mingle or marry each other. This divide continues to play its role even after immigration to Israel. This divide requires serious study as this is reflected today in the absence of political unity and a unified political pressure group of the Indian Jewish community in Israel. The present political status of the Indian Jewish community has a lot to do with the Ashkenazim politics ever since the establishment of the state of Israel. [25]

There is some indication that the converted Jews faced discrimination from the others and often rebelled to no avail. They wanted to build another synagogue but the local British resident opposed it. They tried to worship from some private homes, but that was opposed by the Diwan of Cochin. In spite of this they managed to conduct their worship for some years from a private home on Cochin's Lillie Street. A letter written by a Jewish company in Bombay on October 22, 1845 requests the Diwan to repeal discriminatory rules against converted Jews. Subsequently, the Jewish authorities in Jerusalem ruled that all Jews converted and otherwise should have equal status in the religion.

This led to removal of all vestiges of discrimination in the foreign Jewish church of Cochin. A.B. Salem, known as the "Jewish Gandhi," led sit-ins, hunger strikes, and other forms of "civil disobedience" (satyagraha) against these Paradesi practices which came to an end only recently. [26] This divide is clearly the influence of Indian culture on them. Many of the custom of the *Bene Israel* were inspired by their Hindu neighbours. Not remarrying of widows was the one and another was the discouragement of levirate marriages (a Jewish custom which commands marriage between the widow and her dead husband's brother if the man dies childless). The *Bene Israelis* were also less strict about the kisher laws.

Some Eminent Jews of India

The *Bene Israel* as a community weren't a powerful and influential community but there were many among them who advanced to high ranks in the armies of local rulers. Some of them also got land from the local rulers as reward for their services. After the British arrived in India, many *Bene Israelis* joined the British forces in India and fought for the British Empire in their different wars around the world. Later on, the *Bene Israelis* adopted the profession of building /budding construction contractors and ventured into other new modern professions that emerged in India such as office clerks, law, modern medicine and other professions. [27] There were some *Bene Israelis* who reached high positions as of judges, lawyers, doctors, institute managers and administrative or other high ranking officers in government services and distinguished themselves as officers in the Indian army.

Baghdadi Jews were mostly traders and financiers and quickly became one of the highest earning communities in the city. Their contribution to the industrial growth of Bombay is well documented. Although the Baghdadi Jews are known primarily for their presence in India, they also established themselves in trading ports further east, notably in Yangon (Rangoon), Singapore, Melaka, Bangkok, and Shanghai. The most prominent Baghdadi Jew was Sir David Sassoon who established the Indian House of Sassoon in 1832 and paved the way for the arrival of many other Iraqi Jews in India. Sir David Sassoon was also a well-known philanthropist.

As philanthropists, the David Sassoon family donated their wealth to public structures. The David Sassoon Docks and a Sassoon Library are some of the famous landmarks still standing today. The Sassoon family is the one after whom the Sassoon docks, the Sassoon hospital, and two of Mumbai's well known sites, the Jacob Circle, and Flora Fountain have been named.

Among the Kolkata Jews, David Joseph Ezra is associated with some of the Kolkata's most imposing buildings—Esplanade mansions, Ezra mansions and Chowringhee mansions as well as Ezra street. David Joseph Ezra made his fortune from prime real estate. Elia David Ezra, son of David Joseph Ezra built the city's most magnificent synagogue—the Magen David Synagogue. D.J Cohen and Reverend E.M.G Cohen played a more direct part in civic work and social uplift. Under Reverend E.M.G. Cohen's proprietorship the Hebrew newspaper Pariah had a circulation of 500 copies a week in 1880's.

There have been many among them who rose to national stature. Hannah Sen, was the President of All India Women's Conference and also the first lady director, Lady Irwin College for Women, Delhi. Ezra Kolet did pioneering work for the Government of India, and the secretary of Delhi Urban Arts Commission, strove to make Delhi a beautiful and habitable place. Haffkine, after whom the famous Haffkine Institute in Bombay (Mumbai) has been named. Dr. E. Moses was Mayor of Bombay. Maj. Gen. Samson who was awarded the Padma Bhushan, and a few other Jews reached prominence in the Indian Armed Forces. General Jacobs became the Governor of Goa. An erstwhile Chief of the Naval Staff was also a Jew.

Nissim Ezekiel (December 24, 1924-January 9, 2004) was a poet, playwright and art critic. He was considered one of the foremost Indian writers in English of his time. He joined the Illustrated Weekly of India as an assistant editor in 1953 and stayed there for two years, he also worked as a broadcaster on arts and literature for all India Radio. He also worked as visiting professor at University of Leeds (1964) and University of Chicago (1967). Ezekiel received the Sahitya Akademi cultural award in 1983 and the Padma Shri in 1988. He was professor of English and reader in American literature at University of Mumbai during the 1990s and secretary of the Indian branch of the international writers' organization PEN.

In the Indian film industry actress/dancer Helen, Hindi film actor David, and Sulochana, the Queen of Indian Silent Films, have made an immortal space for themselves in the industry.

Dr. Erulkar was the personal physician/friend of Mahatma Gandhi. His father, also a doctor, Abraham Eurlkar, donated land for the synagogue in Ahmedabad, Gujarat. Dr. Erulkar's daughter became the 1st lady of Cyprus, married to the President of Cyprus. Dr. Jerusha Jhirad was awarded Padma Shri by the Government of India.

Conclusion

The role of the Indian Jewish community though small in size has been significant in the cultural spheres. Their contribution to the local culture has primarily been non institutional and individuals rose to a position to eminence and richly contributed their respective fields. Their role as cultural ambassadors needs more organized study. The materials in Indian archives and in the documents of the companies that dealt with India have unexplored information bout the Indian Jewish community and their role in different facets of social and political life of the period. With the Track II diplomacy taking prominence and India too opening its door and going for dual citizenship, the Indian Jewish community has a bigger role to play. India cannot just rely only on defence and security aspects to deepen the bilateral relations with Israel. Now more and more Indian Jews from Israel are travelling to India to revive their roots and many are seriously contemplating their relocation in India. As the paper tries to trace out the contribution of the Indian Jewish community in different facets of life throughout history; it underlines the crucial roles they can play in building and strengthening the cultural relations between India and Israel.

End Notes

1. Judith T Shuval and Elazar Leshem (1998), "The Sociology of Migration in Israel: A critical View", in Ernest Krausz (ed.), Immigration to Israel: Sociological Perspectives, New Jersey, Transaction Publishers, pp. 10-11.
2. Shalava Weil (2002), "The Heritage and Legacy of the Jews of India", in Shalava Weil (ed.), India's Jewish Heritage, Mumbai: Marg Publications, p. 14.
3. Chitta Ranjan Das, "Israel's Jews From India", *The Eastern Anthropologist,* Vol. 49, No. 3-4, p. 327.
4. Benjamin J. Israel (1984), The Jews of India, New Delhi: Mosaic Books, p. 8.
5. L. Aigdor, "A Problem of Cultural Integration", *Jewish Affairs,* Vol. 9, January 1952, p. 6.
6. Eliyahu, Ben Eliya (1997), Namaya Motta: The Patron of Malabarees, Haifa: Eliyahu Publications.
7. Walter J. Fischel, "The Indian Archives: A Source for the History of the Jews of Asia (From the Sixteenth Century Onwards)", *The Jewish Quarterly Review*, Vol. 57, The Seventy Fifth Anniversary Volume of the Jewish Quarterly Review (1967), p. 196.
8. *The Jewish Quarterly Review*, 1956, Vol. 47, pp. 37-57.
9. Walter J. Fischel, op.cit., p. 201.
10. M.D. Japeth (1967), Jews of India-A brief History, Oxford University Press: London, p. 92.
11. Walter J. Fischel, "The Exploration of Jewish Antiquities of Cochin on the Malabar Coast", *Journal of American Oriental Society*, Vol. 86, 1967, p. 237.
12. Walter J. Fischel, "The Exploration of Jewish Antiquities of Cochin on the Malabar Coast", *Journal of American Oriental Society,* Vol.

86, 1967, pp. 230-234.

13. Walter J. Fischel, (ibid).
14. John, P.K., http://www.ananthapuri.com/kerala-history.asp?page=jew
15. Oren Yiftachel, "Social Control, Urban Planning and Ethno Class Relations: Mizrachi Jew's in Israel's Development Towns", *International Journal of Urban and Regional Research*, Vol. 24, June 2000, pp. 419-432.
16. Elazar, Danial J., http://www.jcpa.org/dje/articles3/rwj6.htm.
17. I myself have been part of some such projects.
18. cbs.gov.il, 2005.
19. Government of India (2005), Report of the High Level Committee on the Indian Diaspora, December.
20. Hindustan Times, New Delhi, "Israeli Beauty Queen to Take Part in Pravasi Diwas", PTI, December 2, 2005.
21. http://timesofindia.indiatimes.com/articleshow/msid-1095781,prtpage-1.cms.
22. http://www.hindustantimes.com/news/5967 584013,001600060001.htm.
23. http://adaniel.tripod.com/beneisrael.htm.
24. Benjamin, J.M. (1999), "Jews of Cochin", New Delhi, Jewish Welfare Association, p. 3.
25. Deborah Bernstein, "Political Participation", *Plural Societies*, No. 5, 1984, pp. 15-32.
26. *Jewish Political Studies Review Abstracts*, Vol. 5, Nos. 3-4 (Fall 5754/1993).
27. Benjamin J. Israel (1984), The Jews of India, New Delhi: Mosaic Books, p. 8.

References

Benjamin, J. Israel (1984), The Jews of India, New Delhi, Mosaic Books.

Benjamin, J.M. (1999), Jews of Cochin, New Delhi, Jewish Welfare Association.

Chitta Ranjan Das, "Israel's Jews from India", *The Eastern Anthropologist*, Vol. 49, Nos. 3-4.

Deborah Bernstein, "Political Participation", *Plural Societies*, No. 5, 1984.

Eliyahu Ben Eliya and Namaya Motta (1997), The Patron of Malabarees, Haifa: Eliyahu Publications.

Government of India, Report of the High Level Committee on the Indian Diaspora: Chapter 9, 2000.

Jewish Political Studies Review Abstracts, Vol. 5, Nos. 3-4 (Fall 5754/1933).

Judith, T. Shuval and Elazar Leshem, "The Sociology of Migration in Israel: A Critical View", in Ernest Krausz (ed.), Immigration to Israel: Sociological Perspectives, New Jersey: Transaction Publishers, 1998.

L. Aigdon, "A Problem of Cultural Integration", Jewish Affairs, Vol. 9, January 1952.

M.D. Japeth, Jews of India: A Brief History, Oxford University Press, London, 1967.

Oren Yiftachel, "Social Control, Urban planning and Ethno Class Relations: Mizrachi Jew's in Israel's Development Towns", International Journal of Urban and Re ional Research, Vol. 24, June 2000.

Shalava Weil, "The Heritage and Legacy of the Jews of India", in Shalava Weil (ed.), India's Jewish Heritage, Mumbai: Marg Publications, 2002.

Walter J. Fischel, "The Exploration of Jewish Antiquities of Cochin on the Malabar Coast", Journal of American Oriental Society, Vol. 86, 1967.

Walter J. Fischel, The Indian Archives: A Source for the History of the Jews of Asia (From the Sixteenth Century on), The Jewish Quarterly Review, Vol. 57, The Seventy Fifth Anniversary Volume of the Jewish Quarterly Review (1967).

Part III
Terrorism, Globalization and Security

10

India-West Asia Co-operation in Fighting Terrorism

Bansidhar Pradhan

Seeking cooperation from certain West Asian countries in its fight against terrorism has emerged as a crucial component of India's West Asia policy in recent years. Mention may be made in particular about Israel and Turkey with whom India has already set up Joint Working Groups (JWGs). With countries like Iran and the Arab League in general, a broad understanding has been reached on cooperation in fighting the menace of terrorisms. To what extent are these endeavours effective in combating the type of terrorism that India faces? This will be the main thrust of my paper.

At the outset, one needs to put India's problems regarding terrorism in proper perspective. India has been fighting terrorism for more than two decades and over 60,000 people have been killed so far. During the 1980s, it confronted the menace in the border state of Punjab in the form of Khalistan militancy. Since the late 1980s, the main problem for India is the cross-border terrorism in the highly sensitive and strategic state of Jammu and Kashmir, as also in some other parts, sponsored by Pakistan. Taking advantage of some internal problems in Jammu and Kashmir, Pakistan has been using terrorism as an instrument of state policy in regard to its perennial conflictual relationship with India.

This has been done through providing finance, training, intelligence and weaponry to those sections of the state that have some grievances against the Central Government. Pakistan's Inter Services Intelligence (ISI) has been the main executing agency of the terrorist operations as part of a prolonged low-intensity, proxy war against India. Thus, the terrorism that India confronts is "typically cross-border and State-sponsored". Even though, numerous initiatives have been taken in the last couple of years to "ease tensions and normalize relations" one cannot say that there is an end to cross-border terrorism in Jammu and Kashmir. The recent decline in infiltration is more as a result of some effective measures taken by the Indian Army than due to any "discernible change of heart, or action, by the Pakistani authorities". In other words, India's strategic environment remains "largely unchanged". This becomes evident from the 2004-2005 annual report of the Defence Ministry.

Even though India has been appealing before the international community at every level to take note of its difficulty in tackling the problem of cross-border terrorism for more than two decades, it "took" the September 11 attacks on the US mainland to "bring the global reach of terrorism into the collective consciousness of the world". The terrorist attacks of 11 September shook the entire American nation as never before and galvanized the Bush administration into action. The US response was swift and decisive in the form of the war on terrorism. The US war on terrorism was later sought to be projected as a global war against terrorism.

The fact that the war was waged in the then Taliban-controlled Afghanistan, that had provided sanctuary to Osama bin Laden and his Al-Qaeda network, made it all the more important for India. As is well-known, the Taliban regime was basically created and sustained by Pakistan. India, naturally therefore, extended full support that included military facilities to the US war on terrorism. The Vajpayee government hoped that now the US would understand the high cost of terrorism that India had been paying for so long and would lend full support to its *efforts* to combat Pakistani-sponsored terrorism from across the border.

In hindsight, it would appear that those hopes were

unfounded as became evident from the US response to the terrorist attacks on the Indian Parliament on 13th December 2001. One is not arguing here that India had any other option except supporting the US war against the Taliban and Al-Qaeda, both on moral and strategic grounds. But the fact remained that the US did not reciprocate in equal measures to India's *efforts* towards retaliatory strikes on terrorist training camps in Pakistan-held Kashmir. In this regard, the whole misconception about the "global war on terrorism" needs to be understood.

There is hardly anything global about the war against terrorism. The predicament is that almost each and every country claims to be a part of it, even though each one has its own perceptions about what terrorism is and who are the terrorists. This is despite the fact that in October 2004, the UN Security Council has unanimously passed a Russian-initiated anti-terror resolution which seeks to somehow come around a broadly accepted definition of terrorism. The said resolution declares "all acts of violence against civilians, unjustifiable by any political, philosophical, ideological, racial, ethnic or religious considerations". In fact, some countries who claim to be part of the global coalition against terrorism are themselves part of the problem. Further, there are double standards on the part of the Western nation, particularly the US, on the issue of terrorism and the rationale behind retaliatory strikes against terrorist hideouts.

Thus, the so-called global war has been reduced to a war against those who challenge US interests. As for now there is very little common ground between the US and India's wars on terrorism. While Pakistan is the main strategically of the US in its war against terrorism, it continues to sponsor terrorism against India. Given the illusive and self-sustaining nature of Al-Qaeda and recent reports about the resurgence of the Taliban, it may be a long time before Pakistan loses its importance in US calculations in the South Asian region. The crux of the matter is that India has to fight against terrorism on its own. What about the West Asian countries, particularly Israel?

Israel tops the list of West Asian countries that India is seeking cooperation from in fighting terrorism. This formed part of the Vajpayee government's consistent effort to build a strong strategic relationship with Israel. Counter-terrorism cooperation was the central focus of all high-level bilateral discussions between the two countries since the September 1999 visit of Brajesh Mishra to Israel. The subsequent visits of L.K. Advani and Jaswant Singh laid a strong basis for this. In fact, a team of Israeli counter-terrorism experts visited the Kashmir valley in October 2000 which was deliberately kept less publicized. However, the terrorist attacks of 11 September and 13 December brought India much closer to Israel leading to the setting up of a JWG on counter-terrorism. India sought to elevate this bilateral cooperation to a broad conceptual framework through a strategic partnership with Israel.

This idea was first mooted by the then Home Minister Advani in the aftermath of 11 September. Then, in May 2003, the then National Security Adviser Brajesh underlined the necessity of creating a viable alliance of democratic societies to combat international terrorism. During the then Prime Minister Ariel Sharon's visit to India, the strategic partnership to fight terrorism was sought to be given a formal shape. The issue of terrorism topped the agenda in all high-level discussions. The Delhi statement on Friendship and Cooperation between India and Israel considered both countries "partners in the battle" against terrorism. It also called upon all countries to "take decisive action against this" and "condemn state and individuals who aid and abet terrorism across borders, harbour and provide sanctuary to terrorist and provide them financial means, training or patronage".

India's strategic relationship with Israel in fighting terrorism has been a highly sensitive and debatable issue within the country. During the Vajpayee government, the main opposition party, the Congress, for instance, opposed this. In fact, the party had cautioned the government not to break the national consensus on foreign policy. What is interesting to note is that after coming to power, the Congress-led UPA has not taken any such step that would indicate a dilution of India's strategic relationship with Israel. The only difference lies in the style of pursuing the policy. While the earlier BJP-led NDA government was more aggressive and outgoing in building a strategic partnership with Israel the present government seems to be doing the same in a more nuanced and subtle manner. This is despite the fact that the left parties are strongly opposed to such a relationship with Israel.

The claims about the gains of Indo-Israeli cooperation against terrorism seem to be overstated because of the following reasons. First, at the conceptual level there are fundamental differences between he situation in Jammu and Kashmir and the Palestine issue. India is fighting a state which is not only occupying almost one-third of Jammu and Kashmir but also using the territory as a springboard for terrorist operation to subvert internationally acclaimed democratic process there. In simple terms, Pakistan is encouraging secessionism in Jammu and Kashmir, Israel, on the contrary, is in occupation of Palestinian land and the Palestinians in West Bank are resisting an illegal occupation.

India is a victim of cross-border terrorism whereas Israel is an occupying authority suppressing the legitimate rights and aspirations of the Palestinians. This is not to deny the fact that in recent years certain Palestinian factions have resorted to methods like suicide bombings, killing innocent Israeli civilians which are terrorists and cannot be justified on any ground; the Palestinian leadership has accepted this. But to equate the whole Palestinian resistance movement with terrorism is erroneous. Therefore, it will be as difficult for Israel to openly declare Pakistan a sponsor of terrorism as it is for India to accept that the whole Palestinian armed resistance against Israeli occupation is another manifestation of global terrorism.

Thus, there can be little common ground between India and Israel in fighting terrorism. The dynamics are extremely complex even though some high ranking Indian officials during the tenure of the Vajpayee government persistently tried to simplify them by using opaque language and abstract ideas such as the solidarity of democracies and free societies. Equating Indian democracy with that of Israel is to draw a false parallel. India is a tolerant, pluralist, secular democracy while Israel is an exclusivist Jewish state even though it practices democracy in other aspects.

Second, at the strategic level, Israel cannot do anything that harms US interest and taking on Pakistan would go against the US war on terrorism. Pakistan provides sanctuary to forces like the Lashkar-e-Taiba which is responsible for most of deadly terrorist operation in recent times in different parts of India. From an Indian viewpoint taking on the Lashkar-e-Taiba is fast emerging as a strategic imperative. It is very difficult to believe that Israel would join hands with India in any future operation against the Lashkar-e-Taiba simply because that would annoy Pakistan which in turn would be strongly opposed by the US. Moreover, it is a question of time when Pakistan and Israel would establish full diplomatic relations; there are strong indications that Pakistan wants to balance the growing Indo-Israeli ties, especially in the defence sector, by establishing diplomatic relation with Israel. The recent landmark meeting between the foreign ministers of Pakistan and Israel in Istanbul is an instance of such indications. Further, Israel considers Iran (as also Syria) as the "epicentre of terrorism" whereas for India it is Pakistan. So where is the common ground?

Third, at the empirical level too Israel can be of very little help to India. In the immediate aftermath of the 13 December attack, Shimon Peres, the then Israeli Deputy Prime Minister and Foreign Affairs Minister, had visited India. Peres did not talk about Pakistani-sponsored terrorism and took refuge in broad generalities by terming the attack on the Indian

Parliament as a strike against democratic institutions. In fact, he considered it unwise to attack terrorist camps based in Pakistan. Similarly, during his visit to India, Sharon diplomatically avoided a question on Pakistan's role in sponsoring terrorism by saying that he was not familiar with the situation there. How can India establish counter-terrorism cooperation with a country whose Prime Minister is not familiar with the situation in a place where all the terrorist operations against India are given final shape?

Further, the most important reason why a strategic ties with Israel is being talked about is the Israeli record in counter-terrorism. At best, the Israeli success in combating terrorism is dubious. The fact that the Israelis today are more insecure than ever before speaks enough about the effectiveness of the Israeli approach to terrorism. The topography of the Kashmir valley is entirely different. This is not to deny that Israel can be of some help to India in terms of supplying sophisticated weaponry to fight terrorism.

India can buy any weapon it wants through bilateral defence deals. Israeli supply of arms and equipment over the years included unmanned aerial vehicles (UAV) for surveillance, fast-attack patrol boats, automated manoeuvring combat instrumentation, large quantities of ammunition including sophisticated anti-tank rounds, thermal imaging system for T-72 tanks and armoured vehicles, the controversial Barak anti-missile system for the Indian Navy, the Phalcom Airborne Warning and Control System (AWACS), etc. In fact, defence and military cooperation between the two countries has been marked by a certain degree of opacity.

For instance, in November 2005, an Israeli source reported that Israel would sell around 50 unmanned spy drones worth US$ 220 millions to India. The Indian Defence Ministry neither confirmed nor denied the report. The point, however, is that any defence deal between India and Israel is a purely commercial relationship between two friendly nations which India and Israel are. Israel wants access to India as a market for advanced weapon system. The relationship, therefore, can very well be kept at that level without giving it the aura of a "strategic relationship in counter-terrorism" which creates avoidable complications.

Finally, at the policy level, India's so-called common cause with Israel in fighting terrorism may send a wrong message to other important allies in the region with which India has substantial relations in diverse fields. Iran is one such country which is concerned with the growing Indo-Israeli strategic cooperation, not least because of the known hostile policies of the US and Israel towards it.

Among the Islamic countries in the region, cooperation with Turkey has been given priority. Being pluralistic, secular and democratic countries, India and Turkey broadly share the concern about terrorism posing threats to the very fabric of their societies. The projected areas of cooperation are wide-ranging from cross-border terrorism to religious fanaticism to obscurantism to drug-trafficking. This has been the focus of bilateral discussions during all the high-level visits from both the sides in the post-Cold War period. During the Taliban regime, both the countries had similar views on the spread of terrorism from Afghanistan. At the specific level, Turkey and India face identical problems with regard to the issues of Kurdistan and Kashmir, respectively, Even though there are differences between the two issues (Kurdistan being an ethnic one).

Turkey has shown greater understanding of India's position on cross-border terrorism in recent years. The fact that it is gradually distancing itself from Pakistan is an indication that it does not approve of Pakistani activities in the Kashmir valley. Pakistan's open support to forces of extremism and terrorism cannot be overlooked by Turkey in the light of its own problem with the Kurdish rebels. Indeed, after the Taliban experience in Afghanistan, Turkey remains gravely concerned about the spreading of forces of religious bigotry and fanaticism into Central Asia where it has huge stakes as much as India. Further, during Prime Minister Vajpayee's visit to Turkey in September 2003 (the first such visit of an Indian Prime Minister in fifteen years after Rajiv Gandhi had visited Turkey in July 1988) when the two countries signed an agreement to set up a JWG on combating terrorism, the Turkish Prime Minister, Erdogan, underlined the dangers involved in a selective approach to terrorism. This was an indication that Turkey, unlike Israel, shared India's focus about the double standards being adopted by certain dominant actors in international politics while dealing with the issue of terrorism.

Iran is yet another country in the region with which India is seeking to develop a common understanding on the issue. Making a common cause with Iran on the menace of terrorism is crucial for India in view of the strong and friendly relationship between Pakistan and Iran in the past. It needs to be pointed out that India and Iran have moved closer to each other during the last few years which had enabled them to recognize the threats to regional peace and stability from the forces of terrorism and extremism. Once again, the nature of the Taliban regime and its external patronage provided a strong basis for the convergence of perceptions between India and Iran. Both the countries were gravely concerned about the dangerous nexus between the illicit trade in narcotics and the forces of terrorism.

Iran's support for India in the war against international terrorism became very clear from the Tehran Declaration that was issued at the end of Prime Minister Vajpayee's visit to Iran in April 2001. It needs to be remembered that the Declaration was issued much before the 11 September attacks. Further, just one week after Vajpayee's visit, Iran signed an agreement with Saudi Arabia to combat terrorism, organized crime, drug trafficking, etc. From India's viewpoint such a pact implied the "further consolidation of the regional coalition against the forces of extremism and narco-terrorism radiating out of Pakistan and Afghanistan". The New Delhi Declaration that was issued at the end of President Khatemi's visit to India in January 2003 went a step further when both the countries agreed that the fight against terrorism "should not be selective or based on double standards".

Their worries about double standards are not misplaced as becomes evident from the differences that India and the US have over the relationship between Iran and Al-Qaeda. India very well realizes that the recent gains which it has made in Afghanistan would not have been possible without the Iranian cooperation. The recent killing of an Indian driver by the Taliban in Afghanistan and the alleged involvement of Pakistan in the episode is a reminder that in the long run, cooperation with Iran would be more rewarding for India in containing cross-border terrorism.

With regard to the Arab-Islamic countries in the region, India has been following a two-track approach to ensure their cooperation. At one level, it has revived its interaction with the wider Arab League focusing on a variety of issues including terrorism. For instance, an MoU was signed in March 2002 with the League which envisaged regular consultation between India and the Arab League ministers and senior officials in New York as also in New Delhi and Cairo alternatively. At another level, India has been making efforts to set up proper legal and institutional mechanisms like extradition treaty, JWG, etc. to deal with the menace at the bilateral level. At the same time, India is also trying to convince each country, through quiet diplomacy as well as high-level discussions, about Pakistan's continuing support to cross-border terrorism.

The response of these countries has been broadly positive, though somewhat slow and cautious. In the aftermath of 11 September specially, these countries have become more sensitive to the threats emanating from the forces of religious extremism and terrorism to their own regime stability. As a result, they seem to have shown a greater understanding of India's concerns and appear willing to make common cause with it in the fight against terrorism. India's efforts are showing modest results as becomes evident from the arrest of Anees Ibrahim, one of the key accused in the Bombay serial blasts, and the deportation of Aftab Ansari, the prime accused in the attack on the American Centre in Kolkata, by the UAE.

However, in order to get wholehearted and timely cooperation from these countries, India needs to dispel the lingering doubts about the moves to identify terrorism with a particular religion, Islam in the present case. The common concern in these countries is that India is gradually moving close to the US-Israel position on the fight against terrorism and thereby according legitimacy to the horrendously coined phrase Islamic terrorism". Terrorism is terrorism; there is nothing Hindu, Jewish or Islamic about it. This is a major challenge for India policy makers in the coming years as far as fighting terrorism is concerned.

In conclusion, two points need to be made. First, in the fight against terrorism, the US because of its own strategic compulsions cannot be expected to rein in Pakistan even though Indo-US relations in techno-economic spheres have shown great improvement. As the Al-Qaeda operations spread across the region, the US will be more heard-pressed to depend on Musharraf's military regime. Viewed in this context, a strategic relationship with Israel would be of very little help. Second, it would not be unwise on India's part to cultivate the Arab/Islamic countries in West Asia more intensely in its fight against terrorism. It needs to be remembered that terrorist fugitives invariably take shelter in these countries like the UAE after creating havoc in India.

There is no need for grandiose security framework or strategic tie-ups; this can be done through quiet diplomacy and, more importantly, by binding these countries with strong economic ties so that they develop heavy stakes in India. In fact, given the strong relationship between India and Russia, the good relations between Iran and Russia, the warming up of ties between Iran and Saudi Arabia in view of the latter's uneasy relationship with the US, it would not be bad idea for

India to develop a broad framework of cooperation along with Russia, Iran and Saudi Arabia to counter Pakistan-sponsored cross-border terrorism. This may well prove to be a better option than the US-Israel-Turkey strategic equation that some are talking about in India. The case of Turkey can probe to be a little complex in view of its close ties with Israel and the US on the one hand, and the burgeoning relationship with India on the other. Needless to say, the Arab/Islamic countries, on their part, need to be more sensitive to India's concerns with regard to terrorism.

11

Impact of Globalization on the Arab World

Akhtar Nazmi

Globalization is the name that has been given to the social, economic and political processes that have, taken together, produced the characteristic conditions of contemporary existence. In particular, globalization refers to the ways in which previously distant parts of the world have become connected in a historically unprecedented manner, such that developments in one part of the world are now able to rapidly produce effects on geographically distant localities. This in turn has made it possible to begin to imagine the world as a single, global space linked by a wide array of technological, economic, social and cultural forces. This general conception of globalization is echoed by all of its major theorists. Globalization has been characterized variously as 'the intensification of world-wide social relations which link distant localities in such a way that local happenings are shaped by events occurring many miles away' as 'time-space compression' as 'the stretching out of the geography of social relations' as 'the receding constraints of geography on social and cultural arrangements' and as 'the compression of the world and the intensification of the consciousness of the world as a whole. However, the human societies across the globe have established progressively closer contacts over many centuries, but recently the pace has dramatically increased.

Jet airplanes, cheap telephone service, email, computers, huge ocean going vessels, instant capital flows, all these have made the world more interdependent than ever. Multinational corporations manufacture products in many countries and sell to consumers around the world. Money, technology and raw materials move ever more swiftly across national borders. Along with products and finances, ideas and cultures circulate more freely. As a result, laws, economies, and social movements are forming at the international level. Many politicians, academics, and journalists treat these trends as both inevitable and (on the whole) welcome. But for billions of the world's people, business-driven globalization means uprooting old ways of life and threatening livelihoods and cultures. The global social justice movement, itself a product of globalization, proposes an alternative path, more responsive to public needs. Intense political disputes will continue over globalization's meaning and its future direction.

Globalization and the Arab World

The special nature of the Arab region today is derived greatly, among other things, from its oil wealth. The oil has been functional, for the second half of the 20th century, in shaping all Arab societies. It had a strong impact on the development of both the oil as well as the non-oil countries through labour migration, which was accelerated during the seventies with the boom in oil prices. However, other factors have influenced the socio-economic formations of the Arab countries, such as their relationship with western capitalist countries, in addition to the radical socio-economic and political changes resulting from the revolutions, which occurred in some Arab countries in the 1950s and the 1960s. The response to globalization by different Arab countries would depend, to some extent, on the initial socio-economic and political conditions of each country: their different levels of development and their actual degree of integration into the global economy.

It has been argued that globalization is not a new phenomenon and that the first wave of globalization began in 1870 through commercial activities and over-seas investments. Thereafter came the second wave of globalization, starting in the 1970s of the 20th century through the MNCs operations within the process of "internationalization of production". Each wave of globalization had a centre from which its influence spread all over the world. The Arab-region, it is suggested, was radiant centre for globalization in that sense more than once throughout history.

However, since the rise of modern western civilization the Arab region became a passive recipient of the influence of globalization. In 1998 two centuries have passed since the first contact between the Arab region and the Modern West through Napoleon's campaign on Egypt. Few years later Mohammed Ali inaugurated a new round of interaction between the Egyptian and the world economy through exporting cotton to Europe and importing; production, knowledge and war arts from Europe. The following decades of the 19th century and the first decades of the 20th century witnessed series of integrations of Arab countries, one after the other, into the world economy through British or French occupation or American hegemony. These processes had strongly affected the Arab region economically, socially, politically and culturally.

Globalization and Arab Satellite Television

Al-Jazeera, a Qatari news satellite television station, scooped the world's media with its coverage of the US attack on Afghanistan and Iraq in the aftermath of the September 11, 2001 attacks on the World Trade Centre and the Pentagon. The growing importance of transnational Arab news media, notably the phenomenon of Al-Jazeera, the Qatari news channel that has become a global cause calibre since airing videotapes produced and featuring Osama Bin Laden, Leader of the al-Qaeda network. However, the Al-Jazeera has become a household name by challenging every imaginable Arab taboo, ranging from interviewing Islamic radicals and Israeli generals, to frontal attacks on Arab government and non-holds barred discussion of social and cultural controversies. In the aftermath of September 11, 2001 and the US attack on the Taliban regime and removal of autocratic rule of Saddam

Hussain, Al-Jazeera played an important role to cover all the facts. The network sold footage to an impressive range of world media, and became a source of fascination, praise and outrage in global public discourse.

In the current conjecture the West Asia is again at the heart of global geopolitics. With the Saudi-American relationship at an historically low ebb, the drums of an Iraqi war beating loudly in Washington, and the Israeli-Palestinian conflict reaching a boiling intensity, the stakes of the post-September 11 era are very high for Arab regimes. As a result, political issues are taking an unprecedented importance on the level of transnational media. While these developments might appear to be unprecedented, they in fact fall in line with history, which provides the willing contemporary observer with important insights on the current situation.

West Asia after 9/11

West Asian's response to the 9/11 incident is complicated and thought-provoking. Some extremist organizations attempted to take this opportunity to drag the whole Islamic world into an all-round anti-Western war. They held that the US military operation in Afghanistan was a surprise attack on poor Muslims, aimed at destroying Islam. So Muslims throughout the world should unite to launch a holy war against the US. Other universalized Muslim elites stood up to clarify their stance on Islamic fundamentalism". They held that "all Muslim developing themselves in a multi-technological, multi-cultural and multi-belief world should defend an Islam advocating tolerance". [1]

When leaders of West Asian countries condemned the terrorist act and expressed their support for the US flight against terrorism, the anti-US sentiments of the masses of people in these countries rose. Besides, almost all these countries held that while the incident occurred in the US, the long pending Middle East issue no doubts was one of the hotbeds of terrorism. A socially extreme trend of thought has risen again, which is being used by terrorists because the region has long been treated unfairly. Western countries have seriously distorted the image of Islam and Arabs, while globalization has subjected it to various negative assaults. It is mere fact that the globalization is mainly an economic process pushed by market forces, but the practical situation is much more complicated. In the Arab World, globalization is still hard to grasp. Its importance lies not only in economic forces, but also in cultural experiences of the Islamic world, that is, the Muslims' way of understanding daily life. Globalization involves nationality, national culture and nationalism; it may become a decisive factor in the fields of culture, politics and economic life and change the mechanism of a people's daily life. Therefore, it poses an unprecedented great challenge to Islamic traditional cultural and lifestyle.

Undoubtedly, many countries in the region have a clear understanding of the advantages and disadvantages globalization may bring to them some countries are making positive preparations for meeting the challenge of globalization in order to guard against any loss of national characteristics and cultural values. But, this cannot offset the dissatisfaction of the Islamic world with the current globalization and Americanization, nor can it impede the swell of socially extreme trends of thought resulting from this dissatisfaction. The criticism of globalization by the Islamic social elite is full of such worries that the undesirable reactions globalization may cause, for example, rise of stubbornly biased sentiments and extremism, increase of desire for revenge, and feelings of isolation. [2]

The radical anti-globalization social trend of thought emerging in Arab World has something to do with its weak position and unfair treatment in the global economic system of Middle East countries (except Israel). To many, the current world economic order is based on the unfair "world system". This systems' structural features are that the prosperity of developed countries at the cost of the poverty of developing countries, and the prosperity of a few countries "depending" on the poverty of most countries. The superpower is working out the rules of globalization, unabashedly insisting on placing its own national interests above other considerations, while eulogizing the merits of globalizations. [3] Such rules of the game will weaken the national role of West Asian countries and put them in an unfavourable position in global competition. Some countries will even be "marginalized" and in realty become victims of globalization.

The rise of socially extreme trends of thought has a bearing on the attempt of the US and the West at large to build a new international order, which represents the interests of the great powers and rich states while ignoring the interests of developing countries in the post-Cold War period. Many Arab countries think that this new international order may widen the gap between various members of the international community. This is because it disregards the interests of developing countries and poor societies, flaunts the banner of trade freedom while stifling the attempts of developing countries, and adopts a dual standard and a non-objective position on human rights. It does as it pleases, sometimes turning a blind eye, sometimes making trouble.

This makes societies, organizations and countries belonging to the Third World, in the past and present, suffer grave oppression and difficulties and to be feared by many peoples. [4] The rise of socially extreme trends of thought is related to the long-term distortion and mortification of the Islamic world and the masses of Arab people. Arab countries see the West's view of them to be based on such "unorthodox" theories as "the end of history" and "the clash of civilizations" and other improper concepts". These wrong theories and irresponsible remarks have sowed seeds of suspicions in the international order and made the West unable fairly to coordinate and lead the world. Especially when it exerts non-objective impact on suspected international organizations, it often regards Islam and Muslims as formidable enemies, and then Arab and people being inclined to support Arabs. [5]

For a long time, Islam has been misinterpreted and reprimanded as a backward and rigid religion by the West and Arabs and Muslims residing in the West also have often been discriminated against. After 9/11, many incidents occurred, in which innocent Arabs and Muslims were attacked in the Western world. The practice of distorting and vilifying Arabs and describing them as terrorists has been long standing and even has become a fixed mode in the media and works of literature, film and television. Amr Moussa, former Egyptian Foreign Minister, pointed out that Arabs are faced with unprecedented huge challenges. These result from the latest equipment made with advanced technology, the most dangerous theories put forward according to Western concepts, and the most severe distortions and slander. [6]

To sum up, the extreme social trend of thought in the Arab world results from many factors which have been brewing over the long-term. The assault of the negative impacts of globalization has added fuel to the flames in this trend of thought. A noteworthy phenomenon is that the extreme trend of thought in the anti-globalization movement has often merged with terrorism in recent years. Violence occurs in the anti-globalization movement not only in West Asia, but also in other parts of the world. The WTO ministerial meeting in Seattle in December, 1999, was suspended due to violent demonstrations. Confusion appeared at the G-8 Summit in July 2001. The IMF and World Bank conference scheduled for September 2001 in Washington shortened its agenda by a wide margin due to an expected large-scale demonstration at the time; after the September 11 incident its date was forcibly delayed. Mohammad Malaek, Iranian Ambassador to China, stated that various passive consequences of globalization obviously are harmful to the spirit of freedom, cultural diversity and pluralism; they can easily incite turbulence and violence. [7] Historical experience tells people that terrorism always looks for support from the socially extreme trends of thought.

Globalization has enlarged the distance between the rich and poor states. For a long time, the advantages of the transnational links contrasted sharply with the social inequality between them. Since the September 11 incident, the new antiterrorism coalition composed of rich states may drive a wedge between developed and developing countries. This geopolitical wedge may enlarge the long bred economic disparity and further estrange the developing countries. [8] All this may become the soil of terrorism.

Moreover, in a sense, terrorism benefits from globalization without effective management. This globalized flow with loopholes of such essential factors as fund, information and personnel has created material conditions for the worldwide operation of terrorism. [9] Therefore, when we are planning to fight and eliminate international terrorism, we must look into its root causes and symptoms and make efforts to remove its source. The issue of development should be energetically resolved to make the people of all social strata in all the countries benefit from the globalization process.

It must be pointed out that Islam, as a worldwide religion, certainly is not the source of terrorism. But like other extreme religious trends, Islamic fundamentalist extremism often becomes a theory in support of terror and other violent activities. In recent years an Islamic force, politically and socially autocratic in colour, has been rising and constitutes some armed gangs advocating a lopsided explanation of Islamic doctrine. [10] Violent and terrorist activities plotted by these armed gangs tend to rise. At the same time, pan-Islamist thought is also reviving in Muslim society.

The Arab countries are often interwoven with the pan-Islamic unity movement. Not only to fundamentalists but also to many Arabs, the sole Islamic community is Muslims Umma—which must be placed above the Arab nation. Individuals should unreservedly support Muslims in Bosnia, Kashmir, Chechen, Cyprus and the Nagornyi Karabakh region. [11] This passage is in fact an annotation on the pan-Islamist thought active in the Arab world.

Pan Islamism rose in the middle of the 19th century, resulting from the invasion and enslavement of the Islamic world by Western colonialists and imperialists and responding to the challenges with which Muslims were faced. It stressed that people of all nationalities who believe in Islam should have common historical and cultural traditions and common interests and unity to safeguard and rejuvenate Islamic belief. Its ideological base originated from Islamic self-understanding as a universal religion without limitations of nationality, colour, language or national boundary.

It called on Muslims all over the world to unite, to form an extensive community on the basis of common belief, and to conduct a holy war against the invading European colonialists under the leadership of a caliph of noble character and high prestige till final victory. [12] The pan-Islamist thought created by Afghani (1838-1897) was strongly anti-imperialist in colour and expressed the dissatisfaction of the lower strata with society because of the Western capitalist's entry into Middle East. [13] This has exerted great impact on arousing the national consciousness of peoples of various Islamic countries; it is one of the most important social thought trends and movements in the modern and contemporary history of Islam.

Though as a movement, pan-Islamism ended in failure, this traditional religious social trend of thought still has extensive influence. This desire for recognition by the belief community of pan-Islamism led to the anti-US sentiments and irrational sympathy for the Taliban and Bin Laden by the masses of Muslims in the Islamic world after the U.S. military operation in Afghanistan. [14] Pan-Islamism is not an extreme trend of thought: it is a social trend of thought easily to be misinterpreted by the West and made use of by Islamic extremists. The reason is that it follows the banners of Islam, anti-imperialism and anti-colonialism, thus having broad influence on the masses of Muslims. Though many people know that Islamic extremism does not represent Islam, the two are often mixed up wittingly or unwittingly, causing confusion in the judgement of ordinary people.

After the September 11 incident, the US Government stressed repeatedly that anti-terrorism was not anti-Islam. Henry Kissinger also warned that the US and its allies must act with caution and cannot represent his new anti-terrorist policy as a clash of civilizations between the Western and Islamic civilizations; even Huntington came out to state that the incident was not a clash of civilizations. But some people still associated the two consciously or unconsciously. Recent polls show that 60 percent of Americans do not trust neighbours of Arab descent, and over 100 racial crimes targeting American citizens of Arab Descent have occurred. This spontaneous racial discrimination is hard to control. President Bush made a slip of the tongue and referred to the US military operation in Afghanistan as "a new crusade". Though the US Government itself remedied the mistake in time, many Arabs still considered that this wording reflected the true mentality of many Americans. Moreover, after the incident the mainstream world's political words were only of condemnation of terrorism and paid no attention to its source.

Western definitions of terrorism are also questionable because they concern only the phenomenon of violence itself, especially individual retaliatory actions targeting developed countries. They seldom explore the in-depth source of the phenomenon of terrorism. Especially, they ignore its cultural and religious meanings and the antagonism caused by the present international system, thus losing historical insight into terrorism. [15] Such definitions certainly are incomplete; often they are mixed up with special interests and value judgements which easily create a misunderstanding of Islam in ordinary people unaware of the truth.

Conversely, careless stated words and deeds of some Americans can enrage the broad masses of Muslims in the Islamic world. For example, someone named the US military operation in Afghanistan and Iraq as an "unlimited just action". However, to Muslims, it is a blasphemy to attribute sacred power to humankind, because only God can ensure unlimited justice. Besides, after the September 11 incident, some angry Americans assaulted and censured Muslims indiscriminately. In so doing, they probably were not at all aware that they had, in fact, done a favour to those terrorists hoping to provoke a struggle between the Islamic and Western worlds.

The 9/11 incident will no doubt exert great and deep impact on trends of Middle East social thought. But as the follow-up on this incident is far from over, the widespread and far-reaching influences it will bring to the Arab society are uncertain and will depend on the results of this incident. From the perspective of the current situation, the incident's direct impact on West Asian social trends of thought may be manifested in the following two aspects: (a) With the development of the fight against terrorism, the international community has paid ever more attention to various issues in the West Asian extremes of social thought. Various countries have gradually reached consensus on issues of improving the West Asian political and social situation and on removing the sources of international terrorism, and (b) The incident has led the Arab and Islamic world to look into many of its issues and to make efforts to overcome the negative impacts of globalization and its own social maladies, thereby achieving peace and development together with the international community.

The above judgement is a mainly positive consideration with a more or less personal emotional colouring, but events may develop in an opposite direction, namely, the visible terrorists are defeated while the invisible extreme trends of thought continue to swell. In the Arab World, the statement that after bin Laden is destroyed many people may turn out to follow his example is not simply alarmist talk. All depends on the follow-up on the incident. This is along and complicated process, in which the international community can play a positive role to push events in a favourable direction.

The international community must help the West Asia root out the sources of terrorism, including attention to the unjust treatment suffered by the Islamic world, removal of poverty and more concern to promote a West Asia peace process while combating international terrorism. Bullying and oppression, compulsion, poverty, despair and life in the shadow of an occupation army can only cause indignation, violence, extermination and sacrifice. [16]

Arab scholars hold that the utmost value for Islamic culture is the pursuit of justice. Muslim can even tolerate limitation of their freedom, but absolutely cannot tolerate unjust treatment. They oppose the treatment of the similar people according to different standards. They consider that this unfair state must be changed, and see US unfairness on the issue of Arabs and Israel to have led to a great extent to the attacks on the US [17] When talking about the US position on the Arab-Israeli issue, Arabs often give the following example: no resolution of the UN Security Council recognizes occupation by force. After the outbreak of the Third West Asia War in 1967 and the Gulf War in 1990, the UN adopted respectively two important resolutions for Israeli withdrawal from the occupied Arab territory and Iraqi withdrawal from Kuwait.

However, the former did not result in force to make Israel withdraw from the occupied territory while the latter resulted in the formation of a US-led multinational force which applied military force. They see this as an unfair US position. On this issue, a Japanese professor wrote after the September 11 incident that if this terror activity is an act of Islamic radicals it is not hard to imagine the following background. In the view of Islamic believers, many unfair events have taken place in quick succession in the past half century. From the angle of the world, fair countermeasures must be taken toward Muslim societies and hostility towards them as a source of terrorist activities must be reduced. If many Islamic believers think that fairness has been achieved, terrorist organizations will lose support and perish by themselves. However, if acts of war unfold, aimed at non-specific Islamic believers, hostility will evoke hostility and the possibilities of a clash of civilizations becoming a reality will increase. [18]

The international community should redress the portrait of Arabs and Muslims in Western eyes and help improve relations between Western countries and the Islamic world. For historical reasons the Islamic and Western worlds have had a long and fundamentally tense relationship. In the 18th century, the West stepped up its infiltration into West Asia, first through trade ties and then with colonialist and aggressive imperialist political and economic policies, bringing bout a qualitative change in the earlier relations between Christian West and Muslim East. The equal relations between the Islamic society and the West were transferred into a relationship in which Islamic society was subordinated, ruled and exploited. Each Muslim social group in all walks of life was affected by the consequences of this change.

From the religious angle Muslims expressed their response to this politically subordinate and economically exploited position, as well as to the social and cultural alienation this caused. In the past half century the West, especially the US, has taken a position partial to Israel on Arab Israeli relations, making its relations with the Islamic world, more tense. In recent years, violent terrorist activities of Muslim "extreme organizations" have been aimed mainly at the US and they regard West at large as anti-Muslim. Meanwhile some Western countries and Western public opinion have often linked terrorism with Islam indiscriminately and some media have not hesitated to vilify Arabs and describe them as terrorists.

Alawi holds that as for the hatred incurred between the Islamic world and the West, the West of course should bear the responsibility, but "we can't also shirk our own responsibility". He thinks that most Muslims hope their religion can coexist peacefully with other beliefs and hope to benefit from the new opportunity offered by the modern world. They do not in the slightest want to force Muslim citizens and non-Muslims in a country to live according to a single way, or to declare war on the world for the sake of publicizing their own religion. The US and the West at large should review their own policies to Arabs and the Islamic world. [19]

The international community must prevent further extension of such wars as Afghanistan and Iraq, especially from evolving into a religious war. All the countries including Israel in West Asia hope not to extend the war into other Arab countries. They see extension of the war only as encouraging extreme West Asian thought trends.

In Islamic countries, people's awareness of Islam is stronger than that of the state. At present, anti-war sentiments of the broad masses of Muslims are closely linked with anti-US sentiments. Though the Taliban terror regime is not attractive in the Islamic world and the Afghan holy warriors' behaviour in the name of Islam is everywhere despised, nonetheless they are Muslim brothers who believe in the same religion. To many Islamic countries, supporting a Western Christian anti-Muslim coalition is a risky action. [20] More and more people in Western countries have begun to suspect that terrorism cannot be destroyed by only military attacks. The *Chicago Tribune* published an article pointing out that, by declaring war on Islamic terrorism without clearly pointing out some particular country and even some particular target, the Bush administration had set foot in a region that was becoming particularly dangerous because of religious conflicts and the history of colonialism and economic exploitation. The long-standing hatreds have incited Islamic extremism; bombs and missiles can only intensify this extreme sentiment. [21]

Conclusion

The impact of globalization on the Arab world culture is not a matter of simple statistics and reports. It is, in essence, a diagnostic line of analysis to consider its pluses and minuses on the Arab general public. Globalization consists of social, economic and political adjustments that people may embrace to epitomize their culture and incorporate it with the world. It is a concept that has it economics, social and political roots and consequences. To a large extent, globalization promotes integration of the world and calls for the removal of all cultural barriers. Although globalization is a vital process toward transferring knowledge and education to the world, it still has its negative effects on most cultures and civilizations. Its impact on cultures, in this case the Arab culture, is relatively controversial.

Many nationalists and cultural trustees of the Arab world, for instance, condemn the influences of globalization on their culture. Conservative Arab nationalists and fundamentalists argue that their culture cannot adhere to many globalized notions. For them any claim to the contrary is just an inspiration to degrade other cultures in favour of a dominant one, or an attempt to certify the domination of one culture, mainly the modern version of Western culture, over the others. While its advocates rationalize that with the support of those momentous technological information devices, such as computers and satellites, Arab culture can be acclimatized to retain most globalized concepts regardless of the variances with Western culture and the distinctions between their respective historical and religious roots. Critics of globalization argue that this cultural invasion will lead to the disintegration of identity and the spirit of culture. In opposition, its cheerleaders consider the decline of cultural distinctions as a substantial sign of enhanced communications, a measure of integration of societies, and a scope toward unification of civilizations.

Actually, the magnification of global media networks and satellite communication technologies enable some dominant powers to have a truly global reach. Distinctly, technological superiority is a definite advantage when it comes to originating a culture as it formulates its universal appeal. Though it is a necessary credit, it is also insufficient. The fact that the internationalization of information has provided networks of communication and interaction between different cultures of the world is clear and certain. However, the great accomplishments of this information age, which shortened time, distances and shrank the world, should not be employed to determine the guidelines of any civilization or reshape the Arab national cultures. Hence, it is a mere fact to say that the tools now obtainable in order to bring cultures closer also drained many cultures of this world. This, however, is because of the organic structures of culture, which are grounded on human intellect, traditions and activities that were implanted in a particular geographical and historical setting.

On the economic level, in 1999, a 262-page annual study commissioned by the UN Development Program counselling the unevenness of globalization revealed that open markets are contributing to cultural insecurity in poorer nations, which have removed barriers against Western imports. This imbalanced flow of Western economic views and lifestyles heading for one direction, from rich countries to the poorer and from giant industrial states to the developing nations, have made in effect these lesser countries under invasion by the global socioeconomic forces of the industrialized West. In fact, this rapid economic, technological, social and political intrusion of foreign culture into the Arab world may put their cultural magnitude in jeopardy and will force people to fear for the loss of their religious and societal characteristics. However, if globalization is introduced with significant educational, social and economic support that could make Arab countries flourish alongside foreign cultures, then it may turn into a universal culture in which Arabs may come under its umbrella as equals.

History shows that bridging cultural gaps and functioning as a home to diverse peoples requires a superior ideology and social structure that have far-reaching economical systems that can adopt foreign cultures and surpass any cultural hindrance, yet, none seems to have all. At large, compelling a Western model on dissimilar countries may harm the economic future and cultural standing of Arab countries as well as that of other worlds. However, alternative approaches harmonizing economical and cultural diversities should be pursued, and not sameness of the culture.

End Notes

1. Abdullah Alawi, "Muslims and World Citizens," *Le Monde Diplomatique*, October 2001, p. 267.
2. Hussain Kamil Bahaeddin (2001), Patriotism in a World without Identity: Challenge of Globalization, Shanghai Foreign Language Education Publishing House, September.
3. Ibid, pp. 61-62.
4. Amr Moussa, Secretary-General of League of Arab States, speech at the meeting celebrating the 10th anniversary of the founding of Middle East Radio and TV Centre, September 20, 2001.
5. Ibid.
6. Ibid.
7. Mohammad Malaek, Speech at the 2001 seminar, "21st Century Forum: Dialogue among Civilizations" sponsored by CPPCC.
8. The Financial Times, September 27, 2001.
9. Yang Mingjie, "International Social Trends of Thought and the September 11 Incident", *Contemporary International Relations,* No. 10, 2001, pp. 88-89.
10. Abdullah Alawi, "Muslims and World Citizens", *Le Monde Diplomatique*, October 2001, p. 268.
11. Ghali (2001), Unvanquished: Ghali's Memoir, World Knowledge Publishing House, January, p. 190.
12. Chinese Encyclopaedia of Islam (1994), Sichuan Dictionary Publishing House, March, p. 148.
13. Contemporary Middle East Political and Social Thought (1992), China Social Sciences Publishing House, February, p. 137.
14. *Die Welt,* 25th September, 2001, p. 78.
15. Wang Yizhou, "How to Define Terrorism?", *Contemporary International Relations,* No. 10, 2001, p. 86.
16. Amr Moussa, Secretary-General of League of Arab States, speech at the meeting celebrating the 10th anniversary of the founding of Middle East Radio and TV Centre, 20th September, 2001.

17. Egyptian Consul General in Shanghai to SIIS scholars.
18. *Tokyo Shimbun*, 25th September, 2001.
19. Abdullah Alawi, "Muslims and World Citizens," *Le Monde Diplomatique,* October 2001, pp. 70-71.
20. *Dei Welt,* 25th September, 2001, p. 79.
21. "Military Force is not the Way of Winning the War against Islamic Terrorism", *Chicago Tribute*, 24th September, 2001, p. 66.

12

India and Saudi Arabia: Retrospect and Prospects

A.K. Pasha

The Gulf coastal area has since times immemorial been a meeting place for people not only from the neighbourhood but also for people as far away as China, Malay, Java and others. Due to its strategic location at the cross roads of ancient trade routes, as also very near to several great river based civilizations, Arab people of the Gulf region have been interacting with traders, seafarers, and others. Around 3400-3000 BC, the great Dilmun civilization flourished in what was then known as Uwal-modem day Bahrain and in the present Eastern Saudi Arabia. Due to its proximity to the Mesopotamian, Sumerian, and Magan centres of civilizations-especially Sohar, Muscat, people in the Gulf area traded with each other. People from the Harappan civilization, Sind, Gujarat, Nile based Pharonic civilization also came to the Gulf for trade.

It is commonly believed that Gulf Arabs had extensive trade relations not only with the immediate neighbourhood but with far off lands like China as well. It must also be mentioned that the Gulf is located very near to the famous Silk Route through which bulk of the Asian supplies reached different centres. There is considerable historical evidence from places in the Gulf like Thaj, al-Hinna, Ayn Jawan, Hatta, Qatif, Dahra, Failaka, Tell Abraq (UAE) Mazyad near Jabal Habit, Tarub in Eastern Saudi Arabia, ed-Dur on the coast of Umm al-Qaiwan, Mleiha in Sharjah, Qalat of Bahrain to suggest that traders came to such places from all over Asia. With the rise of the Sasanians (in Persia) the Gulf became a "Sasanian lake" and cities on the Persian Coast from Tiz, Suez, Huzu, Qays, Najiram, and Rishahr became famous trading centres.

However, the most well known were Siraf and Hormouz and at all the places Arabs were present in considerable numbers. Hormouz welcomed merchants of different religions and from all regions of the world and the city was called the citadel of security. Sassanid monarchs were defeated by the Arabs who spread Islam. In fact, the last Sassanid monarch even sent emissaries to the Chinese Emperor to plead for military help but all in vain. After the rise of Islam, Arab merchants made their presence all along the Persian coast. Soon Arabia became entranced by the magnificence of goods from China. The Chinese city of Canton (Zaitun as Ibn Battuta wrote which he visited) was well known to the Gulf Arabs.

Since Chinese products like silk were famous and unequalled "the lure of China was irresistible" to the Arabs even though the round voyage to China took a year and a half which was also very risky. To this day Arabic porcelain is called 'Chinese'. Even the Red Sea came to be known for the Arabs, as 'Sea of China', because it was from there in the earliest times that ships began their voyages with cargoes of ivory, incense and gold to barter for luxuries in that country. The Emperor of China was known to Arabs as Sahib al Sin. Even Prophet Mohammed advised Muslims to venture out to China for education.

According to Captain Buzurg ibn Shahriyar (Persian), author of the Wonder of India around 1150 AD, Persian and Arab merchants in the East were already numerous enough to launch a sea borne raid on Canton, presumably to avenge some mistreatment. Due to upheavals in China around 880 AD many foreign traders and their families were massacred. Wealthy Jewish merchants from Sohar, Uwal, Hormouz, Uqair, Satun, Julfar, Dibba, Basra, al Zarqa (Qatib) and Muscat brought silk, porcelains, precious stones from China. But by far the most robust or vigorous interaction was between the Gulf Arabs and

Indians from all along the West Coast especially.

Not only basic necessities like rice, textiles went but Indian traders settled all along the coast from Basra to Muscat. Ceylon was well known to the Arabs as Sirandib—the Isle of Rubies. Malay and Sumatra and the Malacca Straits were familiar to Arabs. Although due to the Mongol invasion of Iran and much of the Arab world (Mashreq) especially the destruction of Baghdad in 1258 (also Basra) affected the Gulf Arabs also but they continued their maritime contacts with Asia. It was only with the arrival of the Europeans starting with the Portuguese who reached Calicut in 1498 that the supremacy of the Gulf Arabs disappeared soon after except for Omani influence in East Africa.

The Europeans due to bigger ships mounted with heavy guns evicted the Arabs from many ports and cities all over Asia, even though it was the Arabs who showed the way to all major trading centres in Asia to the Europeans. It is only with the discovery of oil that the Arabs have re-emerged from their long slumber and have resumed their contacts with Asia. India's historical ties with the people of Nile Valley, Mesopotamia and Dilmun civilizations which flourished in West Asia are well known. The commercial, cultural and other relations enabled both the peoples to interact quite vigorously and many settled in both the regions.

With the rise of Islam in seventh century AD, Arab traders spread Islam to coastal towns in Kerala, Gujarat and other areas. Many people converted to Christianity and Syrian Christians settled in Kerala and the West Coast of India. Many Jews also settled in Kerala and along the West Coast of India especially those who escaped persecution from the Romans in West Asia. The Mongol invasion and the subsequent Ottoman domination of the region did not substantially disrupt the links between India and West Asia. But the discovery of a direct sea route to India from Europe by the Portuguese sailor Vasco da Gama (with the assistance of Ibn Majid an Omani Arab Captain) to Calicut in Kerala in 1498 and the subsequent

European colonialism and imperialism disrupted the close interaction India had with West Asia. [1]

India has historical ties with Arabia. Large number of Indians used to go to Arabia to study medicine. The rise of Islam and its spread initially to Indian coastal areas by Arab traders and later to the interior led to visit by Indian Muslims and Christians to Pilgrimage centres in West Asia like Mecca, Medina, Jerusalem, Karbala, Bethlehem, Mashed and many other places. Gradually India's sea trade passed into the hands of the Arabs who came to dominate the Red Sea, Gulf region and the Indian Ocean. Many Indian *Hajees* stayed to trade in the Holy Land, taking local Arab wives. In Jeddah, several hundred Indian families especially Hindus had established themselves in a separate colony retaining their self-identity and distinctiveness in manners, dress and employment.

According to one writer they had taken the place of Jews, who had formerly been the brokers but, having offended the Sheriff of Mecca, had been driven out to Yemen. Large number of Indian ships from Calcutta, Surat and Bombay arrived at Jeddah with cargoes of cotton, textiles, silk, spices, gems and other materials. The Jeddah merchants made huge profits out of Indian goods which were later transhipped to Suez and Europe especially to Venice and Genoa. [2] The Portuguese within a decade since the discovery of the Cape route almost monopolized the highly lucrative spices trade from India to the Red Sea and the Gulf area at the expense of the interests of Muslim traders and the important sea ports of western India like Camby and Chaul.

The Portuguese inflicted a crushing defeat on the allied Muslim fleet near Diu in 1509 and established themselves at Diu, Daman and Goa. The Mughal Ruler Jehangir tired of objectionable practices by the Portuguese especially their religious intolerance, was delighted when the British in 1612 defeated the Portuguese at Surat under the leadership of English Captain Best. The Mughal Ruler unable to build up any credible sea power and having been defeated by the

Portuguese, they were concerned for the safe passage of their Muslim subjects to Haj pilgrimage. The religiously indifferent English were preferable to the crusading Portuguese whose religious intolerance provoked the hostility of several Indian rulers as well. In 1613, Jehangir issued a *firman* permitting the English to establish a factory permanently at Surat.

Since then, English traders were made welcome throughout the Mughal Empire which subsequently led to the colonization of India by the British. But the English as early as in December 1688 turned against the Mughals and blockaded Bombay and the Mughal naval vessels and their captains (who went to Red Sea and Persian Gulf are often) mainly "to arrest the pilgrimage traffic to Mecca". By the middle of the 18th century Indian ships commanded by English officers were a common sight in the Red Sea and the Gulf area especially at Jeddah, Aden and Muscat. Before Gujarat passed into the hands of Sultan Aladdin Khilji of Delhi in 1297, the King of Gujarat Arjuna had the broad-mindedness to endow a mosque erected by a Muslim ship owner of Hormouz and provided for the expenses of certain Shia festivals.

He further laid down that under the management of the Muslim Community of Somnath any surplus was to be made over to the Holy Places of Mecca and Medina. [3] It is interesting to note that Aurangzeb between 1661 and 1667 received "complimentary embassies" from several foreign Muslim powers such as the Sheriff of Mecca and others to neutralize his harsh treatment of his father and brothers. It was also customary for rich Indian prices to lavish gifts on the Sheriff of Mecca and the Holy Places as the Hashimi family had ruled Mecca since the 11th century AD. The Anglo-French rivalry for domination in India sent ripples to the Hijaz. By their conquest of Surat, the English stopped the flow of treasure amounting to ₹ 5,000 a year granted by the Mughal Ruler to the Sheriff of Mecca. The Sheriff complained to the Ottoman Ruler at Constantinople and for a time the port of Jeddah was closed to English ships. [4]

More recently, when Abdul Aziz (known as Ibn Saud) captured Mecca, Medina and the entire Hejaz and later proclaimed himself King of the Hejaz on 8th January 1926, he encountered opposition both internal and external. Moreover, despite quick recognition of King Saud as the King of Hejaz by the European powers, still he had to "Legitimize his position in the eyes of the Islamic world, which had started with a prejudice against Wahhabism and had been vandalized by the violence with which the puritans had suppressed to cult of saints in the conquered holy land". The agitated people of Hejaz especially the followers of Sheriff of Mecca also had to be won over and their economic grievances redressed. Thus, to legitimize his position as the ruler of Hejaz, guardian of holy places and also to reassure the Muslim world he called the Islamic conference. [5]

Ibn Saud made a proclamation to the Muslim world asking for representatives to come to the Hejaz to discuss the future of the Holy Places. The Islamic Congress opened on 7th June 1926 at Mecca during the Haj and was attended by 60 delegates from all over the world including the Indian Muslim Community which was led by the Ali Brothers—the Khilafat Committee members. The Indian members sent to Mecca achieved little as they became embroiled in mediatory efforts to reconcile the Saudis and the Hashemites. [6] The Saudi King apparently disliked the Indian delegation's intervention as the King had declared Sheriff Hussein of Mecca as a traitor for claiming the title of Caliph on 5th March, 1924 made vacant by deposition of the Ottoman Sultan.

Due to objections from the Indian delegation on a number of issues related to Haj, Wahhabi control of Holy Places, the Saudi King according to one writer ordered it to leave Hejaz—clearly an undiplomatic move. It was only after the deportation of the Indian delegation that Ibn Saud felt secure. The Saudi King went on to merge Najd and Hejaz and established the Kingdom of Saudi Arabia on 23rd September, 1932. Some delegates at the Islamic conference had indeed objected to Ibn

Saud's assumption of the unIslamic title of King. It must be added that pilgrims for Haj from the Indian sub-continent formed one of the largest group and the Sheriffs of Mecca and King Ibn Saud, following the traditional practice, continued to purchase large quantities of tents from India to be used to house the Haj pilgrims. [7]

Soon after Independence, Pakistan tried hard to mobilize Arab and Islamic states to its side on the Kashmir and other issues. In this, Pakistan's relations with Saudi Arabia were to prove most rewarding. But soon India established close ties with Egypt's President Gamal Abdel Nasser. Many Arab states resented Pakistan's attempt to raise the Kashmir issue in Islamic meetings. Pakistan's membership in western sponsored military pacts was also denounced. Saudis attacked Pakistan's decision to join the Baghdad pact which subsequently became CENTO after Iraq withdrew from the military alliance in the wake of the Iraqi revolution in July 1958.

In fact, Riyadh was astonished to find that the "Islamic state of Pakistan should accede to those who have joined hands with the Zionists Jews" and spoke of the Pact as a "stab in the heart of the Arab and Muslim states" and urged it "to return to the right path", by withdrawing from the widely unpopular western military pact. Pakistan, which had launched a campaign against India on the issue of treatment of Indian Muslims, also got a setback when Riyadh publicly sided with India on the issue. King Saud bin Abdul Aziz of Saudi Arabia paid tribute to the Government of India for its policy of equality and equity towards the forty million Muslims in India.

Giving impressions of his 17-day long tour of India [from 26th November] in a now famous public statement, the Saudi Kin on 10th December 1955 told the Indo-Arab Society in Bombay: "I desire to say to my Muslim brethren all over the world with satisfaction that the fate of the Indian Muslims is in safe hands. In my capacity as the guardian of Muslim holy places, I desire to express my gratitude to the great Indian leader, Mr. Nehru, and all those lieutenants of his, through whom he executes this policy of equality and equity", A joint statement, issued by King Ibn Saud and Prime Minister Nehru in New Delhi on 12th December, 1995 said that both the countries are resolved to strengthen the existing friendly ties through further cooperation to their mutual advantage in the cultural, political and economic spheres.

The statement said the two countries fully subscribe to the five principles of peaceful co-existence. [8] India's Prime Minister Jawaharlal Nehru on a three-day visit to Saudi Arabia starting from 24th September, 1956, returned the visit where he was received at Riyadh by Crown Prince Amir Feisal, Prime Minister of Saudi Arabia. Nehru was given a great ovation by a huge gathering present at the airport. Thousands of people gathered at the airport lustily cheered and clapped happily as the Indian Prime Minister stepped out of the plane and he was accorded a warn, enthusiastic and rousing welcome with slogans of "Welcome, O! Prophet of Peace" which obviously angered Pakistan. Similar scenes were witnessed when Prime Minister Nehru reached Dhahran airport earlier.

Tens of hundreds of people collected at the airport shouted: "marbhaba Nehru *Rasoul al Salaam*" [meaning, Welcome Nehru, O! Prophet of Peace]. For the first time in the history of Saudi Kingdom, a large number of Arab women in strict purdah came to Dhahran airport, and again at the Riyadh airport to welcome a high dignitary of a foreign country. Sitting in curtained trucks and shining Cadillac's, these women had a glimpse of Nehru from behind their veils as he came down the steps. Acknowledging the greetings, Prime Minister Nehru declared: "I have come as a pilgrim of peace to your famous land". [9] Soon after India's Independence, Prime Minister Jawaharlal Nehru had to tackle amongst other things, Pakistan's relentless propaganda against India over Kashmir and other issues.

Pakistan, by convening and hosting a number of Pan-Islamic conferences since 1949 together with its refusal to recognize Israel and the support it gave to Arab causes had managed to establish close ties with certain Arab and Muslim states especially with Iran, Saudi Arabia, Turkey, Jordan and others. It must be emphasized that more than Islam, it was the cold war politics which enabled Pakistan to mobilize West Asian countries support but could not make much headway. In fact, by the end of 1952 Pakistan's attempt to forge a Pan-Islamic alliance was in shambles and had to be subsequently abandoned.

Among all its allies in the WANA region, Pakistan's relations with Saudi Arabia were to prove most rewarding. King Abdul Aziz Ibn Saud after consolidating his territorial gains and having obtained financial security in terms of oil revenues, charted to follow a more autonomous foreign policy. When King Saud visited Pakistan in 1953, he extended Riyadh's political support to Pakistan on the Kashmir issue. [10] India's recognition of Israel on 17th September 1950 came as a surprise to many in the Arab and Islamic world in view of India's persistent opposition to the partition of Palestine. Pakistan tried to paint India in the darkest colours in the eyes of the Arabs on this issue. But New Delhi's unequivocal support to the Palestine cause and subsequently her diplomatic and moral support to Arab National Liberation Movements in Algeria, Morocco, Tunisia, South Yemen and elsewhere brought it closer even to many conservative Arab states in the area. [11]

The coming to power of Gamal Abdel Nasser in Egypt and the emergence of secular nationalist Arab regimes in Syria, Iraq and later in Libya, South Yemen and Algeria to a large extent neutralized the Pakistani offensive against India in the region, especially over the Kashmir issue. Pakistan's open identification with the policies of the US and the West in the region made it a suspect in the eyes of most Arabs. [12] Pakistan's attempt to seek support on the ground of common religion did not work among the Arabs. In fact, many WANA countries resented Pakistan's attempt to raise the Kashmir issue in Islamic gathering and elsewhere. [13]

Pakistan's membership in the Western sponsored Baghdad Pact led to its isolation in the West Asian and North African (WANA) region (except Iran and Turkey) because with the exception of Iraq of the Arab countries joined the military Pact. Even Iraq withdrew after the 1958 revolution from the Pact which was subsequently re-christened as CENTO. Saudi Arabia denounced the Pakistani decision to join the Baghdad pact. [14] India's support to Egypt during the 1956 Suez crises and opposition to western attempts to pressurize Arab countries which followed non-aligned policies further improved India's credibility among the Arabs. Pakistan on the other hand by siding with the West alienated itself in the region. Egypt went to the extent of declaring that Kashmir was an integral part of India and that "Suez was as dear to Egypt as Kashmir was to India". [15]

Taking the cue from Nasser, the Egyptian media blasted Pakistan and its close alliance with the US-UK with an unprecedented anti-Pakistan campaign and branded the latter as "the number one enemy of Cairo and Arabs" who must be cowed before Egypt could handle the West effectively. [16] The Pakistani Prime Minister Hussein Shaheed Shurawardy whom Nasser refused to receive in Cairo made the well known statement denigrating the Arabs that "the Arab world is divided among themselves and even if they were united, zero plus zero is after all equal to zero".

No wonder Egypt refused Pakistan's offer to contribute a contingent to the United Nations Emergency Force (UNEF) in the Sinai. [17] In a U-turn in Saudi Foreign Policy, King Ibn Saud after his visit to the US (after the Suez crisis) became close to the US and endorsed the Eisenhower Doctrine. The US wanted Arab support in the cold war which it failed to get through the Baghdad Pact. No wonder, Egypt's Nasser denounced the US Eisenhower Doctrine as imperialist attempt to dominate the WANA region. The secession of Syria from the UAR in 1961, Egypt's military intervention in North Yemen after the 1962 revolution, US decision to supply offensive weapons to Israel under President Johnson, emergence of Faisal as Saudi King and his emphasis on Pan-Islamism rather than Pan-Arabism which Nasser advocated, all this brought about radical changes in the region with implications on India's policy towards the region which had come to be identified as Cairo-centric. [18]

In the US-Israeli scheme to contain Nasser and Arab nationalist forces, Saudi Arabia and Pakistan, together with Turkey and Iran (CENTO partners) became prominent players in the game. Moreover, Pakistan's rabid hostility towards Arab nationalism and communism was well appreciated by the House of Saud. No wonder a Saudi-Pakistan alliance virtually came to be established in mid-1960s with Riyadh terming India as an aggressor in the 1965 Indo-Pak war and warned New Delhi not to take undue advantage of its close ties with the Arab and Islamic states. [19] Saudi Arabia at the Arab Heads of States meeting in September 1965 joined with Jordan in demanding a collective Arab disapproval of the Indian stand on the War.

Of course the final communique did not support India or Pakistan, but Saudi criticism of India was mainly due to close Indo-Egyptian friendship and Nasser's support to Indian position especially on the liberation of Goa by not allowing Portuguese ships to cross the Suez canal] at several forums. [20] However, Egypt's humiliating defeat in the 1967 Arab-Israel war, Nasser's death in September 1970 led to a decline in Egypt's influence in the region. Under the changed circumstances, Saudi Arabia gradually became the leading Arab state influencing the policies of several Arab states partly due to its huge financial resources. The Saudi's under king Faisal quickly seized the opportunity by asserting their leadership in the region by reacting strongly to the damage done by the burning of the *Al Aqsa* mosque in Jerusalem (under Israeli occupation)—the third holiest shrine of Islam on 29 August 1969 and calling for a conference of Islamic heads of state or government. An Islamic Conference to discuss the

Al Aqsa issue was held in Rabat (Morocco) on September 22-25, 1969.

The summit was attended by 23 Arab and Islamic heads of states and the PLO as an observer. India was officially invited to participate in the conference at Saudi [King Faisal's] request but Pakistan staged a walk out from the conference against the presence of Indian delegation which was led by industries Minister Mr. Fakhruddin Ali Ahmed. The Rabat Summit paved the way for the establishment of the Organization of Islamic Conference (OIC) in May 1971. Thirty eight states became founding members of OIC. Saudi Arabia wields considerable influence in the OIC not only due to the location of head quarters in Jeddah but also due to its major contribution towards the OIC budget. In the OIC Secretariat large number of Pakistani nationals work with some holding key positions.

Pakistan which had been taking keen interest in organizing Islamic conferences where it had routinely denounced India and raised the Kashmir issue along with its declaration of world Islamic solidarity found in Saudi Arabia a very useful partner. Pakistan with Saudi Arabia's support always attempted at OIC conferences to get the Islamic world use its pressure in favour of its stand on Kashmir especially since the eruption of militancy in the Kashmir valley in 1989. [21] The Bangladesh crisis and the Indo-Pak war of 1971 had a major impact on Indo-Saudi ties. Riyadh's position on the crisis at the UN was that the developments in East Pakistan were Islamabad's internal affair and that no other country had any right to interfere in the same.

However, India managed to convince the Saudi rulers of New Delhi's sincere desire to live in peace with Pakistan and respect its territorial integrity. The 1972 Shimla Pact signed by Indian Prime Minister Mrs. Indira Gandhi and Pakistani leader Zulfikar Ali Bhutto and the subsequent release of Pakistani prisoners by India helped the atmosphere, as Saudi concerns for Pakistani territorial integrity had become an issue in India's bilateral ties. [22] The 1979 Iranian revolution, Soviet intervention in Afghanistan and the Iran-Iraq War [1980-88] brought about closer Saudi-Pak ties, which the US also supported. This made General Zia ul Haq, Pakistani ruler say: "If Saudi Arabia's security was threatened and help was sought from Pakistan he would personally lead Pakistani forces in the defence of Saudi Arabia". [23]

In the wake of the 1793 Arab-Israeli war, Riyadh (mainly due to the oil embargo and financial resources) emerged as the leader of the Arab/Islamic states especially due to mounting isolation of Egypt under President Sadat due to his separate peace policy with Israel under US auspices. In view of limited military capability (which made them conscious of their vulnerability to external and internal challenges), the Saudis developed close security relations with Pakistan with the blessings of the US. Several hundred Pakistani military advisors had been stationed in the Kingdom to bolster the security of the House of Saud. The US-Saudi-Pakistani triangular relationship-which worked effectively to evict the Soviets from Afghanistan to give one instance-has to be kept in mind while discussing the Kashmir issue and the OIC. [24] The United States came to rely increasingly on Iran and Saudi Arabia for its oil and commercial interests in the Gulf area.

The twin pillar policy gave Pakistan ample room to manoeuvre in the region's politics. The downfall of the Shah of Iran in 1979 and the Soviet military intervention in Afghanistan aggravated Saudi concern for their national security. Notwithstanding the Carter Doctrine, Rapid Deployment Force and later the Central Command and US assertion that it will not allow the repetition of Iranian revolution in Saudi Arabia, to enhance Saudi security, the United States was well disposed to Pakistan's decision to volunteer military training and trained men to Riyadh. [25] In return, Pakistan received Saudi funding for its arms purchases especially from Washington. Saudi Arabia's military aid to Pakistan became a major irritant in relations between New

Delhi and Riyadh. Pakistan also exploited the issue of communal riots in India by propagating that Muslims were not safe in India. [26]

The rhetoric from Islamic Iran and the Iran-Iraq War among other issues posed a dilemma to the House of Saud. These events coupled with the ongoing Arab-Israeli conflict especially Israeli invasions of Lebanon and with Soviets fully entrenched in Afghanistan; the Saudis gradually realized that their close ties with Pakistan need not come in the way of establishing good ties with India. Added to all these events in early April 1981, Mr. Eric Gonsalves, Secretary in the Indian Ministry of External Affairs in an interview published in *The Washington Post* said among other things, the sale of US arms to Saudi Arabia and other Gulf States could provide these states with a false sense of security that could lead to their royal families being toppled as the Shah of Iran. He gave the interview on the eve of Saudi Foreign Minister's visit to India. This created a ripple in India's ties with Arab Gulf monarchies. [27]

End of Communication Gap

No Indian Prime Minister had been to Saudi Arabia since Jawaharlal Nehru visited the Kingdom in 1956, until Mrs. Indira Gandhi paid an official visit to Riyadh in April 1982. The only exception was the visit by Fakhruddin Ali Ahmed, President of India, who attended King Faisal's funeral in March 1975. It was the first time an Indian President personally represented India at the funeral of another Head of State, since the practice had been to depute the Vice President or senior Cabinet minister. It indicated the importance India attached to relations with Saudi Arabia. During the period 1956-1982, India's relations with Saudi Arabia had never been unfriendly but at the same time they were not close either. A variety of factors worked at: such as close Indo-Egyptian ties, treaty relationship between India and USSR, close Indo-Iraqi ties, Indian support to the Iranian revolution and policies and on top of it the Indo-Pak 1965 and 1971 Wars.

However, what materially affected Indo-Saudi ties was the close Saudi-Pakistan relationship. Interestingly, despite the lack of political understanding, Indo-Saudi economic ties quietly flourished. [28] It is in this backdrop one should see Mrs. Gandhi's visit which ended the 26 years long "communication gap" between the two countries. Her visit paved the way for better relations and "heralded a new era" in Indo-Saudi ties. She praised the Kingdom's "constructive role" in the global arena and its contribution in solving many international problems. She supported the Fahd Peace Plan on the Arab-Israeli issue saying "we have welcomed it. It is in line with our basic principles to which we must adhere to resolve the crisis in West Asia". She also described the Fahd Plan as "new hope, conforming to India's stand". Mrs. Indira Gandhi also sought Riyadh's cooperation to strengthen peace and stability in the South Asian region. [29].

Indo-Saudi Economic Ties

While political relations have been far from bonhomie as a result of Cold War alignments and Saudi-Pakistani affinity, Indo-Saudi economic cooperation took a more realistic form and flourished. Mrs. Gandhi's visit to the kingdom paved the way for a new chapter in economic cooperation. The most tangible gain was the setting up of an Indo-Saudi joint commission to promote economic and technical collaboration. The assumption that a combination of Indian technology, skilled manpower and Saudi money could work to strengthen South-South Cooperation yielded tremendous economic gains during the last 25 years, forcing a rethink on the political front, which saw a new dawn with the visit of King Abdullah in January 2006, the first by a Saudi head of state to India in 50 years. The Joint Commission was established under an economic and technical cooperation agreement signed in April 1982. The commission has been meeting regularly since 1983 in Riyadh, and in New Delhi. [30]

The year 1997 was witness to a tragedy at Mina (Mecca) in which over 343 people, including over a hundred Indians, died in a fire. But it is not the first incident involving *Hajees* in Saudi Arabia. Large number of *Hajees* from Yemen, Egypt, Iran, Indonesia, Turkey and other countries have lost their lives in such incidents in the past. But what brought Indo-Saudi relations into sharp focus was the statement by the Indian Consul General in Jeddah, Afzal Amanullah, pan IAS officer from Bihar] in which he said that the lives of the Indian *Hajees* could have been saved, had the Saudi authorities been alert. He was referring to the decision of the Saudi guards to lock the entrance of the area where the tents caught fire. India quickly disowned this assessment, describing it as "premature". The Indian Ambassador in Riyadh, Mohammed Hamid Ansari, also promptly contradicted the Consul General's statement.

The Indian Minister of state for Home affairs, Mohammed Maqbool Dar, who led the Haj delegation, also gave a clean chit to the Saudi authorities for the facilities extended to the Haj pilgrims. The four members whom India sent after the fire tragedy made a statement announcing that the medical facilities provided by the Saudis to the injured were "excellent". Maqbool Dar went to the extent of saying that to die at a holy site should be in its own way compensation enough for the believers. This statement was not very different from what the Saudi Interior Minister said when he claimed that the Haj fire was "God's will".

Indian responses to fire tragedy have been variously described as "pathetic gestures" to appease the Saudis. Others have claimed that South Block decision makers perpetually appease the Saudis, that Saudi Arabian behaviour continues to be "crude", and that it has "(for a) long period (displayed) hostility" towards India. Despite growing economic relations, Indo-Saudi relations became strained in the wake of the militancy in Kashmir and the Iraq-Kuwait conflict. Saudi Arabia called for a solution to the Jammu and Kashmir issue on the basis of the UN resolutions saying that the long standing problem had cast a shadow over Indo-Pakistani ties. Riyadh helped Pakistan build up support at the UN Human Rights Commission at Geneva meeting in March 1994.

Its financial muscle gives a great deal of influence to the lending of its name as a sponsor because it would not have to vote on the resolution, not being a member of UNHRC. Moreover, Saudi Arabia wields considerable influence in the OIC being the leading state in its establishment, giver of a major portion of the OIC budget, and with the location of OIC headquarters in Jeddah. [31] The Saudis, who co-sponsored the Pakistani resolution at the UNHRC in March 1994 on alleged Human Rights violations in Jammu and Kashmir by India, compelled India's Minister of State for External Affairs Mr. Salman Khurshid to say that India was not asking for special rapporteurs to be sent to investigate the condition of women in the Kingdom who were denied basic human rights. Dinesh Singh India's External. Affairs Minister called the Saudi step at UNHRC "quite wrong", and said that the issue should not be given a communal colour.

"It would only create difficulties for the Muslims in India", he added. [32] in view of India's lack of sensitivity to Saudi national security concerns, whether with Nasser's Egypt, Yemen, Iraq or Iran the Saudis have always looked upon India's close ties with the Kingdom's enemies in the region with deep suspicion which, in fact, has partly driven them to support Pakistan on Kashmir and other issues, affecting India. The reaction to the plague scare in 1994 by the GCC was perhaps taken at the initiative of Saudi Arabia. Earlier, the GCC at Saudi initiative described the Babri Masjid demolition [1992] as, "sacrilege and an unpardonable act". The severest condemnation of India came from Saudi Arabia on the Babri issue. The Saudi financed Jeddah based *Rabita-e-Alami,* or the League of the Islamic World, also accused India of being "fully responsible" for the destruction of the Babri Mosque. [33]

All this clearly indicated that the time had come for India to take the initiative on a summit meeting to prevent stagnation in Indo-Saudi ties. No exchange at the highest governmental level had taken place since Mrs. Gandhi's visit to the Kingdom in 1982. India's strategy was to strive to ensure that Saudis took a more balanced view of its relations with India and Pakistan. A directive for opening out towards the Saudis had to come from the top leadership. [34]

There was a growing perception that India under the BJP led NDA government due to the Kashmir issue, Indo-Pak tensions, US support to Pakistan and US economic sanctions after the May 1998 nuclear explosions looked at closer cooperation with Israel in a number of fields as additionally useful to reach out to the US. One need not underestimate the importance of Indo-Israeli relations, but one has to assess its impact on India's traditional ties with the Islamic countries. In the wake of the end of the Cold War, disintegration of USSR, and the Gulf War over Kuwait, it became obvious that the US was openly welcomed by the Gulf monarchies for security and stability in the region.

The US has shown (as in Iraq) its determination as to the extent it can go to safeguard its interest in the Gulf especially concerning oil and the stability of GCC family rule. In the coming years, the US would be preoccupied with the security of the GCC monarchies which is vital for its status as the sole superpower. It is in this context that we have to see the significance of Indo-Saudi ties. If New Delhi can engage the US in a dialogue over security measures in the Gulf area, and achieve a breakthrough especially in assuring the Saudis and other GCC States of India's willingness to help them in concert with the US, then in that case Saudi Arabia could hold the key for not only better Indo-US relations but more significantly for stability in south Asia as well including the resolution of the thorny Kashmir issue.

The emergence of militancy in Kashmir in 1989 and especially since the demolition of Babri Masjid in 1992, India worked hard to improve ties with the Kingdom. The opportunity to cement that effort came following 9/11, when Saudi Arabia responded to Indian overtures, realizing that both countries face the common scourge of terrorism. Since then, Riyadh has condemned all forms of extremism and terrorism, including the attack on Indian Parliament in 2001, while making its fervent appeal for peace in the Indian subcontinent.

The heading process was demonstrated by the quick aid dispatched to the victims of the Gujarat earthquake the same year. Further, much of the political rapprochement comes amid the Saudi shift in position on Kashmir over the last five years. Saudi Arabia's position on Kashmir now emphasizes the bilateral process with a dialogue with Pakistan based on existing Shimla and Lahore agreements, which confirms with New Delhi's stand. Since then the Kingdom has condemned all forms of extremism and on several occasions made a fervent appeal for peace, between India and Pakistan. The appeal was again made during Crown Prince Abdullah's meeting with Najma Heptullah, Deputy Chairperson of Rajya Sabha in Jeddah in 2002.

Despite growing Indo-Saudi economic ties, the political ties have not progressed and bilateral visits were few. Mr. Jaswant Singh, India's Foreign Minister visited the Kingdom in January 2001. The then Finance Minister Manmohan Singh visited Saudi Arabia for the meeting of the Indo-Saudi Joint Commission in 1994, which was followed by the visit to India of Prince Khalid bin Sultan bin Abdulaziz in October 1996. However, in 2005, there were many bilateral visits at the ministerial level with Finance Minister P. Chidambaram visiting Riyadh in April; and India's Petroleum and Natural Gas Minister Mani Shankar Aiyer visiting the Kingdom three times since taking charge.

He was also the first Indian oil Minister to visit the Kingdom. Saudi petroleum minister Ali Al-Niami visited New Delhi in January 2005 to attend the first round table of Asian oil ministers on regional cooperation in the oil and gas economy. Saudi Arabia is not only a major economic partner of India; it is also a major power in the Gulf region, with substantial influence on other GCC states. It is also a major player in the Organization of Petroleum Exporting Countries [OPEC] by virtue of being the largest oil producer in the world at over 10 million barrels a day. Mr. Omar Abdullah, India's Minister of State for External Affairs led a delegation to the Kingdom to sign the Hajj agreement in Jeddah on 22nd August 2001. A five-member delegation led by the Chairman of Indian Oil Corporation visited Saudi Arabia from 6-8 April 2001 to renew a term contract with Saudi Arabia for the supply of crude oil and other petroleum products to India for 2001-2002.

A 12-member team from the National Defence College [NDC] paid a 5-day visit to the Kingdom from 21st May 2001. This was the first visit of an NDC team after a gap of ten years. The team visited major defence and economic institutes and held discussions with Saudi officials in Riyadh, Dammam and Jeddah. While the campaign undertaken by the Saudi ministry of labour to achieve full Saudization in the sectors of gold and tourism [travel agency] have continued to test Saudi-Indian relations during the last two years, India has to look beyond given that Riyadh is bound to further intensify its unemployment alleviation drive. The Saudi Arabian General Investment Authority has given licenses to Indian companies to setup joint ventures in different areas.

Saudi King Abdullah was the chief guest at the Republic Day celebrations in New Delhi on 26th January 2006. Indian Prime Minister Manmohan Singh broke all protocol and went to the airport to receive the King. He became the first Saudi king to get that honour. The tradition of inviting a head of state as chief guest at the Republic Day parade every year is now considered a measure of the importance India attaches to that country, apart from serving as an opportunity to showcase the country's military might as well as secular and democratic traditions. Saudi King referred to India as his "second home". When India suggested that it would draw a list of eminent

Muslims who could meet the King in Delhi, the King instead favoured meeting a group of eminent Indians, not just Muslims, which was a secular message. Setting the stage for economic agreements during King Abdullah's visit to India, the first India-Saudi Arabia joint Business council meeting was held on 21st November 2005.

The meeting acted as a "Catalyst" in furthering economic ties between the two countries. Saudi Ambassador in New Delhi Mr. Saleh Mohammed Al-Ghamdi announced that India and Saudi Arabia had concluded 15 agreements: memorandum of understanding on meeting challenges such as crime and terrorism; to promote bilateral investments, avoidance of double taxation and security matters; agreement relating to youth and sports; and 11 commercial agreements between Saudi and Indian firms, covering sectors like pre-engineered buildings, health sector [opening India's Apollo hospitals], water services, pipe manufacturing, finance and oil and gas equipment. The total investment in these joint projects will exceed US$ 270 million. King Abdullah was conferred with an honorary degree by the Jamia Millia Islamia, New Delhi.

Meanwhile, a high-level Saudi business delegation to India urged the Indian companies and the investors to take advantage of the tremendous opportunities in the Kingdom and put in their expertise and resources to develop strategic partnerships with Saudi companies. Further, Saudi Arabia is playing a key role in the talks for a Free Trade Agreement between GCC and India that began in January 2006. Based on its new diplomacy of promoting cooperation between importer and exporters of crude oil, India and Saudi Arabia are encouraging cross investments in the industry, mining and energy sectors. In an interview to NDTC the King said that Riyadh had the ability to meet any requirement that India may have for its energy security in the long term. He felt current oil prices are too high and his is damaging to developing countries.

As seen before there are over 1.8 million Indian workers

gainfully employed in the Kingdom who sends valuable remittances in foreign exchange which form a good part of the trade bill for India. Additionally, more than one and a half lakh Indian Muslims go on Haj pilgrimage annually to the kingdom besides several hundred thousands making the Umra-lesser pilgrimage every year. The visit of King Abdullah has given a boost to the tourist traffic between the two countries with Saudi visitor arrivals in India already up by 16 percent in 2004 to about 15,000 and likely to go up further by six percent in the first half of 2006. Those figures are bound to rise further as Saudis discover India as a viable destination for medical treatment, education and sight-seeing. India's official international carrier, Air India, now generates about 19 percent of its revenue from the Gulf, with the Saudi sector accounting for 30 percent of the figure.

Clearly relations are likely to see upswing in the coming years. In the broader context of rapidly improving Indo-US ties, closer Indo-Saudi ties are likely to be upgraded which could include security cooperation to meet common challenges. King Abdullah's visit should kick-start a process that will look beyond religion, oil and employment, as well as remain independent of its close ties with Pakistan. On Pakistan, King Abdullah had this to say: "Our relationship with India is not related with Pakistan. Both the countries are friendly countries with great ties, the relationship between us and India is not affected with regard to any other country. It is our hope and I believe of everyone else in that region that these two great nations of India and Pakistan manage to resolve their differences for mutual benefit and the benefit of others". As noted earlier the Kingdom has been appreciative of Indian stand on the Kashmir issue and has repeatedly signalled that its ties with Pakistan need not come in the way of better ties with India.

Saudi Arabia seen as the most conservative Arab country and until recently a close ally of the US-where family rule is total and absolute, is perhaps the most vulnerable to US manipulations in post-Saddam scenario. The US has identified Saudi Arabia as the breeding ground for religions extremism in the region and the Saudi rulers are apprehensive that the US will keep them in focus until it undergoes basic transformation to satisfy US-Israeli concerns. No wonder the Saudi ruler have now (after 9/11) taken initiative for democratic transformation in the Arab world. Saudi King Abdullah [while he was Crown Prince] had proposed a charter to reform the Arab condition which called for an "end to the silence that has gone on for too long" and urged "internal reform and enhanced political participation (which are essential steps towards building Arab capabilities] and providing condition for comprehensive Arab revival".

If the Arab regimes both monarchic and military led authoritarian dictators are reformed, modernized and genuine political transformation takes places through which people's participation in the decision making process is guaranteed under constitutional supervision, then the regimes can avoid the incoming cataclysmic changes and effectively marginalize the extremists religious elements and hence terrorism. In the absence of this, there could be an upsurge in terrorism not only in the West Asian region but also in South Asia and generally around the globe. India should actively encourage the process of political change and modernization because once the Arab regimes become democratic and responsive to popular demands, not only their legitimacy would be enhanced but more significantly their dependence on outside states especially the US would come down and this may lead to reduction in outside military and political intervention which has periodically undermined peace, security and stability in the region thereby affecting India's interests as well.

Genuine political reforms would give the politically oppressed people a stake in the running of the political system as also the much needed political stability and smooth transition. The abundant oil resources could then be used to advance economic development so as to engage the Arab people in the process of political stability and smooth transition. The abundant oil resources could then be used to advance economic development so as to engage the Arab people in the process of political and economic progress. Undoubtedly for India, the threat of religious extremism and terrorism from the West Asian region would be contained if this democratic process takes shape.

Along with these steps towards democratic transformation, steps to resolve the thorny Arab-Israeli issues would also be debated, discussed, at all forums thereby allowing Arab countries to take initiatives for meaningful steps along with serious US-Israeli steps (which are very essential) to tackle the Arab-Israeli disputes. Both these steps would reinforce the momentum for change and India could then look forward to greater peace, security and stability in West Asia in the future. In certain Arab countries like Lebanon, Bahrain, Jordan, Morocco and elsewhere the Islamic parties/groups have gained seats in legislatures or come to share power through democratic process but such groups have learnt how to be responsible and accountable.

It is far easier to control terrorism and religious extremism in liberal democratic political systems which have high level of legitimacy and strong domestic control than the present political set up where the rulers want to remain in total control of all state affairs. The long over due change has now become inevitable but if its not coming soon internal/regional terrorism may be directed against such autocratic regimes unwilling or unable to initiate reforms. Instability, religious extremism and terrorism in West Asia could spill over into South Asia as security and stability in both the regions are mutually interlinked through a number of factors. The most credible option to tackle these twin menaces which are posing a new challenge to India's composite culture, liberal democratic structures and also national security is to adopt a political course that prevents alienation of any segment of the population—especially religious minorities so that they do not take recourse to unlawful activities or terrorism. In India certainly the rising tide of Hindutva militancy has led to the emergence of certain Muslim groups as happened in Sri Lanka in which Israel was also involved.

End Notes

1. The Muslim ruler of Gujarat, commonly known as, Mahmud Bagarsha, who came to power towards the middle of 15th century in alliance with Qwansauh-al-Ghauri, Sultan of Egypt, tried to check the rising power of the Portuguese in the Indian seas. The Egyptian fleet, under the command of Amir Hussein, the Kurd, Governor of Jeddah, and the Indian Contingent, under the command of Malik Ayaz, a Turk, who had found employment in the court of Gujarat, defeated a Portuguese squadron commanded by Dom Lourenco, son of the Portuguese Viceroy, Francesco de Almeida, near Chaul, South of Bombay, in 1508. Subsequently after his defeat at the hands of the Portuguese, in 1509, Mahmud granted them a site for a Factory at Diu. Begarsha died on November 23, 1511. For details, see R.C. Majumdar et al., An Advanced History of India (Delhi: Macmillan, 1978), p. 346. After they took over Constantinople in 1453, and renamed it as Istanbul, the Ottomans lost naval supremacy in the Mediterranean in 1571, when they were defeated at the Battle of Lepanto. The Europeans began to dominate trade in the Indian Ocean and Arab Mudarabah or speculative trade declaimed, as the former came to dominate the territories as well. Historian Bernard Lewis quotes from Umar Talib, one of the Turkish elite, who complained in 1625 AD that: "The Europeans have become acquainted with the whole world sending their ships everywhere and seizing the harbours. The goods from India, Sind and China previously came to Suez and were distributed by the Muslims to the whole world. Now, however, these goods are transported by the Portuguese, the Dutch and the English to the Frankish countries, from where they distribute them to the world. The goods they don't need, they bring to Istanbul and the Islamic countries, selling them at five times their value, thus, reaping great profit. For this reason, both gold and silver have become scarce in Islamic countries." Quoted from Bernard Lewis, "Some Reflections on the Decline of the Ottoman Empire", *Studies Islamica 9,* 1959, p. 118.

2. K.N. Chaudhari, *Trade and Civilization in the Indian Ocean: An Economic History from the Rise of Islam to* 1950 (Cambridge: 1985); See also Wrike Freitag and William G. Clarence Smith, (ed.); *Hadhrami Tradlers, Scholars and Statesmen in the Indian Ocean, 1750's-1960's* (Leiden: EJ Brill, 1997); and A.K. Pasha, "Tipu and the Ottoman Empire", in B. Sheik Ali (ed.), Tipu Sultan: A Great Martyr (Bangalore: Prasaranga, 1993), pp. 219-32; and A.K. Pasha (ed.); *Perspectives on India and the Gulf States* (New Delhi: Detente Publications, 1999) pp. 1-23; See also Khaldoun Hasan al-Naqeeb, *Society and State in the Gulf and Arab Peninsula: A Different Perspective*, [London: Routledge, 1990] pp. 31-42.
3. R.C. Majumdar, Ibid., p. 175; see also M.A. Salem Khan, *Early Muslim Perception of India and Hinduism* (New Delhi: South Asian Publishers, 1997): See also K.N. Chaudhuri, *The Trading World of Asia and the English East India Company 1660-1760* (New Delhi: Cambridge, 1978); and Shafaat Ahmad Khan, *The East India Trade in the 17th Century, in its Political and Economic Aspects* (New Delhi: S. Chand and Co.)
4. Michael N. Pearson, *Pilgrimage to Mecca: The Indian Experience, 1500-1800* (Princeton; Markur Wiener, 1996); See also Document: Relations between India and Arabia before the Birth of Islam. Early Contacts, *Indian Journal of Secularism* (Mumbai) Vol. 2, July-September 1998, pp. 73-89.
5. Soon after the abolition of Caliphate in 1924. by the new leader of Turkey Mustafa Kamal Ataturk, an international Muslim congress was held in Cairo in May 1926 at the initiative of Al Azhar ulema to discuss the Caliphate issue. Muslim leaders from nearly thirteen countries participated, including representatives from British India-Maulana Shaukat Ali and Mohammed Iqbal were two of the four Indian delegates who attended. All of them took part in their private capacities with nongovernmental representation. Other delegates were from Egypt, Libya, Tunisia, Morocco, South Africa, the Dutch East Indies (Indonesia), the Yemen, the Hejaz, Palestine, Iraq and Poland. Interestingly, Turkey, Iran, Afghanistan, the Nejd, and Russia were not represented. The conference decided to meet soon as the feasibility of appointing a Caliph at the moment was found incapable of realization, in view of the situation in which the Muslims found themselves. For details see S.A.M. Pasha, *Islam*

in Pakistan's Foreign Policy, [New Delhi: Global Media Publications, 2006].

6. See Uri M. Kupferschmidt, "The General Muslim Congress of 1931 in Jerusalem", *Asian and African* Studies (Haifa), Vol. 12, No. 1, March 1978, p. 126; See also A.K. Pasha, *India and Turkey: Past and Emerging Relations,* [Delhi: Academic Excellence, 2006].
7. S.M. Burke, *Mainsprings of Indian and Pakistani Foreign Policies* (Minneapolis, University of Minnesota Press, 1974), p. 134; Abdullah Ahsan, *The Organization of Islamic Conference: An Introduction to the Islamic Political Institution* (Hendon, Virginia: The International Institute of Islamic Thought, 1988), pp. 11-12 and p. 109; see also Arnold J. Toynbee, *Survey of International Affairs, Vol. 1: The Islamic World Since the Peace Settlement, 1925* (London: OUP, 1927) p. 89; H.A.R. Gibb. "The Islamic Congress at Jerusalem in 1931", *Survey of International Affairs* (Oxford: RIIA, 1934), p. 99 and pp. 105-106; see also Sisir Gupta, "Islam as a Factor in Pakistan's Foreign Policy", *India Quarterly,* Vol. 18, No. 1, July-September 1956, pp. 230-258. For details, see Jacob M. Landau, *The Politics of Pan Islam: Ideology and Organization* (Oxford: Clarendon Press, 1990], pp. 240-241. John Sabini, *Armies in the Sand: The Struggle for Mecca and Medina* (London: Thames and Hudson, 1981], pp. 134-135; see also Arnold J. Toynbee, "The Proclamation of Sultan Abdul Aziz B. Saud as King of Hejaz and the Islamic Congress at Mecca (1926)", in *Survey of International Affairs*, (London: RIIA), Vol. I, 1927.
8. The Hindu, 12-13 December, 2005.
9. The Hindu, 26th September, 2006.
10. Harpal Singh Bedi, *'India and the Pan-Islamic Conferences: A Case Study of Rabat Conference* "M. Phil disst. SIS JNU, New Delhi, 1997; see also Noor Ahmed Baba, OIC. *Theory and Practice of Pan-Islamic Cooperation* (New Delhi: Sterling Publishers, 1994).
11. Ranjit Kaur, *Islam, Cooperation and Unity* (New Delhi: Deep and Deep Publications, 1993); See also A.K. Pasha, "Nehru and Crises in West Asia", *Detente,* Vol. 9. No. 1, May-June, 1990, pp. 4-9.
12. See A.K. Pasha, *India and OIC: Strategy and Diplomacy* (New Delhi: Centre for Peace Studies, 1995); See also A.K. Pasha,

"Security and Stability in the Gulf/West Asian Region", in A.K. Pasha (ed.); *Contemporary Gulf: State, Society, Economy and Foreign Policy* (New Delhi: Detente Publications, 1999).

13. Mujtaba Rizvi, "Pakistan-Saudi Arabian Relations: An Example of Entente", *Pakistan Horizon,* First Quarter 1981, p. 83; S.M. Burke, *Pakistan's Foreign Policy* (London: OUP, 1975), p. 204; See also, A.K. Pasha, "Indo-OIC Relations: Perspective and Trends", *Journal of Peace Studies,* Vol. 1, Nos. 3-4. March-June 1994, pp. 22-50; and M.S. Agwani, "Pakistan and Pan Islamism", in Surendra Chopra (ed.) *Perspectives on Pakistan's Foreign Policy* (Amritsar: 1983), p. 292; Cuyler Young, "Pan-Islamism in Modern World" in Harris Proctor (ed.), Islam and International Relations (London: Full Hebb Press, 1965).
14. Pasha, n.12, p. 3; see also M.S. Agwani, "India, Pakistan and West Asia", *International Studies,* Vol. 8, July 1966-April 1967, p. 159; and Shaukat Ali, *Pan Movements in the Third World: Pan Arabism, Pan Africanism and Pan Islamism* (Lahore: United Publishers Ltd. 1976); see also Pasha, n.5, pp. 140-153.
15. *Round Table* (London) March 1957, p. 172.
16. *Dawn* (Karachi) December 1, 1956, cited in Pasha, n. 12, pp. 3-4.
17. National Assembly of Pakistan Debates (Islamabad) 25th February, 1959, p. 1088; Zulfikar A. Khalid, "Evolution of Saudi-Pakistan Strategic Relations 1947-1990; Military, Security and Economic Factors", *Strategic Studies,* Vol. XII, No. 1, Autumn 1989, p. 58; Naved Ahmed, "Pak-Saudi Relations", *Pakistan Horizon,* No. 4, 1982, p. 51; Ajay N. Jha, "Pakistan as a Factor in Indo-Saudi Relations", *Journal of Political Studies* (Jallandhar) September 1984, pp. 38-51; and Verinder Grover (ed.), *International Relations and Foreign Policy of India,* Vol. 4, *West Asia and India's Foreign Policy* (New Delhi: Deep and Deep Publications, 1993), pp. 309-325.
18. Noor Ahmed Baba, "Nasser's Pan-Arab Radicalism and the Saudi Drive for Islamic Solidarity: A Response for Security", *India Quarterly,* Vol. XLVIII, No. 1-2, January-June 1992, pp. 1-22; and "Saudi Drive for Islamic Solidarity: A Quesi for Security", *Political Science Review,* Vol. 24, Nos. 1 and 2, January-June, 1985, pp. 34-35; Abdullah M. Sindhi, "King Faisal and PanIslamism", in Willard A. Beling, e.d, *King Faisal and the Modernization of Saudi Arabia* (London: Croom Helm, 1980); see also Nizar Madani, *The Islamic Content of the*

Foreign Policy of Saudi Arabia, King Faisal's Call for Islamic Solidarity, Thesis submitted to the American University, Washington DC, 1977; see also James P Piscatori, "Islamic values and national interest: The case of Saudi Arabia", in Adeed Dawisha (ed.) *Islam in Foreign Policy* (Cambridge: CUP, 1983).

19. *Dawn,* 11, 18, 24 September 1965; and UN General Assembly official Records, session 20, Plenary meetings, Vol. 2, p. 16, as cited in Pasha, n. 5, pp. 166-167.
20. *Dawn,* 20th September, 1965, ibid, p. 165.
21. *Pasha,* n. 12, pp. 98-100.
22. Baba, 9-10, p. 78; *Asian Recorder* (New Delhi) 1971, p. 10473.
23. Z.A. Bhutto called Pak-Saudi ties as "Indestructible solidarity"; King Khalid called for a settlement of the Kashmir problem in accordance with relevant UN resolutions. The Saudi King was on a visit to Pakistan in October 1976. See also Anwar H. Syed, "Pakistan in 1976: Business as Usual", *Asian Survey* (Berkley) Vol. 17, No. 2, February 1977, pp. 187-188; and Rashid Jamal, "Pakistan as the Central Command", Middle *East Report* (Washington DC) July-August 1986, p. 31 and 43.
24. Anthony Hymen, "Pakistan: Towards a Modern Muslim State"? *Conflict Studies,* (London) No. 227, January 1990, p. 19; Pasha, n. 5, pp. 296-297.
25. POT (New Delhi), Vol. VII, Part 265, December 15, 1980, p. 2241-2242; Part 16, January 21, 1981, p. 131; Vol. 143; July 20, 1984, p. 2255 as cited in Pasha, n.5, pp. 294-296, See also Howard W. Wriggins, "Pakistan's Search for a Foreign Policy after the invasion of Afghanistan", Pacific *Affairs* (Vancouver), Vol. 57, No. 2, Summer 1984; See also A.K. Pasha, "India and Israel: Growing Cooperation", *World Focus,* Vol. 14, No. 8, 164, August 1993, pp. 19-22.
26. Riyaz Punjabi and A.K. Pasha (ed.), *India and the Islamic World,* New Delhi: Radiant Publishers, 1998; *The Washington Post,* 13th April 1981.
27. See A.K. Pasha, *India and West Asia: Continuity and Change* (Delhi: Gyan Sagar, 1999); *Dawn* (Karachi) 16th April 1981; *The Washington Post,* 13th April 1981.
28. A.K. Pasha "Communal Revivalism in India: Its Impact on Ties with West Asia and North Africa", in Muchkund Dubey (ed.), *Communal Revivalism in India: A Study of External Implications*

(New Delhi: Har Anand, 1994), pp. 54-88; and A.K. Pasha, "India's West Asia Policy: Continuity and Change", Strategic *Analysis,* Vol. XVI, No. 6, September 1993, pp. 783-804.

29. A.K. Pasha, "Perspectives on Indo-Saudi Relations", *Asian Affairs* (London), Vol. I, No. 11, September 1997, pp. 24-26.
30. A.K. Pasha, "India and the Gulf States: Challenges and Opportunities", in Rajen Harshe and K.M. Seethi (ed.): *Engaging with the World: Critical Reflection on India's Foreign Policy* [New Delhi: Orient Longman, 2005].
31. See A.K. Pasha, "Security and Safety aspects of Hajj", *The Pioneer,* May 24, 1997; Mohan Guruswamy, "Dealing with Saudi Arabia: Beware of Unholy Bias", *Indian Express,* May 9, 1997; *Times of India,* April 24, 1997; *The Pioneer,* 24-25, 28 April 1997; and 7 May 1997. See also Muhammad Azhar, "GCC Aid to India" in AK Pasha ed: *Perspective on India and the Gulf* States (New Delhi: Detente Publications, 1999).
32. A.K. Pasha, n. 12, pp. 54-118.
33. A.K. Pasha, "India and the GCC", in n. 26, pp. 34-48.
34. A.K. Pasha, "Indo-Saudi Arabian Summit is Long Overdue", *The Pioneer,* 3rd August, 1992; A.K. Pasha, "India's policy towards the Arab world in 21st Century" in V.D. Chopra (ed.), *India's Foreign Policy in 21st Century* [Delhi: Kalpaz, 2006] pp. 25-26.

13

India and the 1956 Suez Crisis

Fazal Mahmood

Events Leading to the Nationalization of the Suez Canal

The Suez Crisis started with the nationalization of the Suez Canal Company by the Egyptian President Jamal Abdul Nasser. Nasser took this step in response to the US Secretary of State John Foster Dulles's speech announcing the withdrawal of American assistance pledged for building the Aswan High Dam. [1] The Aswan High Dam Project was the most important project launched by the Revolutionary Command Council. The purpose of this ambitious scheme was to improve the irrigation of the Nile Valley and develop hydro-electricity to meet the growing need of the country. [2] The Suez crisis was the culmination of many events, and trends the most important of them being the Baghdad Pact, Arab-Israeli hostility and the loan for Aswan High Dam. It was not simply a local regional crisis but its impact was felt internationally. Nasser's opposition to Baghdad Pact, the arms deal with Czechoslovakia, the growing cultural and trade relations with the East European countries and communist China were perhaps some of the developments that created apprehensions among the Western powers.

In May 1953, US Secretary of State John Foster Dulles made an extensive tour of the West Asia and presented the concept of "northern tier" consisting of the countries bordering the Soviet Union. [3] In the American view, the Soviet danger to the West Asian Countries particularly to Iran and Turkey was growing and this could be contained only by building a bulwark through a pact of the northern tier countries against the Soviet Union. On February 24, 1955, Iraq and Turkey signed a mutual security pact to which Pakistan, Britain and Iran adhered in the course of the same year. This series of treaties come to be known as the Baghdad Pact. [4]

From the very beginning the pact became a focal point of international friction and conflict. It provoked Egypt's sharpest opposition who came to the conclusion that military alliances with foreign powers were totally incompatible with national independence and real interests of the nation. [5] Nasser expressed the determined opposition to big power participation in the Middle East security arrangement. He was of the view that the defence of the area must rest primarily with the inhabitants of the area. He said that Arab League Collective Security Pact was the only alternative and efforts should have been made strengthened it. [6] The Egyptian-Western relations further deteriorated when on April 19, 1956, United States became an associate member of the Baghdad Pact.

Arab Israel Hostility and Egypt

The second source of tension between Egypt and the West was the Arab-Israeli conflict which was aggravated by an incident in early 1955. On February 26, 1956 Israel launched a massive military attack against Egyptian troops stationed in the Gaza Strip. This attack brought home to the Egyptian the bitter truth that they were militarily week and could be harassed by Israel easily. Egypt was short of arms and even after the Suez Canal Base Agreement of 1954 Britain, the normal supplier continued to refuse, on the grounds of Tripartite Declaration of 1950, to meet Egypt's requests for increased deliveries of arms. [7]

The Revolutionary Command Council gave high priority to procuring modern military equipment. Moreover, after the Gaza raid, Nasser was under great pressure to obtain modern armaments to offset Israeli strength. The United States in order to defuse the Arab hostility particularly of Egypt towards Israel was conditionally willing to make Egypt eligible to military and economic aid. The conditions as laid down by the

US congress were:

1. Association with the American led Western mutual security programme.
2. Acceptance of an American military and economic aid. Nasser and the Revolutionary Command Council accepted the US$ 40 million economic aid but refused to consider any sort of alliance with the West. [8] Meeting with virtual refusal Nasser turned towards the Soviet bloc. On September 27, 1955 he announced the conclusion of a barter deal with Czechoslovakia whereby Egypt's cotton was to be exchanged for an undisclosed quantity of heavy armaments. The deal became a decisive event in the development of the Suez Canal crisis. It increased the Western-Egyptian tension and particularly raised question of the status quo in West Asia as envisaged by the Western Tripartite Declaration of May 25, 1950. [9]

Aswan High Dam Development

After the revolution, the Revolutionary Command Council launched a number of reforms in the country in order to improve the agricultural produce in the country. The Aswan High Dam project was one of them. The scheme was expensive and Egypt was not in a position to finance it out of her resources. The Egyptian government had sought financial aid from the World Bank in this connection but without success. [10] Soviet government made tempting overtures to Egypt. Soviet had undoubtedly helped in precipitating the Western decision to make offers to Egypt, as the US and other Western countries did not want to see the Soviet influence expand in Africa. [11] On December 17, 1955, the US and Britain together with the International Bank for Reconstruction and Development (IBRD) offered a total of US$ 270 million financial help on easy instalments. To this they had attached three restrictive conditions. First, that Egypt should reach a fair agreement with the Sudan about Nile water rights. Second, that Egypt should give this project priority over other schemes.

Third, that Egypt should not accept aid from communist sources. [12] Meanwhile, some events took place which deteriorated the Egyptian-Western relations. [13]:

1. The dismissal of General Glub from the command of the Arab Legion. This shattering blow to the British position in the region was widely credited to Nasser's influence.
2. Egypt continued its supports for the Algerian rebels in defiance of French threats and protests.
3. The controlled Egyptian press continued carried propaganda campaign against the US and the West for their sponsorship of the Baghdad Pact.
4. Failure of General Temple mission in Jordan in December 1955. The purpose of the mission was to persuade Jordan of the advantages of joining the Baghdad Pact.
5. On 16th May 1956, the Egyptian government broke off diplomatic relations with nationalist China and recognized the communist China.
6. In June 1956, the Soviet Foreign Minister visited Cairo to attend the ceremonies marking the evacuation of the British troops. Moreover, the cultural and trade relations with the East European countries and communists China increased.

These developments had created apprehensions among the Western powers, and influenced the US decision regarding the Aswan Dam Scheme. On July 19, 1956 the US Secretary of State John Foster Dulles issued a statement withdrawing the US offer, due to developments "unfavourable" to the success of the project. [14] The statement noting that: (a) Egypt had not reached a settlement with Sudan on the distribution of the Nile Waters; (b) that Egyptian willingness and ability to concentrate its economic resources upon the vast reconstruction programme was in doubt as development within the succeeding seven months (of 1956) had not been favourable to the success of the project, and (c) that the US government had concluded that it was not possible in those circumstances to participate in the projects. The British government on 20th July also withdrew its offer to finance the Aswan Dam on the same ground. The IBRD too followed the suit. [15]

Nationalization of Suez Canal Company

The withdrawal of loan offered by Washington, London and IBRD changed the whole situation and further deteriorated the Western-Egyptian relations. President Nasser considered the refusal of loan by the West a great insult to him and his country. He condemned Washington's insinuations that Egypt would be unable to carry her share of the financial burden for the project. The US, he said, had lied about Egypt's economic conditions. "Cairo would go ahead with the project on its own" he declared. [16] Nasser further stated, "our answer to them is that we Egyptians will not permit any imperialists or oppressors to rule us militarily, politically or economically". [17] Nasser on July 26, 1956 in a long speech at Alexandria announced publicly the nationalization of the Suez Canal Company. [18].

About the construction of the Aswan High Dam he declared, "We shall build the High Dam as we desire, we are determined". [19] The revenues of the Suez Canal Company henceforth would be used for the benefit of Egypt, he announced. [20] About the Suez Canal, Nasser stated. [21] "Today...the Suez Canal has been nationalized...we declare that our property has been returned to us. The rights about which we are silent have been restored to us". At the end, he declared, [22] "all of us will fight to the last drop of our blood for the construction of our homeland and for the construction of Egypt".

Western Reaction

Nasser's decision was enthusiastically welcomed in Egypt. In the Arab countries there rose a wave of admiration and jubilation "that is our man (Nasser) telling off the West, snubbing the West fearlessly, showing we are a force in the world. [23] The sense of exhilaration was felt throughout the east, and was encouraged by the Soviet bloc. The Western countries considered the nationalization of the Suez Canal as an act of humiliation. It created a new and highly inflammable situation. Within days the issue assumed world wide proportions and got involved in an intricate mesh of conflicting international policies. [24]

The nationalization of the Suez Canal Company by the Egyptian government created uproar in the Western capitals, particularly in London and Paris and the news was received with shock and indignation. Immediate consultations between British, France and the US began and hasty emergent meetings were followed in London with the representatives of the French and American government. [25] It was decided that Nasser could not be allowed to seize control of the Canal in defiance of international agreement and that British essential interests in this area must be safeguarded, if necessary, by military actions.

The Chief of Staff, therefore, were instructed to get ready a plan and a time table for an operation designed to occupy and secure the Canal, should other methods fail. [26]. Further, on 30th July in the House of Commons, British Prime Minister Eden declared, [27] "No arrangements for the future of this great international waterway could be acceptable to Her Majesty's Government, which would leave it in the unfettered control of a signal power".

On July 31, it was announced that certain precautionary measures were being taken in the form of troop movements. The British foreign Secretary Selwyn Lloyd expressed doubt about the safe functioning of the Canal under the Egyptian administration. [28]

Reaction in France was more hysterical and militant. She, fearful of the repercussions which Nasser's might have in North Africa, pressed for immediate joint military action against Egypt. It was suggested that the "Hitler of the Nile" should be checked, preferable by joint military action. On 27th July, the French government declared that Egyptian action was contrary to the international law.

India's Response

India supported the action of Nasser and stated that Egypt had acted entirely within her sovereign rights. India's reaction was obvious because it still looked toward Asia as its prime concern. Nehru, during first Asian Relations Conference held in Delhi in 1946, declared that Asia could "no longer be used as pawns by others". [29] The conference focused on Asian solidarity, economic development and de-colonization. He strongly opposed the Western colonialism in Asia and emphasized the importance of Asia in World affairs. [30]

However, the sudden decision of Nasser to nationalize the Suez Canal Company surprised Nehru. Nasser did not inform him before taking such a major decision. Mohammad Heikal, a confidant of Nasser and former editor of Al-Ahram, asserted that Nehru had no prior information of Nasser's decision to nationalize the Suez Canal Company. In July 1956, the three leaders Tito, Nehru and Nasser met at Brioni in Yugoslavia to reaffirm their support for the "ten principles" outlined at the Bandug Conference. [31]

At Brioni, the three leaders of non-alignment also discussed the Arab-Israel conflict and other issues related to West Asia. From Brioni, Nehru and Nasser flew back to Cairo together and on the flight Nasser received formal announcement of Dulles's decision regarding the withdrawal of American aid for the Aswan High Dam Project. [32] At Cairo, both the leaders discussed the matter in detail and agreed to give emphasis on large number of smaller projects rather than to concentrate on one major scheme i.e. Aswan High Dam. At this stage, no reference was made by Nasser about the nationalization of the Suez Canal Company. [33]

Nehru, in a statement to the Lok Sabha on 31st July, admitted that the knowledge of Nasser's decision to nationalize the Suez Canal Company first came to him through reading reports in the press after his return to Delhi. [34] He in a letter to Nasser expressed his anguish, "I thought that decision (to nationalize the Suez Canal Company) must have been taken after I left Cairo". [35]

Being the leaders of the newly independent countries of Asia and the founder members of non-alignment, both the leaders (Nehru and Nasser) had development good working relationship. India was in friendly relations with Egypt. To the Indian government, Nasser was a nationalist standing up to Western imperialism. Both the Indian and Egyptian governments were firm supporters of Afro-Asian solidarity and of the policy of non-alignment. Despite such affinity, Nehru felt that the decision to nationalize the Suez Canal Company had been made without giving due consideration to international repercussion. [36] Nehru made it clear to Nasser that Egypt had crated this crisis on its own and India's support in this situation could not be taken for granted. Nevertheless, the nationalization of the Suez Canal was the legitimate right of Egypt—it had been done without formal support of the non-aligned countries. [37]

Nehru was concerned for peaceful settlement of the crisis and wanted to act in accordance with the strict codes of non-alignment, against the Western colonialism. He was anti-imperialist and wished to support Nasser, but at the same time did not want to give impression that he had been influenced by blind anti-imperialist emotion in supporting Nasser. India's close relations with Britain and membership of commonwealth deterred Nehru to oppose Eden critically. (He made efforts to maintain balance approach in dealing the Suez issue). [38] Motivated by these feelings he decided to maintain balance and adopted cautious approach. Regarding India's relation with Egypt Nehru categorically stated in the Lok Sabha as follows. [39], "She (India) is in friendly relations with Egypt and associated with her in the acceptance of the Bandung Declaration and the Five Principles [Panchsheel]. India also had good and close relations with the principal Western counties involved [the United States, Great Britain and several European countries]. Both these relations are held in great esteem by us".

Nehru was, in fact, not against the nationalization of the Suez Canal Company nor considered it illegal or contrary to law, but felt that it had been done in a manner, which could escalate the international tensions. Therefore, he resisted himself being influenced by emotional sympathy and fraternal solidarity.

Nehru's attitude, and his lack of public support to Nasser, however, deluded the official opinion of Britain. It was inferred that Nehru would not oppose the action against Egypt. Encouraged by Nehru's attitude, the British government contemplated to discuss international control of the Canal in a conference and was prepared to implement the plan forcibly. The movement of troops by Britain and the decision to use force both by Britain and France created a very grave situation in West Asia. [40]

Nehru supported the idea of an international control of the Canal but was against the used of force to secure this goal and warned that military confrontation would not serve the purpose rather propel tension in Asia. [41]

Nasser, in response of the decision to use force both by Britain and France, announced that the government had decreed general mobilization throughout the country and martial law in the Canal Zone. He declared that Egypt intended to meet force with force, aggression with aggression, offence with offence. [42] Nasser warned the West that to interfere with the Egyptian act of nationalization was to invite "obstruction of navigation" in the Canal. [43]

The US too regarded the use of force as high handedness and extremists step, persuaded Britain and France from taking any strong measures. The US suggested the proposal of international control of the Canal though the international authority. [44] They agreed after hectic discussion, to hold a conference of major users of the Canal on August 16, 1956 at London, and invitations were issued to twenty four countries including Egypt. Egypt refused to attend proposed conference. Nasser said that the conference had no right in any way to discuss any issue concerning the sovereignty of Egypt or the sovereignty of any of its parts.

Regarding the freedom of navigation, Nasser had sent notes to all government and to the Secretary General of the United Nations, in which he guaranteed the freedom of navigation of the Canal. Nasser realized that the success of nationalization would depend on smooth functioning of the Canal. He, thus, assured that the Canal would continue as an open international waterway. He charged the West that it was attempting to convert the internal question of nationalization into an international problem. However, later Nasser agreed to send his political adviser Ali Sabry to London to act as an observer. [45]

Nehru did not regard the nationalization of the Suez Canal as the major issue. He was mainly concerned with the question of the Egyptian sovereignty. [46] On 8th August in the Lok Sabha, he clearly mentioned, "the Canal itself is in Egypt and an integral part of Egypt. The sovereignty of Egypt is thus beyond question". [47] Nehru further asserted that the Indian government "would equally decline participation in any arrangements for war preparations or sanctions or any step which challenged the sovereign right of Egypt". [48]

However, it was India's own "national interest" which concerned Nehru most. India's economic interests ultimately dominated during the Suez Crisis. In 1956, India had initiated the Second Five Year Plan, which focused on rapid industrialization based on basic and heavy industries. Much of India's principal exports and imports were passing through the Suez Canal. The outcome of India's Second Five Year Plan was dependant on the free and uninterrupted movement of India's trade through the Canal. The Suez route was, of course, shorter and cheaper. The trade via the Cape of Good Hope route was costly and 40 percent longer, resulting increased in freight charges and shipping delays. [49] Highlighting economic significance of the Suez Canal Nehru stated in the Lok Sabha, [50]

"India is not a disinterested party. She is a principal users of this waterway [the Suez Canal] and her economic life and development is not unaffected by this dispute India is passionately interested in averting a conflict".

Faced with that situation, India wished widely accepted arrangement with regard to smooth functioning of the Canal. Nehru, thus, decided to attend the London Conference and outlined India's motives as follows. [51], "India had to take a decision in the situation as it confronted them...The considerations and the criteria on which the [Indian] government had to base their decision [to attend the London Conference]—and not an easy one—is how best they could serve the cause of averting conflict and obtaining a peaceful settlement before it was too late".

Nehru assured Nasser that India would in the conference, work for conciliatory approaches and prevent to take unilateral action by one nation or any group of nations. The conference began on August 16, 1956 and it was attended by twenty-two countries. The Indian delegation was led by Krishna Menon, who deplored Egypt's absence at the conference and categorically mentioned that final solution to the Suez Crisis was not possible without Egypt's participation. India and the Soviet Union were basically against the Western domination of the conference. They were anxious to avoid anything in nature of a decision by the conference. They raised the question that conference was only a selected group and did not represent the principles of universality as the UN did. [52]

The Western maritime powers by and large were in favour of international control over the Canal. Dulles introduced a four-point plan for an international regime for the Canal. American Draft contained the following. [53]

1. The operation of the Suez Canal, in accordance with the 1988 Treaty and the principles therein set forth, would be made the responsibility of an international board to be established by treaty and associated with the United Nations—Egypt would be represented on the board.

2. Egypt would have the right to an equitable return which would take into account all legitimate Egyptian rights and sovereignty.
3. Fair compensation would be paid to the Suez Canal Company.
4. Any difference over the second and third points would be settled by an arbitral commission to be made by the International Court of Justice.

The Indian representative Krishna Menon viewed American plan as a scheme to take the management of the Canal out of the Egyptian hands. He stated that the Western plan was an infringement on Egypt's sovereign rights. Menon tabled a counter-proposal which called for the recognition of the sovereign rights of Egypt and for the "recognition of the Suez Canal as an integral part of Egypt. Indonesia and Ceylon (Sri Lanka) continued to support the Indian plan". [54] Finally, on 21st August, the American draft with minor modifications was adopted by the eighteen out of the twenty-two delegations attending the conference. A five-member committee under the chairmanship of the Australian Premiere R.G. Menzies was appointed to convey this proposal to Nasser. [55]

Nasser made it clear to Menzies' Committee that the existence of such a body operating the Suez Canal, in the view of Egypt, will infringe Egyptian sovereignty. He warned that any attempt to impose an international authority on the Canal would indeed be a signal for incalculable strife and would plunge the Suez Canal into the turmoil of politics. He, thus, refused to accept the proposal and pointed out that an international authority would mean the restoration of "collective colonialism". [56]

The failure of Menzies' mission and the developments at the London Conference disillusioned Nehru. He was convinced that it was politically impossible for Nasser to undo the act of nationalization and unthinkable to impose a solution on Egypt.

Meanwhile, military units and paratroopers of Britain and

France landed in Cyprus. This Western step created a tense atmosphere as threats to use force became more open. [57] Nehru was against the use of force, as peaceful solution was still possible. On Nehru's advice, the Egyptian government on 10th September proposed for a new Suez Conference to discuss the issued of freedom of passage, future development and equitable tolls, without prejudice to Egypt's sovereignty or dignity. Nasser was ready to safeguard the legitimate concerns of users' interests without acceptance of international authority on the Canal. [58] The Egyptian proposal provided an opportunity for peaceful settlement of the crisis and created base for negotiations and dialogue.

In the mean time Dulles's idea of Suez Canal User's Association (suggested on 4th September) reached London on 10th September. He proposed the formation of Suez Canal User's Association (SCUA) on the basis of 1988 Convention. On 12th September Eden announced the formation of the Suez Canal Users Association unilaterally. [59] Eden's announcement shocked Nehru. The unilateral decision of Eden created a new situation and met with a markedly poor world reaction. Nehru was against the unilateral formation of SCUA and pointed out that since it was to be taken unilaterally and was not the result of agreement, cooperation or consent, it was in the nature of an imposed decision. He appealed to Eden not to impose decision on Egypt. He was in favour of an emergency meeting of Commonwealth Prime Ministers on this issue. [60]

Nasser refused to accept the plan and calling it nothing but an act of provocation in order to wage war against Egypt. He in an interview said: [61] "We shall not allow the Western proposed Canal Users Association to function through the Canal we Egyptian shall run the Canal smoothly and efficiently and if, in spite of this Canal Users Association forces its way through the Suez Canal then it would mean aggression and would be treated as such".

The second conference was held on 19th September at

London in order to give the official shape to SCUA. The Britain Foreign Secretary Selwyn Lloyds in the opening session of the conference said that to protect the rights of the users, some form of international control was essential. He insisted that they could not accept the unrestricted control by one government or one man over the vital waterway of the Suez Canal. [62] Dulles emphasized the smooth and free navigation of the Canal and proposed that the membership of the Association should not be compulsory but should be voluntary. Finally, on 21st September, a resolution was passed with majority vote. This resolution frustrated Britain and France because they wanted to exert economic pressure on Egypt by denying the Canal dues. [63] Now the economic pressure through the Canal Users Association held out little prospect of success.

Nehru was not satisfied with the outcome of the Conference and advised Nasser for immediate reference to the Security Council. The Egyptian government only informed the UN, did not lodge complaint before it. Nehru knew that there was very little chance of settlement of the crisis in the Security Council, but at least it could provide an opportunity for further negotiations. [64]

In the meantime the Suez Canal crisis entered into a new phase. On September 23, 1956, France and Britain lodged complaint to the Security Council. They maintained that the action of the Egyptian government brought to an end the system of international operation of the Canal which was confirmed and completed by the Suez Canal Convention of 1988. [65] The next day Egypt lodged counter-complaint to the Security Council that the actions against Egypt by some powers, particularly France and the UK, which constitute a danger to international peace and security and were serious violations of the charter of the UN. [66]

As the Security Council meetings proceeded, private meetings were held between the Foreign Ministers of the UK, France and Egypt and the UN Secretary General. Finally, an agreement was reached which was unanimously adopted by the Security Council on October 13, 1956. The resolution had a second part which was rejected as it was designed to offend Egypt. Britain and France were not satisfied with the outcome in the Security Council, Later, Egypt, UK and France had agreed for direct negotiations which were scheduled to begin on October 29, 1956. [67] Meanwhile, India also attempted to bring about reconciliation between Egypt on the one hand and Britain and France on the other. The Indian proposal went very far towards satisfying the British and France case. [68]

The Suez War

The attack on Egypt by Israel, in fact, was not sudden. The clouds of the war had already started gathering as soon as Egypt had nationalized the Suez Canal on 26th July 1956. During the long period of over three months between 26th July and 29th October when Israel invaded Egypt as a prelude to the British-French attack, the two western powers were engaged in military preparations and movements while at the same time they were attending the London Conference and the UN sessions. From October 22-24, 1956, the Anglo-French Israeli secret negotiations were held at Severe near Paris. In the meeting the Israeli Premier Ben-Groin was assured of France's protection of Israel and of the Franco-British intervention in Egypt following Israeli's attack on Egypt. On 29th October, Israeli armoured units crossed the Egypt-Israel armistices Demarcation Line and Israeli planes dropped a paratroops battalion at the eastern end of the Mitla pass in Sinai. In this way the Suez war had begun. [69]

The Israeli attack on Egypt and the subsequent Anglo-French ultimatum surprised Nehru and others. He immediately condemned the aggression and assured Nasser of India's full political and diplomatic support. He also suggested Yugoslavia and the Bandug Countries for public condemnation against the Israeli invasion. Nehru called for immediate UN action against the attack, and urged the US to intervene for immediate halt of

Israeli action. It was not possible now for India to continue the balancing act after Israeli attack on Egypt—rather it compelled Nehru to public criticism of the British government. Nehru was deeply hurt and expressed his anguish over the British action against Egypt. He communicated to Eden that Britain, with her record of liberal policies, after attack on Egypt, now had become again the symbol of colonialism.

Nehru's main motives at this moment were to prevent the hostility and military escalation, to safeguard the sovereignty of Egypt, and to save the commonwealth. He did not agree with proposal made by Soviet Union and supported by Egypt and China for holding a meeting of the Bandung countries. Nehru was interested to call a meeting of the Colombo powers which was held on 14th November 1956 after cessation of war on 6th November 1956. He was against the building of an Afro-Asian or even a regional bloc.

He regarded the action through the UN most appropriate and legal and preferred to act through the General Assembly of the UN. In the UN, Nehru supported the proposal of stationing the US contingent to re-establish armistice lines between Israel and Egypt and, of an observer team manned by Czechoslovakia, Canada and India. He was prepared to participate in the UN Emergency Force as and when set up by the UN. Nehru also suggested the Soviet Premier Marshall Bulganin to act through the UN who expressed Soviet determination to crush the aggressors by the use of force. Finally, on 6th November 1956, France, Britain and Israel agreed to cease all military action against Egypt and troops began to withdraw from the Suez Canal area. The unit of UN emergency force took over police duties from them and Canal was opened for world navigation after its clearance on 8th April 1957.

Conclusions

The Indian policy, throughout the crisis, was largely dominated by the efforts to resolve the dispute by peaceful means. India made genuine efforts to avert a military confrontation between Egypt and the Western powers, which were opposed to Egypt's unrestricted control of the Canal. It may not be wrong to say that Britain France and Israel had committed themselves to the military operation in dealing with Nasser. Nehru had a legalist attitude and had strong commitment to the UN charter, which went against any resort to the use of force.

The encouragement given by Indian went a long way in sustaining Nasser during the crisis. India wanted some institutional arrangement of the Canal without violating the sovereignty of Egypt and also to uphold Egypt's right to nationalize the Suez Canal Company. India was among the few countries which supported Nasser in the London Conference.

Nasser had an exceptional by strong feeling for his people's aspiration. He was a charismatic leader who commanded full confidence of his people. The planner of the aggression failed to consider this important fact.

Moreover, Nasser was rubbing shoulders with Nehru, Tito, Chou Enlai and Sukarno, the Tallest leaders of Afro-Asian and non-aligned worlds. This was the period when the new world of Afro-Asian countries was coming into its own after centuries of subjugation by the West. Thus, Nasser was taken as a challenge both, by the declining imperialism of Western Europe and the rising influence of the US.

End Notes

1. Weinberger, S.J., "The Suez Canal Issue 1956", *Middle Eastern Affairs*, (New York), February 1957, Vol. VII, No. 2, p. 46.
2. Bowie, R.R. (1974), Suez 1956: *International Crisis and the Role of Law,* (Oxford), p. 11.
3. Hurewitz, J.C., *Diplomacy in the Near and Middle East: A Documentary Record 1914-1956,* (New York), 1956, Vol. II, p. 337.
4. "The Baghdad Pact", *Round Table*, (London), June 1957, Vol. XLVII, No. 187, pp. 216-217.
5. Khaduri, Majid, "The Problem of Regional Security in the Middle East:" An Appraisal An Appraisal", *Middle East Journal* (Washington), 1957, Vol. II, No. 1, pp. 12-16.

6. Nasser, G.A., "The Egyptian Revolution", *Foreign Affairs*, (New York), January 1955, Vol. 33, No. 2, p. 210.
7. Bagley, F.R.C., "Egypt under Nasser", *International Journal* (Toronto), 1956, Vol. XI, No. 3, p. 203.
8. Hanna, P.L., "American in the Middle East", *Middle Eastern Affairs*, (New York), 1959, Vol. X, No. 5, p. 183.
9. Bagley, No.7, p. 203.
10. Bowie, No. 2, p. 11.
11. Dean, V.M., "Aswan and Suez", *Foreign Policy Bulletin*, (New York) September, 1956, p. 6.
12. Herbert, F., "Suez Scenario: A Lamentable Tale", *Foreign Affairs* (New York), 1960, Vol. 38, No. 4, p. 598.
13. Perlman, M., "The Voice of Cairo", *Middle Eastern Affairs*, (New York), 1956, Vol. VII, Nos. 8-9, p. 296.
14. Weinberger, No.1, p. 46.
15. Tom, L., "Nasser and Cold War Strategy", *Middle Eastern Forum* (Beirut), 1959, Vol. XXXIV, No. 4, pp. 22-26.
16. Weinberger, No.1, p. 47.
17. Perlman, No. 13, p. 297.
18. Nolte, R.H., and Polk, W.K., "Towards a Policy for Middle East", *Foreign Affairs* (New York), 1958, Vol. 36, No. 4, p. 655.
19. Watt, D.C., *Documents on the Suez Crisis:* 26th July to 6th November 1956, (London), 1957, p. 44; For the text of Nasser' speech, see Appendix, no. D.
20. Ibid.
21. Ibid.
22. Ibid.
23. Perlman, No. 13, p. 297.
24. Barraclough, G., *Survey of International Affairs,* (London), 1962, p. 4.
25. Eden, A., Full Circle, (London), 1960, 424.
26. Barraclough, No. 24, pp. 6-7.
27. House of Commons Debate, Vol. 557, V Series, Column 1715.
28. Ibid, Cols., 1662-1663.
29. Nehru, Jawaharlal, India's Foreign Policy: Selected Speeches September 1946-April 1961, (Delhi), 1961, Ministry of Information and Broadcasting, Government of India, p. 253, hereafter cited as I.F.P.
30. Bishku, M.B., "Personalities and Perceptions: Political and Economic Factors Which led to India's Involvement in the Suez

Crisis of 1956", *Journal of South Asian and Middle Eastern Studies*, (Villanova), 1987, Vol. X, No. 4, p. 27.
31. Ibid, p. 29.
32. Heikal, M.H. Nasser: The Cairo Documents, (New York), 1973 pp. 64 and 68.
33. Gopal, Servepalli, "*India, the Crisis, and the Non-Aligned Nations*" in Roger Louis, W.M. and Owen, R. (ed.), Suez 1956: The Crisis and its Consequences (Oxford), 1989, pp.173-174.
34. Bishku, No. 30, pp. 29-30.
35. Heikal, No. 32, p.281.
36. Bishku, No. 30, pp. 17-18 and 27.
37. Gopal, No. 33, pp. 175-177.
38. Ibid.
39. Nehru, I.F.P., pp. 527-532.
40. Watt, No. 19, p. 6.
41. Gopal, No. 33, pp. 175-176.
42. Herbert, No. 12, p. 600.
43. "The Strategy of Egypt's Defence", *Egyptian Political and Economic Review*, (Cairo), 1957.
44. Finer, H., Dulles over Suez, (London) 1964, p. 99.
45. Ibid, pp. 123-125.
46. Ibid, p. 134.
47. For Full text of Nehru's Speech of 8th August 1956 to Lok Sabha, see I.F.P., pp. 527-532.
48. Ibid.
49. Gupta Subratta, India's Five Year Plans, (Calcutta), 1975, pp. 47-58.
50. I.F.P., No. 29, pp. 527-532.
51. Ibid.
52. Finer, No. 44, pp. 147-150.
53. Eden, No. 25, pp. 450-451
54. Barrachough, No. 24, pp. 24-25.
55. British and Foreign State Papers, (London) 1955-1956, Vol. 162, p. 755.
56. Ibid, pp. 781-785.
57. "Lond Haul at Suez", *The Economist*, (London), 11th August 1956, p. 453.
58. Gopal, No. 33, pp. 180-181.
59. Nutting, Anthony, No End of a Lesson: The Story of Suez, (London), 1967, pp. 60-65.

60. Gopal, No. 33, pp. 182-183.
61. Quoted in Finer, No. 44, p. 248.
62. Barraclough, No. 24, p. 37.
63. Hanna, No. 8, pp. 178-190.
64. Gopal, No. 33, p. 182.
65. Corbett, Percy, E., "Power and Law at Suez", *International Journal* (Toronto) 1956-57, Vol. XII, No. 1, pp. 7-8.
66. United Nations Document, No. S/13654.
67. UN Security Council Official Records, No. S/3675.
68. Watt, No. 19, pp. 77-80.
69. "Why Britain and France Went to War in Egypt", US News and World Report, (Ohio, 1956) Vol. 4, No. 19, pp. 29-23.

Index

Index